Mastering
Value at Risk

FINANCIAL TIMES
Prentice Hall

In an increasingly competitive world, it is quality
of thinking that gives an edge – an idea that opens new
doors, a technique that solves a problem, or an insight
that simply helps make sense of it all.

We work with leading authors in the fields of
management and finance to bring cutting-edge thinking
and best learning practice to a global market.

Under a range of leading imprints, including
Financial Times Prentice Hall, we create world-class
print publications and electronic products giving readers
knowledge and understanding which can then be
applied, whether studying or at work.

To find out more about our business and professional
products, you can visit us at www.business-minds.com

For other Pearson Education publications, visit
www.pearsoned-ema.com

Pearson
Education

market editions

Mastering
Value at Risk

A step-by-step guide to
understanding and applying VaR

CORMAC BUTLER

FINANCIAL TIMES

Prentice Hall

An imprint of Pearson Education

London · New York · San Francisco · Toronto
Sydney · Tokyo · Singapore · Hong Kong · Cape Town
Madrid · Paris · Milan · Munich · Amsterdam

PEARSON EDUCATION LIMITED

Head Office:
Edinburgh Gate
Harlow CM20 2JE
Tel: +44 (0) 1279 623623
Fax: +44 (0) 1279 431059

London Office:
128 Long Acre
London WC2E 9AN
Tel: +44 (0)20 7447 2000
Fax: +44 (0)20 7240 5771

_____

First published in Great Britain 1999

© Pearson Education Limited 1999

The right of Cormac Butler to be identified as author
of this work has been asserted by him in accordance
with the Copyright, Designs, and Patents Act 1988.

ISBN 0 273 63752 5

British Library Cataloguing in Publication Data
A CIP catalogue record for this book can be obtained from the British Library.

10 9 8 7 6 5 4 3

Typeset by Northern Phototypesetting Co. Ltd
Printed and bound in Great Britain by Redwood Books, Trowbridge, Wiltshire

The Publishers' policy is to use paper manufactured from sustainable forests.

About the Author

Cormac Butler has considerable international experience as a freelance training consultant in Hong Kong, Croatia, Poland, Estonia, London, and Dublin. Specializing in risk management derivatives trading, he has worked with major banks including Salomon Brothers, Banque Paribas, Commonwealth Development Corporation, Allied Irish Banks, as well as acting as a consultant with Lombard Risk Systems (producers of Oberon), ABB and Arab Banking Corporation.

He has also worked as a lecturer to students of the Institute of Chartered Accountants and to traders sitting the examinations of the Institute of Investment Management and Research.

He graduated from the University of Limerick, Ireland, with a degree in finance. Apart from merchant banks, Cormac Butler has worked with Coopers & Lybrand and Peat Marwick. Mr. Butler has also acquired some experience in the area of options and equity trading. He has recently completed two workbooks: *Treasury Risk Management* and *Portfolio Risk Management*.

CONTENTS

PREFACE

There is little doubt that, over the past four years, the profession of Financial Risk Management has grown considerably. Banks have set up specialist risk divisions whose function is not only to measure risk, but also to control it. Value at Risk has an important role to play here. Those who have a sound grasp of its principles, and who understand the unique nature of derivative risk, are in a better position not only to trade properly, but also to avoid contributing to the huge losses that many major banks have suffered in the last few years. Value at Risk is not only of interest to risk practitioners, but also to traders who want to trade profitably and, of course, to graduate and post-graduate students who want to become derivative traders, or who want to specialize in risk management. Recently, the Futures and Options Association has recommended that directors of major banks become actively involved in policies of risk management, rather than to delegate them, which is the current practice of many banks. A good grasp of VaR is, therefore, essential for this sector as well.

Mastering VaR is designed for the practitioner. Today, most practitioners recognize the importance of an interactive book, which encourages active as opposed to passive learning. *Mastering VaR* uses Excel spreadsheets to achieve this. If you have Excel available, you will be guided toward setting up a simple but illustrative VaR system. If you do not have Excel, the examples are designed so that you can follow them with relative ease and so at least understand how VaR systems operate.

A common complaint among practitioners is that, although there are many books on VaR, few are accessible to the non-academic. As one colleague put it, "It seems as though all writers in risk management are academic professors trying to impress more senior academic professors." In a practical world, many of the articles and books on VaR will lose the attention span of busy traders and practitioners who do not have a post-graduate degree in mathematics or statistics. Clearly, there is a gap in the market for a book which sets out, in digestible blocks, what VaR is, its limitations, and how to apply it.

The book is designed to give readers a practical insight into VaR and what this latest risk-measurement system is trying to achieve. In the first chapter, the concept of VaR is explained. You will be introduced to the concepts of volatility, normal distribution, and correlation. There are a number of practical but simple examples of each of these concepts. By the end of the chapter, you will have an intuitive understanding of the basics of VaR.

In Chapter 2, we examine why regulators and banks have found it necessary to develop a VaR system. We give you the regulators' perspective and the need for banks to "self-assess" their own risk with a view to calculating capital adequacy. We examine the role of the capital adequacy and why the existing framework is not the most suitable for measuring risk. The chapter also gives some insight into the Basle Committee and the evolution of self-assessment in terms of risk measurement.

In Chapter 3 we get down to the practical issues of risk measurement and build your knowledge of volatility and correlation (already introduced in Chapter 1). The idea behind this is to show you various approaches to the measurement of VaR and to illustrate the computational challenges of dealing with large portfolios. This chapter is to a large extent an interactive chapter where you can (if you have spreadsheets) build up a VaR measuring system which almost incorporates the broad features inherent in real VaR packages. Those who do not have spreadsheets will nevertheless to be able to follow the examples without any difficulty. Although the chapter appears very mathematical, we assume only a basic knowledge and direct nonmathematical readers to two small appendices which explain in simple terms how matrices operate.

In Chapters 4 and 5 we illustrate how fixed income products are "decomposed" and mapped onto weighting matrices for the purpose of risk measurement. Swaps, swaptions, and forward rate agreements are discussed in detail, in order to illustrate the complexities and how we can exploit natural hedging. We also compare VaR risk measurement with the more traditional forms of risk measurement, such as duration and convexity.

Chapters 6, 7, and 8 concentrate on risk measurement for options. In Chapter 6 we illustrate the unique risk nature of options and emphasize the "Greeks". In Chapter 7 we outline some of the popular strategies in which option traders engage and their risk implications. Chapter 8 then illustrates the weaknesses with the standard variance covariance approach and introduces a new method of risk measurement: Monte Carlo simulation. The principles of VaR are not just confined to market risk. In Chapter 9, we show how we can apply VaR principles to the estimation of credit risk. In particular, we look at CreditMetrics and the growth in the use of credit derivatives.

In Chapter 10, we concentrate on volatility forecasting and estimation. We illustrate the unique nature of volatility and the various models used by practitioners. In particular, we talk about GARCH and compare this method to the exponentially weighted moving average method, as adopted by RiskMetrics. Finally, in Chapter 11, we look at the particular problems with modeling risk in general and in, particular, the pitfall of overreliance on models to measure risk.

Questions & answers

We have launched a new website, **answerback.org**, to deal with the most popular questions and queries that readers have raised, after reading *Mastering Value at Risk*. If you are stuck on any area, please send your question to us via the website. You will also see questions and answers from other readers.

ACKNOWLEDGMENTS

I would like to thank the following people for their assistance: Professor Richard Flavell of Lombard Risk, Richard Stagg and Martin Drewe of Financial Times Prentice Hall, Penelope Allport and Helene Bellofatto for their editorial work, and John Vernon of Renaissance Training.

An Outline of Value at Risk

Introduction

What is risk? In simple terms risk measures how volatile an asset's returns are. Given the substantial losses that major banks and corporations have suffered, risk departments are becoming more prominent. Risk consultants are in demand, but the desire to understand risk is not simply confined to the regulators and risk managers of various banks. Traders can enhance their performance if they have a better understanding of how risk arises and, more importantly, how it can be averted. Regulators and risk managers need to have as many tools as possible to control risk and even to exploit it! Value at Risk is an attempt to identify what causes risk and what policies are effective at reducing risk.

To the layman, and to many traders Value at Risk (VaR) is often regarded as "some mathematical model" dreamed up by rocket scientists – which probably doesn't work anyway. VaR models certainly have their flaws. Nevertheless, the concept has attracted some of the best names in risk management who have worked alongside highly qualified mathematicians to build up a system which is designed to monitor and reduce risk. The system has many critics both from experienced traders and mathematicians who have found problems with some of the assumptions – but that does not mean we should ignore it. Although Value at Risk may not be the perfect solution, it signposts the way that risk is developing and, to that extent, it is worth knowing. More importantly, from the trader's point of view, knowledge of the internal workings of VaR is very useful, particularly when devising trading strategies. The world of financial engineering is advancing at a rapid pace and those with a good grasp of it are not only finding ways to reap the rewards of taking on risk, but also finding ways of offsetting or reducing that risk. With sophisticated models, this is how traders will make most of their profits in the future.

Value at Risk is an attempt to identify what causes risk and what policies are effective at reducing risk.

In this first chapter, we give an overview of what VaR is. We formally define VaR and then show in intuitive terms how VaR measures and interprets volatility. We also reveal the importance of correlation in risk determination and the role of statistical models such as the normal distribution curve in estimating the amount of risk that an institution is exposed to.

Regulators

To a large extent, Value at Risk has emerged because of the dilemma facing regulators and supervisors of central banks. On the one hand, they want a comprehensive set of rules and regulations which can identify and, where necessary, penalize banks that take on excessive risks. On the other hand, if they introduce too rigid a system, they may end up compounding as opposed to eliminating risk. Today, regulators are looking very closely at VaR as a means of self-regulation. In Chapter 2, we examine the role of the regulator, the problems with measuring risk, and how developments in VaR are paving the way for self-regulation.

Matrices and variance covariance calculations

In Chapter 3, we get down to the technicalities of how VaR is calculated. Readers will, of course, appreciate that there are various ways of calculating VaR. In Chapter 3, we examine the variance covariance method (adopted by JP Morgan). This chapter is very interactive, and though not confined to readers with access to spreadsheets, those who work through this chapter will end up with a firm grasp of how VaR operates and what VaR is trying to achieve. The chapter places particular emphasis on "diversified" VaR, and illustrates how banks can allocate resources in a way which preserves profits but substantially reduces risk.

> *Today, regulators are looking very closely at VaR as a means of self-regulation.*

Fixed income products

Risk managers must, of course, fully understand the products that they are dealing with. In Chapters 4 and 5, we present most of the popular products such as forward rate agreements (FRAs), interest rate and currency swaps, and bonds. Those risk managers who measure risk on a portfolio basis need to be fully aware of how such instruments react to, say, changes in interest rates. We show how FRAs and swaps are priced, how they are "marked-to-market," and the various risk implications. We also show how VaR models break down the various fixed instruments, so that risk management can be better coordinated. Traditionally, interest rate exposure involved calculating an instrument's sensitivity to interest rate changes (duration). We compare this traditional approach with the improved VaR method and illustrate the importance of examining the yield curve slope as part of risk estimation.

Options

Many experienced risk mangers and traders have challenged VaR on the grounds that it cannot cater for the complex world of options. Indeed, many providers of VaR models accept that their programs should only be used for non-option based products. Nevertheless, more and more banks are becoming heavily dependent on options, and past experience has shown that options are extremely risky. In fact, they were responsible for heavy

> *Traditionally, interest rate exposure involved calculating an instrument's sensitivity to interest rate changes (duration). We compare this traditional approach with the improved VaR method and illustrate the importance of examining the yield curve slope as part of risk estimation.*

Many providers of VaR models accept that their programs should only be used for non-option based products. Nevertheless, more and more banks are becoming heavily dependent on options, and past experience has shown that options are extremely risky.

losses incurred by banks such as NatWest, Barings and nonbanking enterprises such as Procter & Gamble. In Chapters 6 and 7, we examine options in detail and focus specifically on variables such as changes in volatility and changes in the underlying asset. We also examine the latest developments in measuring option risk. In particular, we illustrate the delta gamma approach and give some practical guidelines on Monte Carlo simulation. We also signpost new developments in option-risk measurement and how VaR is incorporating such developments.

Volatility estimation

Value at Risk is really a measure of how volatile a bank's assets are. There are some characteristics in volatility that traders, regulators, and risk managers need to know when estimating future volatility. In Chapters 9 and 10 we illustrate how volatility is forecast, and presenting various methods, along with the relative advantage and disadvantage of each. We also consider at length volatility trades and how volatility risk can be reduced by sensible trading strategies.

Modeling risk analysis

Value at Risk is really a measure of how volatile a bank's assets are. There are some characteristics in volatility that traders, regulators, and risk managers need to know when estimating future volatility.

We conclude the book with an evaluation of model risk and how effective VaR is in measuring risk and providing warning signals. Clearly, the regulatory world, the academic world, along with traders and regulators are divided on how well VaR can be relied upon. Nevertheless, Value at Risk looks like it is here to stay, and while risk managers may incorporate the VaR system in their banks, they also need to be aware of its limitations. We emphasize such limitations and indicate how financial institutions can introduce risk controls, which compensate for any pitfalls in VaR.

Credit assessment

Although VaR was designed to measure market risk, its applications are now being extended to credit risk. Banks need to measure the riskiness of loans at the time they are taken out, and not wait until the loans default before realizing the risk they took. Also, new developments in credit derivatives mean that it is in banks' interest to measure credit risk exposure so that they can hedge themselves. CreditMetrics is a new technique for treating credit exposure on a portfolio basis and borrows from the VaR principles already developed. We examine credit in detail in Chapter 9.

What is Value at Risk?

Definition

Value at Risk measures the worst expected loss that an institution can suffer over a given time interval under normal market conditions at a given confidence level. It assesses this risk by using statistical and simulation models designed to capture the volatility of assets in a bank's portfolio.

VaR measures the volatility of a company's assets. The more volatile they are, the greater is the risk of bankruptcy. A portfolio manager might for instance hold £100 million in a portfolio with relatively low volatility. This means that the risk of making huge losses is quite low. On the other hand, if the investment manager invested in shares whose value fluctuates by large amounts, then although the portfolio manager has a chance of making significant profits, he also runs the risk of making huge losses. In a single figure, VaR measures those potential losses. It also indicates the probability of making more than those losses and the time period over which the losses might occur. In the next section we look at how that volatility is measured.

What VaR does not do

1 VaR does not give a consistent method for measuring risk. Different VaR models will give different VaR figures.
2 VaR only measures risks that can be captured through quantitative techniques. It does not measure political risk, liquidity risk, personnel risk, or regulatory risk.
3 VaR does not measure operational risk.

What VaR can and can't do

1 Metallgesellschaft lost a lot of money because it was unable to meet its margin calls on oil futures. The problem stemmed from the fact that it failed to cash budget properly. VaR would not have been able to pick up this risk.

2 A major British bank used a wrong model when pricing interest rate derivatives and ended up losing £70 million. Again, VaR does not test operational risk exposure and so would not have been able to pick up this risk.

3 A rogue trader has lost £100m and concealed it from his superiors. Rather than admit the loss and lose his job, the trader decides to increase his exposure in the hope that the markets will turn in his favor and recover earlier losses. As long as the trades are "booked" properly, VaR should be able to send warning signals to senior management that a single trader has enhanced the bank's risk exposure.

Volatility and how to exploit it profitably

Definition

Volatility is a measure of how much the price of an asset fluctuates. The more volatile the asset, the greater is the potential to make large profits or large losses. Since VaR is concerned with risk, it uses volatility to estimate the maximum loss that a bank may suffer, over a particular time period.

There are two reasons why a trader should have a good understanding of volatility:

1 They can price options more accurately and indeed use a combination of options to "trade volatility." Many traders have made vast sums through a combination of options known as "straddles" "strangles" and "butterflies," where they have taken a view on whether an asset is going to become more or less volatile. The Black and Scholes model relies on volatility measures when determining option premiums.

2 Volatile assets are risky assets and so require a risk premium. This in fact is the essence of the capital asset pricing model that suggests that "high beta" share, that is those shares that are very volatile, should attract a higher risk premium than low beta shares.

Risk is a measure of how volatile the future value of a portfolio is. Consider Table 1.1, which shows the annual returns of two portfolios taken each year over a five-year period.

	A	B	C
5	Observation	Portfolio	Portfolio
6	period	A	B
7			
8	1	11.5%	7.0%
9	2	11.2%	9.0%
10	3	11.0%	11.0%
11	4	10.3%	13.0%
12	5	11.0%	15.0%
13			
14	Mean	11.00%	11.00%
15	Standard deviation	0.0044159	0.0316

Table 1.1 above shows two portfolios and five observations for each portfolio. The first has returns that are very close to the mean. If the past is any guideline, then the future returns can almost be predicted to be very close to the mean. It would contain a relatively low risk because volatility is low. The standard deviation for this portfolio is low. The standard deviation is simply a statistical term that measures how volatile the portfolio is. In the second portfolio, although the mean return is the same, at 11 percent, each of the observations varies considerably from the mean, and so the standard deviation measure is higher. The second portfolio is considered to be a higher risk portfolio, and so would have a higher VaR.

For Excel or spreadsheet users, the formulas for the mean and standard deviation are shown in Table 1.2. Assume that the data is contained in cells B8–B13 and C8–C13.

	A	B	C
14	Mean	=SUM(B8:B13)/5	=SUM(C8:C13)/5
15	Standard deviation	=STDEV(B8:B12)	=STDEV(C8:C12)

Table 1.2 Standard deviation

The procedure that Excel uses to calculate the standard deviation is shown in Table 1.3, which illustrates that the standard deviation is basically a measure of how far each observation moves away from the mean. The greater the distance, the greater the standard deviation.

	A	B	C	D	E
24	Observation	Portfolio	Mean	Difference	Difference
25	period	A			squared
26					
27	1	11.5%	11.00%	0.50%	0 .025%
28	2	11.2%	11.00%	0.20%	0.0004%
29	3	11.0%	11.00%	0.00%	0.0000%
30	4	10.3%	11.00%	-0.70%	0.0049%
31	5	11.0%	11.00%	0.00%	0.0000%
32					
33	Total			0.00%	0.0078%
34	Standard deviation				0.00441588
35	Mean	11.00%			

Table1.3 Method for calculating standard deviation

Table 1.3 uses the formula:

$$\sigma = \sqrt{\frac{(x - \bar{x})^2}{(n - 1)}}$$

Where x (bar) = mean and n = the number of observations. Therefore, 0.00441588 =(E33/(A31-1))^0.5 or 0.445188% =

$$\sqrt{\frac{0.78\%}{(5-1)}}.$$

Assume that the boxed area represents cells A27 to E31. The cell A31 contains the figure of 5. A general rule with statistics, of course, is that the larger the sample size, the more accurate the volatility estimate will be.

Implied volatility

The above calculation is fine as long as we have a large series of historical data to choose from. Some traders prefer to calculate volatility by looking at option prices. This is known as implied volatility. When option traders are pricing call and put options, they must first calculate volatility and input it into their pricing model. It is possible to work in reverse, that is to look at the option price that the trader calculates and then calculate the implied volatility on the underlying asset. The Black and Scholes (or some other pricing model) is frequently used by risk managers to see what volatility was used to calculate the option premium price in the first place. There are three problems with this approach.

Some traders prefer to calculate volatility by looking at option prices. This is known as implied volatility.

First, option prices, as with all products, are regulated by the laws of supply and demand. Therefore, the relationship between the option price and the true volatility may not always hold. Second, the Black and Scholes formula is not suited to American-style options. American-style options can be exercised at any point up to maturity as opposed to European-style options, which are exercisable at maturity only. The Black and Scholes formula, although sometimes used to price American options, was designed for European options only. A third problem is that traders take a profit margin when calculating option prices. Therefore, the implied volatility will probably be much higher than the volatility which the trader pricing the option believes it is. Despite these small weaknesses, many experts believe that, where possible, we should use implied volatility as an estimate of current volatility rather than historical data.

Problems with implied volatility estimation

1 Option pricing models are not perfect.

2 Options prices are influenced by the laws of supply and demand, as well as volatility estimation.

3 Implied option prices contain a profit margin and so will normally be higher than realized volatility.

Misleading the investor

In the USA there is growing concern about the way that some mutual funds (unit trust) companies can mislead the small investor. Consider a mutual fund company that has two portfolios. Portfolio A has high volatility and has high beta shares (a high beta share is one whose volatility is greater than the index). Portfolio B has low beta shares and so would have a low Value at Risk figure. If the stock market is doing well, the company simply advertises its high beta portfolio indicating that it has outperformed the stock market. Needless to say, the wording of the advertisement encourages the reader to conclude that good management was responsible. In reality, because high beta shares were chosen, a mild increase in the stock market would lead to a significant increase in the portfolio value. If the stock market were going downhill, the company would advertise the past performance of the low-beta portfolio. Again, the advertisement would encourage the reader to believe that good management was responsible for the fact that the portfolio only fell slightly when the stock market fell significantly. The reality is that, since low beta shares were chosen, we would only expect a small decrease if the stock market index fell.

Value at Risk can to some extent highlight this shortfall. If unit trust managers were forced to disclose their volatility, then an astute investor might see that the high returns were due to the selection of high volatility or high beta shares, and not necessarily because the right share was selected.

If we assumed that volatility remained constant over time, we would probably end up underpricing options, particularly options that are out-of-the-money and with a long time to maturity.

Problems with volatility

A major weakness of option pricing models like Black and Scholes is that volatility is assumed to be constant. Empirical research has suggested otherwise. Indeed, if we assumed that volatility remained constant over time, we would probably end up underpricing options, particularly options that are out-of-the-money and with a long time to maturity. As we will see later, there are special models used to analyze volatility over a particular time period. For the moment, we can conclude that traders who price options or attempt to calculate risk on the assumption that volatility remains constant will probably end up with a very inaccurate result.

The normal distribution curve

Definition

A distribution is said to be *normal* if there is a high probability that an observation will be close to the mean and a low probability that an observation is far away from the mean. The normal distribution curve is used frequently in VaR models and also plays an important function in the Black and Scholes model for valuing options. It has certain features and characteristics that are helpful when modeling market risk. An important characteristic of the normal distribution curve is that it peaks at the mean and tails off at the extremes. In layman's language this simply means that an observation is more likely to be closer to the mean or average than far away.

Consider a well-diversified portfolio that is currently producing an annual return of 10 percent. The likelihood that this return will deviate away from 10 percent to, say, 2 percent over the next month is low. Similarly, the likelihood that it will go up to 25 percent is also very low. In other words, the possibility of reaching extreme values is rare. On the other hand, the likelihood that the portfolio moves from 10 percent to 9 percent is much higher and similarly, the likelihood that the return will move from 10 percent to 11 percent is also high. We can see, therefore, that the possibility of reaching extreme values is very rare, while the possibility of reaching values that are close to the mean is quite high. This is summarized in Figure 1.1.

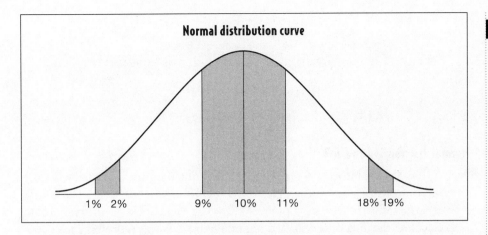

The shaded area represents the probability that an observation will fall between the two values listed on the scale below. The portfolio, which is well diversified, is currently producing a return of 10 percent. The likelihood that the return will stay between 9 percent and 11 percent is very high, and the likelihood that it will go to extreme values, that is 1 percent–2 percent or 18 percent–19 percent, is quite low. Share prices tend to follow a normal distribution, although some mathematical adjustments are necessary. For instance, the current BskyB share price is £4.40. There is a strong likelihood that one month from now the share price will be between £3.60 and £5.20. There is an extremely low probability that in one month's time the share price will be below £2 or above £6.80.

Many VaR models use the normal distribution curve to estimate the losses that an institution can make over a given time period. Normal distribution curve tables (contained in Appendix 11.2) show the probability of an observation moving a certain distance from the mean. Samples from the normal distribution table appear in Table 1.4 below.

Number of standard deviations	−1.645	−1.000	0.000	1.000	1.650
Probability	5.0%	15.9%	50.0%	84.1%	95.1%

Table 1.4 Extracts from normal distribution table

In the first case, the table shows that there is a probability of 5 percent that the value of an observation will be at least 1.645 standard deviations below the mean. This is the standard statistic much used in VaR models. In the second case, there is a probability of 15.9 percent that an observation or event will be at least 1 standard deviation below the mean.

Table 1.4 can be easily set up on Excel as shown in Table 1.5.

	A	B
40	Number of std. deviations	−1.645
41	Probability	=NORMSDIST(B40)

Table 1.5 Formulas for Table 1.4

Where the cell B40 contains −1.645.

Normal distribution and VaR

A portfolio has a value of £10m and its current annual return (assumed to be the mean is 10 percent) what is the probability that its return will fall to 6% within a year, if the standard deviation of the returns is 2 percent? What we want to do is to calculate the area of the shaded region Figure 1.2 (this represents the probability that the portfolio's returns will fall below 6 percent). Figure 1.2 summarizes the results and Table 1.6 shows how this can be set up on Excel.

	A	B	C	D	E	F
46	Observation	1	2	3	4	5
47	Mean return	10%	10%	10%	10%	10%
48	Target return	6%	7%	8%	10%	12%
49	Standard deviation of return	2%	2%	2%	2%	2%
50	Number of standard deviations	-2	-1.5	-1	0	1
51	Probability	2.28%	6.68%	15.87%	50.00%	84.13%

Table 1.6 Normal distribution examples

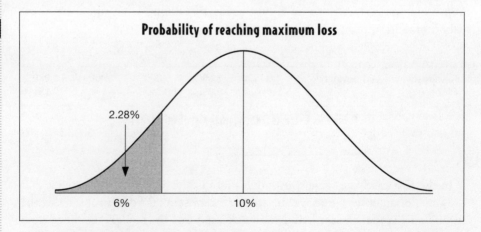

Probability of reaching maximum loss

2.28%

6%   10%

Readers who do not have Excel handy can easily calculate the probability from the normal distribution tables contained in Appendix 11.2.

	A	B
46	Mean return	10%
47	Target return	6%
48	Standard deviation of return	2%
49	Number of standard deviations	=(B47–B46)/B48
50	Probability	=NORMSDIST(B49)

Table 1.7 Formulas for Table 1.6

Table 1.6 above shows the mean return of the portfolio as before. Under column B we see that the mean return is 10% and that the target return is 6%. The size of each standard deviation is 2%. The number of standard deviations that will fit between 10% and 6% is (10%–6%)/2% = 2. In the second observation, the target return is 7 percent, and the normal distribution curve suggests that there is a 6.68 percent chance that the return of the portfolio will fall below this target. Obviously, the return has a greater chance of falling below 7 percent than 6 percent. In observation 3, the target return of 8 percent is even easier to reach. Observation 4 simply states that there is a 50 percent chance that the return will drop below its current level, 10 percent, and by implication, a 50 percent chance that it will go above 10 percent. Finally, observation 5 states that there is an 84 percent chance that the observation will lie below 12 percent. Obviously, the probability is greater than 50 percent because 12 percent lies above the mean, which is the half-way point.

The normal distribution curve assumes complete randomness. In reality, when share prices fall, people sell and risk managers, who are using shares to hedge their derivatives, are forced to offload their hedge. This extra surge of selling will push the share price into the extremes a lot quicker than the normal distribution curve suggests.

Weakness of normal distribution

One major weakness with the normal distribution function is what is known as the "fat-tails syndrome." Loosely put, a share price has a higher probability of reaching the extreme values than the normal distribution curve suggests. The normal distribution curve assumes complete randomness. In reality, when share prices fall, people sell and risk managers, who are using shares to hedge their derivatives, are forced to offload their hedge. This extra surge of selling will push the share price into the extremes a lot quicker than the normal distribution curve suggests. Given that VaR is a measure of risk, the likelihood is that if the normal distribution curve is used without any modifications, the VaR figure will be understated.

This weakness with normal distribution curve has influenced the way that traders price options. Black and Scholes rely on the normal distribution tables to calculate the delta of the option N (d1), and to calculate the probability that the option will be exercised N (d2). The formula is more precise for in-the-money options than it is for out-of-the-money options. In fact, if traders tried to use Black and Scholes option-pricing models to calculate the implied volatility on the underlying asset, they would find that volatility increases the longer the time period to maturity. This increase is independent of the fact that volatility is automatically greater with a longer period to maturity.

Fig 1.3

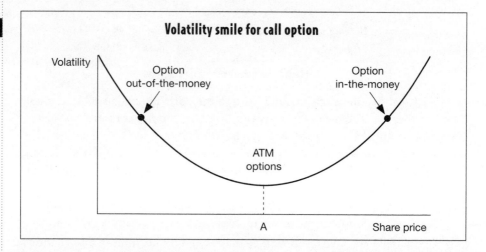

Volatility smile for call option

The curve in Figure 1.3 shows that the implied volatility for an at-the-money option is a lot lower than the implied volatility for a deeply in-the-money or deeply out-of-the-money option. The concept underlines the fact that if the normal distribution curve is not adjusted, we end up underestimating the probability of making large losses.

Case profile

Penalties for underestimating risk

In 1996, NatWest discovered pricing errors in its out-of-the-money interest rate options. This stemmed mainly from the fact that the volatility used in the pricing models was incorrect. In March 1997, the bank announced to the London Stock Exchange that it was writing-off £77 million against pre-tax profits. The problem arose because NatWest failed to forecast properly the volatilities for deeply out-of-the-money options.

Practicalities

There are, of course, other practical factors that we must take into consideration, the risk for which is not exposed in even the most advanced of VaR models. One is liquidity. Liquidity refers to the ease at which a bank can convert its securities to cash at the prevailing market price. Nonliquid assets tend to be more volatile than liquid assets. Therefore, if a security like a corporate bond has a large bid/offer spread, it is an indication that there are very few buyers and sellers. In situations where prices fall, nonliquid assets tend to fall at a much faster pace than liquid assets. Thus, the probability of hitting an extreme value is again greater than what the normal distribution and most VaR models would suggest.

Every experienced trader will confirm that theory is a lot different from reality. When a share price is going up, for instance, traders will jump on the bandwagon and buy. Technical analysts will often see a mild increase in a share price as the prelude to a long and sustained increase, and so will buy. Often, too, traders impose limit order strategies and stop-loss strategies. All of these have the effect of distorting the randomness of market and can push a share price, or commodity price to the extremes a lot quicker than a more random process.

> *Liquidity refers to the ease at which a bank can convert its securities to cash at the prevailing market price. Nonliquid assets tend to be more volatile than liquid assets.*

Naturally, the normal distribution is nothing more than a statistical model, and so cannot capture a lot of other risks. A bank or financial institution can in theory be hedged against market risk, but that does not mean it is exposed to movements in market risk. In fact, major movements in market risk, even in a perfectly hedged portfolio, can lead to problems such as funding and liquidity risk. In the following case profile for instance, Metallgesellschaft undertook risk-reduction policies to cover itself against market risk; ironically, it was a major movement in the market that brought Metallgesellschaft down. Funding and credit risks are other problems not always captured in the VaR models. Where a bank starts to make mild losses, there is the risk that it may run short of funds to meet those losses. Risk managers must, therefore, make sure that there is sufficient funding to meet potential liquidity problems.

Funding mismanagement

Case profile

In December 1993, Metallgesellschaft – a large diversified metals, mining, and industrial conglomerate – suffered major liquidity problems and later announced losses of approximately $1.3bn. The company implemented a hedging strategy whereby it could fix the price of oil for customers worried about price volatility. The company then used futures to offload the risk. The strategy worked as follows:

Customers locked into a fixed price for oil delivery for a specific time period. Metallgesellschaft then went long on oil futures as part of its hedge transaction. If oil prices rose, the futures would produce a profit and this would subsidize the loss of buying oil at the current market price and selling it to the customer at the agreed fixed price. On the other hand, if oil prices fell, the customers were legally bound to pay the fixed price, and so Metallgesellschaft made a profit on this leg of the transaction. However, because Metallgesellschaft was long futures, a fall in oil prices meant a loss on the futures contract, and so any profits made from the customers were used to finance the shortfall on the futures contract.

The strategy made good sense. However, poor planning, particularly with funding, caused problems. For a time, the price of oil fell dramatically, so the ▶

futures position made a loss. Although Metallgesellschaft was adequately hedged to meet the shortfall, there was a timing difference in the cash flows that created a liquidity crisis. Future traders will know that losses on futures must be paid to the exchange on a daily basis. Metallgesellschaft was able to do this for small losses, but for large losses there was a strain on funding. The company simply had to wait for its customers to buy the oil at an agreed fixed rate before it could fund the losses. In the end, people started to panic and the mayhem that followed, led to considerable losses.

A typical VaR model would not have been able to pick up this funding and liquidity problem. This is because VaR tends to concentrate on market risk only and fails to pick up mismatches that can arise through poor cash flow planning. In fact, the likelihood is that any VaR model would have given Metallgesellschaft a clean bill of health. VaR packages should, for this reason, contain a warning that a low VaR figure does not necessarily mean a clean bill of health!

Correlation – its role in risk reduction

Measures of correlation between variables are important to portfolio managers who wish to reduce risk through diversification. Correlation measures the degree to which the value of one variable is related to the value of another. If a strong relationship exists, there is said to be a strong correlation. Property shares, for instance, are related to interest rates in that when interest rates are high, property shares tend to be low. We might conclude from this that there is a strong positive relationship between bond prices and property shares because both rise when interest rates fall.

Correlation measures the degree to which the value of one variable is related to the value of another. If a strong relationship exists, there is said to be a strong correlation.

The first diagram in Figure 1.4 shows strong correlation between variables X and Y. X might be advertising expenditure and Y sales revenue. There is a weak correlation between X and Y in the second diagram that the two variables are completely unrelated, i.e. interest rates at atmospheric temperature. In the third diagram there is a strong negative correlation, that is sale of heating oil and average daily temperature.

One important contribution of VaR is that it encourages traders to diversify and thus not expose themselves to the fortunes or troubles of one particular asset. The ideal situation is where a trader is aware of how much risk each of his trades contributes to overall banking risk. If, while being rewarded for the extra profits he generates, he is penalized for the extra risk he is taking on, he will try to minimize that risk even if he suffers a small drop in profits. Diversification offers him an opportunity to reduce risk.

In 1959, Harry Markowitz produced a study that has had a significant impact on the way portfolio selections are made. His publication *Portfolio Selection:*

Efficient Diversification of Investment formalized the concept that an investor should not put all his eggs in one basket. The objective of any portfolio manager is to be rewarded for undertaking risk and at the same time diversifying that risk away. VaR recognized the importance of diversification, not just on an individual portfolio basis, but also on a global banking basis.

Graphic representation of correlation

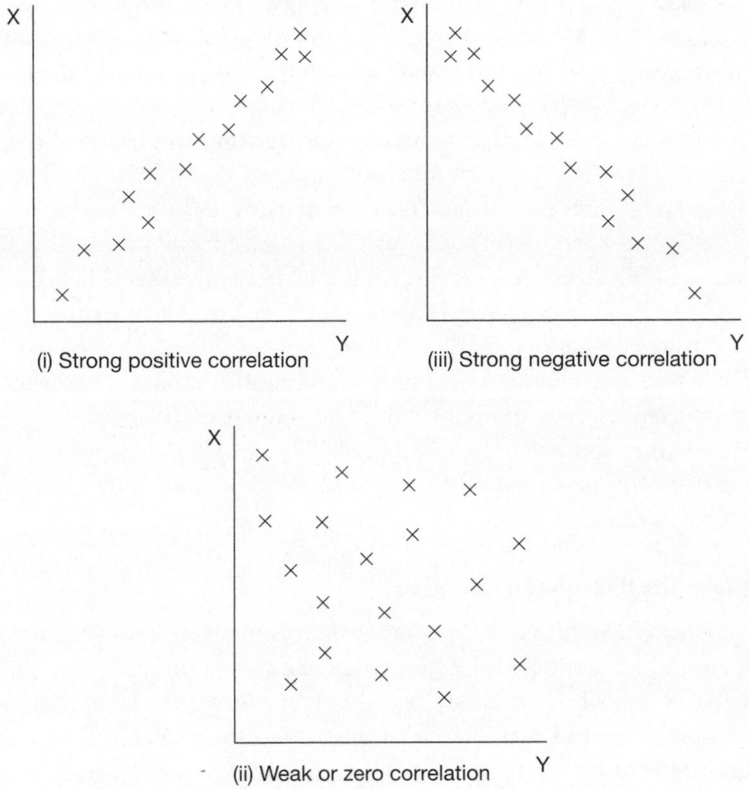

(i) Strong positive correlation

(iii) Strong negative correlation

(ii) Weak or zero correlation

Fig 1.4

> *Without a VaR system in place a situation could arise where an individual trader, in hedging his individual portfolio, may end up reducing the risk of his portfolio but increasing the risk of the bank. VaR methodologies have devised mathematical techniques which identify how a single transaction, whether it is a forward, a swap, or a purchase of shares, can contribute to or even reduce risk.*

Coordinating risk control

The benefit of adopting a VaR system is that it coordinates risk control across the bank and in doing so reduces overall risk. Without a VaR system in place a situation could arise where an individual trader, in hedging his individual portfolio, may end up reducing the risk of his portfolio but increasing the risk of the bank. VaR methodologies have devised mathematical techniques which identify how a single transaction, whether it is a forward, a swap, or a purchase of shares, can contribute to or even reduce risk. Information from VaR models is very important when setting limits. In the past, banks setting limits used a "gut feeling" approach. Now, they can be more scientific and more objective. However, we must not get too carried away. Many VaR experts and regulators acknowledge that reducing the VaR figure to reflect diversification may be dangerous. This is because VaR is strictly a measure of risk and how exposed a bank is when assets lose value. In a crash situation, there is always an element of confusion and panic and people will simply convert all nonliquid assets to cash. Many risk specialists argue, therefore, that the benefits of diversification should not be overemphasized when measuring risk. The simple but relevant example below illustrates the advantage of diversification and more importantly how VaR encourages diversification.

Example

Reducing volatility through diversification

A trader is undecided between investing in shares in an ice-cream company or shares in an umbrella company. Assume that the return on ice-cream shares is 13 percent and that of umbrella shares 12 percent. If the trader was rewarded on profits only, it would make sense to buy ice-cream shares in their entirety and to ignore the umbrella shares with lower profits. Obviously, he is exposing the bank to risk. If the weather is very poor, ice-cream shares will fall in value. This does not matter to him personally because he is not being penalized for the risk that he is taking.

Now suppose the bank introduces a bonus scheme, which is positively related to profits but negatively related to risk. The trader in this case while interested in maximizing profitability would also be keen to reduce the volatility of his portfolio. Therefore, rather than going for maximum profits of 13 percent, the trader would settle for 12.5 percent by splitting his portfolio's resources, investing half of the portfolio in ice-cream shares and half in umbrella shares. If the weather proves bad, the umbrella shares will do well and the ice-cream shares will do badly, and vice versa. Therefore, the overall volatility of the portfolio will be significantly reduced and so too will the VaR figure.

Correlation coefficient

Definition

The correlation coefficient takes a value between −1 and 1 and measures the degree of correlation between two sets of variables.

- A correlation of −1 implies perfect negative linear association.
- A correlation of 1 implies perfect positive linear association.
- A correlation of 0 implies no linear association.

Example

	A	B	C	D	E
64		Company One	Company Two	Company Three	Company Four
65	Observation				
66	1	8%	28%	7%	15%
67	2	9%	24%	10%	9%
68	3	10%	11%	11%	13%
69	4	11%	11%	11%	11%
70	5	12%	8%	12%	12%
71	6	13%	7%	14%	7%
72	7	14%	2%	13%	14%
73	8	15%	3%	15%	14%
74					
75	Average return	12%	12%	12%	12%
76	Correlation with Company One		−0.928	0.943	0.011

Table 1.8 Correlation calculation

Table 1.9 shows how the average return and the correlation is calculated for Companies One and Two in Excel. The data of returns within Table 1.8 is contained in cells B66 to E73. In the correlation formula, dollar symbols surround the cells containing B. This is simply to freeze the cells when we copy the formulas across.

	A	B	C
75	Average return	=SUM(B66:B73)/8	=SUM(C66:C73)/8
76	Correlation with Company One		=CORREL(C66:C73,$B$66:$B$73)

Table 1.9 Spreadsheet function for correlation

Correlation of −1

Company One has a negative correlation with Company Two. Therefore, when Company One is making returns below average, Company Two is making returns above average and vice versa. For the sake of simplicity, imagine that Company One is a sunglasses retailer and Company Two sells heating fuel. When the weather is good, Company One will do quite well and when the weather is poor, Company Two will do well. For the purposes of portfolio diversification, it makes sense to have 50 percent of the portfolio in Company One and 50 percent in Company Two. This means that, in theory, one company will do well while the other is doing badly and vice versa. The overall portfolio, therefore, remains constant and its VaR will be low.

Regulators believe that while this approach may be sound for resource allocation, it is dangerous to use as a risk measure. The reason is that if the stock market is going to fall, shares in Company One and Company Two will both fall, while the VaR calculation assumes that only one or the other will fall but not both. Risk managers can get around this problem by calculating two different types of VaR: a *diversified VaR* and an *undiversified VaR*. The diversified VaR takes into account the lower volatility that can arise if share returns behave differently. It would be used for asset allocation and setting limits. The undiversified VaR assumes that there is no benefit from diversification and calculates the loss on the assumption that both shares can fall in value at the same time.

Correlation of 1

Where a correlation of 1 exists there is no benefit from diversification. In the case of Company One and Company Three, the correlation is close to 1. That means that both companies are in the same sector, probably producing the same product and subject to the same risks. This is clearly evident from the observations. Both have returns below the mean at the same time and both have returns above the mean at the same time. This is more or less the equivalent of putting all your eggs in one basket.

Correlation of 0

Where the correlation coefficient is equal to zero, there are benefits from diversification, but they are not as strong as when the correlation is equal to -1. Company One and Company Four have a correlation coefficient of zero. This simply means that there is no relationship between the returns of one company and another. Company one, therefore might as before, produce sunglasses while Company two might be an electricity generating company and another. If we look at the observations in the box, there is no visible pattern of any relationship. There is absolutely no connection between sales of sunglasses and electricity usage, and so we would expect a correlation of close to zero. A portfolio that comprised Company One and Company Four would have a VaR which is lower than a portfolio comprising of Company One and Company Three and higher than a portfolio comprising of Company One and Company Two.

Table 1.10 illustrates how the correlation coefficient is calculated for Companies One and Two using the standard formula for covariances:

$$\frac{\sum_{i=1}^{n} (xi - \bar{x})(yi - \bar{y})}{(n - 1)}$$

where $(xi - \bar{x})$ = the distance from each value of x from the mean
$(yi - \bar{y})$ = the distance from each value of y from the mean
n = the number of observations.

	B	C	D	E	F	G
83		Company One	Difference from mean	Company Two	Difference from mean	Covariance
84	Observation					
85	1	8%	–4%	28%	16%	–0.569%
86	2	9%	–3%	24%	12%	–0.306%
87	3	10%	–2%	11%	–1%	0.011%
88	4	11%	–1%	11%	–1%	0.004%
89	5	12%	0%	8%	–4%	–0.019%
90	6	13%	2%	7%	–5%	–0.071%
91	7	14%	3%	2%	–10%	–0.244%
92	8	15%	4%	3%	–9%	–0.306%
93						
94	Total					–1.500%
95	Covariance					–0.214%
96	Correlation coefficient					–0.92693
97	Mean return	12%		12%		
98	Correlation coefficient			–0.9269		
99	Standard deviation	0.0245		0.0944		

Table 1.10 Covariance and correlation

The total of column G is –1.5%. The covariance is therefore –1.5%/(8–1) = –0.214%.

The formula for the correlation coefficient is:

$$\text{Correlation coefficient} = \frac{\text{covariance } (1, 2)}{Sd_{(1)} \times Sd_{(2)}}$$

Therefore in this case it is –0.214%/(0.0245 × 0.0944) = –0.9269 (subject to rounding). The formulas behind Table 1.10 are shown in Table 1.11.

	B	C	D	E	F	G
83		Company	Difference	Company	Difference	Covariance
84	Observation	One	from mean	Two	from mean	
85	1	0.08	=C85-$C$97	0.28	=E85-$E$97	=D85*F85
86	2	0.09	=C86-$C$97	0.24	=E86-$E$97	=D86*F86
87	3	0.1	=C87-$C$97	0.11	=E87-$E$97	=D87*F87
88	4	0.11	=C88-$C$97	0.11	=E88-$E$97	=D88*F88
89	5	0.12	=C89-$C$97	0.08	=E89-$E$97	=D89*F89
90	6	0.13	=C90-$C$97	0.07	=E90-$E$97	=D90*F90
91	7	0.14	=C91-$C$97	0.02	=E91-$E$97	=D91*F91
92	8	0.15	=C92-$C$97	0.03	=E92-$E$97	=D92*F92
93						
94	Total					=SUM(G85:G93)
95	Covariance					=G94/(B92-1)
96	Correlation coefficient					=G95/(C99*E99)
97	Average return	=SUM(C85:C92)/8		=SUM(E85:E92)/8		
98	Correlation coefficient			=CORREL(E85:E92,$B$66:$B$73)		
99	Standard deviation	=STDEV(C85:C92)		=STDEV(E85:E92)		

Table 1.11 Spreadsheet functions for Table 1.10

VaR volatility

	A	B
128	Average return	12%
129	Standard deviation	2.40%
130	Required VaR	95%
131		
132	Number of standard deviations	−1.6449
133	Volatility or VaR	−3.95%

Table 1.12 VaR volatility

	A	B
128	Average return	0.12
129	Standard deviation	0.024
130	Required VaR	0.95
131		
132	Number of standard deviations	=NORMSINV(1-B130)
133	Volatility or VaR	=-B132*B129

Table 1.13 Formulas behind VaR volatility

Table 1.12 shows how we would calculate the VaR for an individual share or security. We simply calculate the standard deviation using either the implied volatility or the historical volatility. We want the VaR figure at the 95 percent level. This means that we want 5 percent in the left-hand tail, as shown in Figure 1.5. The normal distribution tables reveal that if a variable is to reach the bottom 5 percent, it must be at least 1.645 standard deviations below the mean. (Readers can check this by looking up −1.645 in the normal distribution tables in Appendix 11.2.) The Value at Risk is, therefore, 1.645 × 0.024 = 0.040 and this represents the Value at Risk at the 95 percent level. If a portfolio consisted exclusively of £1 000 000 of the above asset, the VaR would be £1 000 000 × 0.04 = £40 000. This is the maximum loss we would expect over a given time period, say one year, 95 percent of the time.

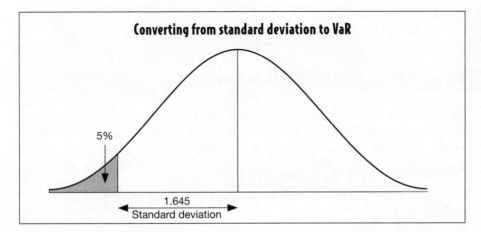

Converting from standard deviation to VaR

5%

1.645
Standard deviation

Fig 1.5

Value at risk of a portfolio

Now that we know how to calculate the standard deviation of an individual security, the next step is to calculate the VaR of an entire portfolio. We start with a two-asset portfolio and in later chapters move onto a multiportfolio asset. The variance of a two-asset portfolio is as follows:

$$Var(p) = w1^{2*}\, \sigma1^2 + w2^{2*}\, \sigma2^2 + 2^*w1^*\, w2^*\, \sigma1^*\, \sigma2^*\rho$$

where $w1$ = the weighting on the first asset
  $\sigma1$ = the volatility or standard deviation of the first asset
  $w2$ = the weighting of the second asset
  $\sigma2$ = the volatility or standard deviation of the second asset
  $\rho12$ = the correlation coefficient between the first and second asset.

The VaR is simply the square root of the variance.

We can now look at a few examples to illustrate this:

	A	B	C	D
		A	B	C	D
113	First security	Example 1	Example 2	Example 3
114	Volatility	2.45%	2.45%	2.45%
115	Weighting	50.00%	50.00%	50.00%
116				
117	Second security			
118	Volatility	9.44%	9.44%	9.44%
119	Weighting	50.00%	50.00%	50.00%
120	Correlation coefficient	− 0.927	0	1.000
121				
122	Portfolio variance	0.13%	0.24%	0.35%
123	Diversified VaR	3.61%	4.88%	5.94%
124	Undiversified VaR	5.94%	5.94%	5.94%

Table 1.14 Undiversified VaR

Table 1.15 illustrates the formulas behind Table 1.14.
The undiversified VaR is simply the weighted average of the indiviudal VaRs.
$5.94\% = 50\% \times 2.45\% + 50\% \times 9.44\%$

The variance of the first portfolio is: 0.13% =
$0.13\% = 50\%^2 \times 2.45\%^2 + 50\%^2 \times 9.45\%^2 + 2 \times 50\% \times 50\% \times 2.45\% \times 9.45\% \times (-0.927)$

The diversified VaR is the square root of the variance i.e. 3.6%.
Diversified VaR is $3.91\% \times £1,000,000$ (portfolio value) = £39,100.

	A	B
113	First security	Example 1
114	Volatility	0.02446
115	Weighting	0.5
116		
117	Second security	
118	Volatility	0.09436
119	Weighting	0.05
120	Correlation coefficient	=C106
121		
122	Portfolio variance	=B114^2*B115^2+B118^2*B119^2+2*B114*B115*B118*B119*B120
123	Diversified VaR	=B122^0.5
124	Undiversified VaR	=B115*B114+B119*B118

Table 1.15 Formulas behind undiversified VaR

A portfolio manager has £1m to invest and decides to split it evenly between two securities. The first security has a volatility (or VaR) of 2.45 percent. Therefore, if the portfolio manager invests £500 000 in this asset alone, the VaR is £12 250 at the 95 percent level. The second asset has a volatility of 9.44 percent or £47 200 if £500 000 is invested. We now examine this portfolio under three different assumptions. In the first case, the correlation coefficient is –0.924. You can see that the diversified volatility of the portfolio is much lower than the undiversified volatility. This is due to the fact that as one security is doing well, the other is doing badly and vice versa. The diversified VaR is, therefore, 3.91 percent of the portfolio, that is £39 100 in total. In the second case, the correlation coefficient is zero and so, although there are still benefits in diversification, these are not as strong as the first case. Finally, in the third case, with the correlation coefficient =1, it is an indication that both shares have the same underlying risks, and so there is no diversification benefits at all. In fact, the portfolio volatility of 5.94 percent is simply the weighted average of the two individual volatilities, namely 50 percent × 2.45 percent + 50 percent × 9.44 percent = 5.94 percent.

In practice, risk managers compute both diversified VaR and undiversified VaR. The diversified VaR is used when deciding limits. Limits are set so that resources can be allocated in a manner that minimizes risk while at the same time maximizing returns. The trade-off between risk and reward will depend on policies set by the bank's board of directors. In general terms, the risk manager will look for opportunities where he or she can diversify so that all of the assets are not exposed to the same risk.

The risk manager will also calculate undiversified VaR to measure his or her risk exposure if an event like a stock market crash occurs. In the panic that usually follows a crash, banks tend to liquidate whatever assets they can in order to stem potential losses. Usually, when there is a crash, little attention, if any, is paid to diversification; obviously, it gives speculators an ideal opportunity to make close to arbitrage profits. However, if there is a selling spree, all assets will fall in value, so it makes sense to assume that in times of crises, there is a one-to-one relationship between asset prices.

Conclusion

Up to now, we have looked in a very basic way at how VaR operates. VaR is simply a standard deviation calculation, which illustrates how volatile a portfolio is. A very volatile portfolio will generate a high VaR figure, and this will indicate to the investor or regulator that the institution concerned has a very high probability of making significant losses. VaR, as we will see in the next chapter, contributes to the science of risk management in three ways:

1 It helps to allocate resources more efficiently, in other words, to avoid being overexposed to one source of risk.

2 It makes traders and risk managers more accountable for their actions where they introduce risk or fail to hedge risk.

3 It helps regulators when deciding capital adequacy requirements for individual institutions.

While there is no dispute about the contribution that VaR makes to the science of risk management, there are several practicalities that we must take into account before we become overreliant on a single VaR figure. Foremost among these are the assumptions upon which VaR is based. Most models rely heavily on the normal distribution curve, which has many flaws. The normal distribution curve fails to capture unique characteristics of asset prices, namely the ease at which they can reach extreme values in times of market turbulence. There are also concerns about the way that volatility is calculated. We cannot assume that volatility remains constant and certainly cannot relax in the belief that past volatility is a guide to future volatility. In later chapters we address how risk managers are developing techniques to overcome these weaknesses. One important thing to remember is that when a bank decides to implement a VaR system, minds automatically become focussed on risk reduction, in the same way that audited annual reports focus minds on profitability. However, just as shrewd boards of directors have found creative accounting techniques to mislead the shareholder, VaR suffers from the same concept. Traders who are anxious to take on risk but not be held accountable for it can do so quite easily by structuring trades where the risk is not captured in the VaR model.

> *We cannot assume that volatility remains constant and certainly cannot relax in the belief that past volatility is a guide to future volatility. In later chapters we address how risk managers are developing techniques to overcome these weaknesses.*

Value at Risk as a Tool in Supervisory Regulation

Regulation: what it is and why it's necessary

There are three important contributions that Value at Risk and CreditMetrics (a version of RiskMetrics dedicated to the measurement of credit risk) can make toward risk management. First, they can encourage performance measurement. Traders, therefore, are not only rewarded for the profits that they earn, but also penalized for the risk they expose their banks to. Second, VaR and CreditMetrics can encourage a more efficient allocation of resources. This means that banks will diversify as much as possible in the hope of reducing risk or at least overexposure to one particular area. Third, VaR and CreditMetrics can help regulators to do their job. Regulators want to make sure that there is little chance of a financial institution going bust. If banks are forced to expose their risk profiles, regulators can assess the danger and then calculate whatever capital adequacy (or cushion) a bank must hold in order to prevent default. In this chapter we concentrate on the role of VaR as a method of assessing the risk of an organization and how it may help regulators to assess capital requirements. In Chapter 9, we look at how VaR principles can be extended to a bank's credit exposure (CreditMetrics) and how those risks can be reduced.

Reasons for regulation

There is always a very strong case for minimal government intervention in any industry. Indeed, the trend in all major international financial centers is toward self-regulation, with government intervention only where absolutely necessary. Regulation is nevertheless necessary to cure what economists call "externalities." Loosely speaking, the term "externalities" in this context refers to the damage that companies cause but are not necessarily accountable for. The standard example in economics is the company which produces chemicals that cause considerable pollution. The company is only accountable for the costs of producing the chemicals, that is to say the raw material costs but, in the absence of regulation, it is not accountable for the pollution it causes. The net result is that the company produces goods which cost more to society than the revenue or benefit it generates. That doesn't matter to the company, however, because it does not have to pay the full costs.

Banks are in a similar situation. A bank may take on huge levels of risk knowing that the rewards will be high. The worst that can happen is the bank itself going bankrupt. Shareholders lose the money they invested, but even this may not discourage the rational investor from taking risks, if the rewards are high enough. The "externality" arises because if one bank fails, it could create a crisis in the financial system, particularly if it is a retail bank. This, of course, will have a domino effect on other banks and could, if the troubled bank were large enough, cause the entire financial system to collapse in a manner similar to the

Wall Street crash of 1929. To overcome this potential problem central banks around the world impose certain conditions upon all licensed banks. These conditions are more severe on commercial banks and more lenient in certain aspects on merchant or investment banks. That said, central banks are less likely to bail out merchant banks compared to commercial banks.

Linear relationships: traders and risk

The reward system of banks and particularly of traders is often known as a non-linear relationship and this relationship normally concerns regulators. Consider a trader who is rewarded with a generous bonus scheme for profits that he or she contributes to the employing bank. The pay structure encourages the trader to take as many risks as possible. Whatever happens, the most a trader loses is his or her job. It makes more sense to take a lot of risks and achieve a high reward than to take low risks and achieve a low reward. This is because traders are not held fully accountable for the losses they make, in the sense that the most they lose is a job. A rational, if unethical, trader would, therefore, recognize that he or she has more to gain by exposing the banks to greater risks and not less. The trader's approach would be different, of course, if he or she were held accountable for **all** the losses.

Option traders will of course realize that this nonlinear relationship is the equivalent to a call option on the assets of a bank. A trader can participate in the profits but his "premium" is simply the cost of being fired if the assets go down in value. Option traders who are long call options are long volatility and hope, therefore, that the underlying asset becomes more volatile (or more risky). The most dangerous situation is the trader who has the ability to make the assets of the bank more volatile and more risky in order to suit his or her own ends.

Fig 2.1

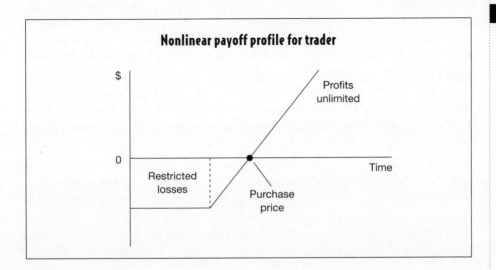

Nonlinear payoff profile for trader

Banks are in a similar situation. Suppose a bank knows that if things get bad the regulators will bail it out. The bank is encouraged to increase the volatility of its assets knowing that it is only held partly accountable for the losses it makes. Like the option trader, the bank has a "call option" on its own assets, and so will increase volatility in the hope of achieving higher profits. Nonlinearity also encourages lenders to go for the high premium but risky loans as opposed to the safe loans with low profit margins. Merchant banks are, by their nature, risk takers. This is why central banks are less willing to rescue them, compared to commercial or retail banks.

Correcting nonlinearity

The previous section illustrates the problem of externalities that regulators must try to correct. Where a nonlinear relationship exists and those who are long volatility have the power to influence it, this is a recipe for disaster. Value at Risk can, to some extent, overcome these problems, but it certainly cannot eliminate them. Under a VaR system, a trader who increases volatility will, in theory, alert the attention of his or her superiors because the VaR figure will increase. In an ideal system, the trader's bonus is linked to VaR and would have the effect of penalizing the trader for the extra risk he or she takes on. The result is that the trader thinks rationally and sensibly when taking on extra risk. In short, the trader will consider the risk–reward relationship rather than simply the reward side only. VaR can to some extent, therefore, cure this non-linear problem.

Similarly, regulators can (in theory) use VaR to reduce the "nonlinear" risk. Instead of simply giving a concrete guarantee that it will rescue banks that go into default, a central bank could instead implement an insurance system whereby the "premium" payable by those seeking protection is directly related to the risks that the bank undertakes. The idea behind good regulation is that only banks that take on excessive risks without hedging them should pay the penalty in the form of increased premium. The most undesirable situation is where the central bank imposes a uniform premium on all banks regardless of risk. Value at Risk can help regulators to achieve this objective by linking a bank's VaR with its capital adequacy payments. The more unhedged risk that a bank takes on, the greater its capital adequacy should be. This to some extent cures what insurers term "moral hazard." An example of moral hazard is where a car owner takes chances with his speed, knowing that if he crashes the car the insurance company will bail him out.

Barings Bank

When investigating the collapse of Barings Bank, the Bank of England's report placed a lot of emphasis on the lack of controls within Barings Bank. An important breakdown in this control was the fact that Barings was making payments to various future exchanges to cover losses by a single trader, Nick Leeson, but still believed that Leeson was making profits. In addition to being chief trader, Leeson controlled back-office duties on his own trades, which allowed him to hide those which were producing losses.

To some extent, Leeson faced a nonlinear situation. At one stage, he clocked up losses of $100 million and took the rational view that it was better to double the bet rather than to admit the original loss. He continued to gamble, perhaps anticipating that there was no difference (for him) between losing $100 million and $800 million, the most he would lose was his job. His gamble was, therefore, a one-way bet. He could recover existing losses by trading heavily or lose his job. Circumstances went against him, however, and he ended up losing $800 million which caused the collapse of Barings, and, of course, he also lost his job.

Poor regulation

One of the difficulties of regulating banks, as with any other type of enterprise, is that it can become costly to implement and may impose restrictions on banks unnecessarily, thus reducing their competitiveness. Obviously, where large profits are at stake, banks will use whatever power they have to get around the legislation. This means that those banks which are unwilling or unable to break the spirit of the legislation are left in a disadvantaged position. The consensus among most regulators is that regulation should not apply to banks which manage their risk well, but should only be directed at those banks which are at risk of collapse and a risk to the banking system in general. Regulation Q is an example of poor regulation. Under this regulation the American government placed a cap on the maximum amount of interest that banks could pay, in the hope that this would make banks less prone to collapse. The regulation cost the banks a lot of money in terms of opportunity cost, so they tried to devise ways around the law. For instance, they encouraged more customers to place deposits in their offices abroad (outside the scope of the regulation). Indeed, the growth in the Eurodollar market is partly due to Regulation Q. Value at Risk has an important role to play in helping regulators to devise a system which reduces the possibility of banks collapsing. If banks can become self-regulating, that is if they can produce a risk-measurement system that complies with the requirements of the regulators, then they can determine how much risk they are prepared to take and how much capital adequacy they are prepared to pay. In theory, therefore, banks that are careless with their risk controls, namely those that enter into deals which are risky, would be penalized because their VaR or credit at risk system would show a very high figure, and so the regulators would demand higher capital adequacy.

Capital adequacy and the Basle Accord – what it is trying to achieve

Regulatory history	
Basle Accord 1988	Committee set out procedures to establish a minimum standard of capital to cover credit risk.
Basle 1993 Proposals	Committee set out procedures to deal with market risk. These proposals introduced risk-measurement techniques to cover movements in interest rates, foreign exchange, equity, and commodities.
Basle 1995 Proposals	Encouraged banks to implement their own risk-measurement system. Capital adequacy calcaulations would then be based on this system.

Table 2.1 Summary of the Basle Accord and Proposals

The role of the capital adequacy rules is to identify how much risk the bank is exposed to and then to make sure that if it loses money it has enough in reserves to cover these losses. By imposing capital adequacy rules, the regulators force banks to keep enough money in reserves to meet potential losses. This means that depositors are protected. The downside for the banks concerned is that they are restricted in the amount of money they can lend out, so their earnings potential is restricted.

In 1988, regulators from the Group of Ten countries met to design an inter-national system for supervisory regulation. This committee became known as the Basle Accord, and its main objective was to design a system which protected the financial systems of individual countries, but at the same time was not too imposing on individual commercial banks. One area of agreement that they did reach was a common measure of solvency, which later became known as the Cooke ratio. This measure was designed to identify the level of credit risk that banks were exposed to the higher the credit risk exposure: the greater the capital adequacy requirement.

Measurement of credit risk

This system operated by examining each individual category of asset and then assigning a weighting system which recognized the level of credit risk of each instrument. For instance, rates of zero percent were allocated to assets that were considered to be credit risk free, that is government bonds and treasury bills. Cash and gold bullion were also included in this category. At the other extreme, weightings of 100 percent were imposed on assets such as equity, cor-porate bonds, and government debt from less developed countries.

Once the total risk was estimated, the Basle Accord calculated 8 percent and then looked at the financing structure of the bank. It divided the capital into two components: Tier 1 and Tier 2. Tier 1 represented cash that the bank raised from stock issues and certain reserves. Loosely speaking, reserves represent profits retained by the bank to cover certain eventualities such as future bad debts. Tier 2 capital consists of "supplementary" capital. These include liabilities to external parties. They comprise perpetual securities and subordinated debt. Long-term debt is also included.

Calculation of capital adequacy

Table 2.2 illustrates how capital adequacy was calculated.

Example

Balance sheet of Bank XYZ			
Assets	Weighting	Value	Credit risk capital
US Treasury Bills	0%	$100	$0
Cash	0%	$200	$0
Claims on other banks	20%	$500	$100
Loans to less developed countries	100%	$1000	$1000
Corporate bonds	100%	$1000	$1000
TOTAL		$2800	
			$2100
Capital charge 8%			$168
Liabilities and shareholders' funds			
Owners' funds			
Issued shares	$80		
Reserves	$40	$120	
Liabilities			
Long-term loans	$500		
Deposits	$2180	$2680	
TOTAL		$2800	

Table 2.2 Calculation of capital adequacy

In this case the assets of the bank are $2800 million. These assets are financed by "owners' funds," which means money raised from shares and money raised by retaining some profits to cover expected losses. The second source of finance is loans that include long-term loans and deposits from customers. The overall aim of the capital adequacy rules is to protect the depositors. On the asset side, some are deemed to be a credit risk and others are virtually risk free. The weighting system illustrates the level of risk. The total capital at risk is $2100. We then take 8 percent of this figure to get $168. The Basle rule is that 50 percent of this $168 must be from Tier 1 capital. In the example above, the Tier 1 capital is $120, and as this exceeds $84, the first requirement is satisfied. The second test, that both Tier 1 capital and Tier 2 capital must be greater than

$168 is also satisfied. Tier 1 capital is $120, and Tier 2 capital is $500, giving a total of $620.

Restrictions on lending

If the bank in the above case had failed either of the two tests, it would have had to restrict its lending. Suppose, for instance, that the Basle Accord had stipulated 20 percent instead of 8 percent. Then the capital adequacy figure would change from $168 to $420. Half of this figure is $210, and so the Tier 1 rule would be broken. The bank in this case would have either to sell risky assets or raise cash, either through issuing more shares or retaining more profits to keep within the rules.

Weaknesses of the Basle Accord

There are two very important weaknesses inherent in the above approach: market risk and portfolio risk.

1 Market risk

The Basle Accord concentrated almost exclusively on credit risk and its very simplified procedure failed to take sufficient account of market risk. For instance, depositors are at risk if interest rates go up and the value of all bonds held by the bank drops. There is, of course, an inverse relationship between bond prices and interest rates. A bank could hold a lot of bonds, which are very sensitive to changes in interest rates, and so those customers who held money on deposit would suffer. Depositors at Barings Bank, for instance, suffered, not because of a credit default, but because the market went against the position taken by Nick Leeson.

With the introduction of derivatives, the issue of market risk becomes more pronounced. Futures and options can show very violent swings for relatively small changes in the underlying asset. Option prices are well noted for their volatility. A bank with unhedged options could very easily find itself going bankrupt when the underlying asset changes by a relatively small amount. Value at Risk can offer potential solutions to this problem because it is, of course, designed to see how exposed a bank is to changes in stock market indices, interest rates, and foreign exchange. However, as we will see later, many VaR models have difficulty in dealing with nonlinear instruments such as options. In later chapters we examine how statistical approaches, such as Monte Carlo simulation, can be used to identify the VaR associated with options.

Unfortunately, given the complexities of many financial instruments, the calculation of capital at risk is no easy task. Regulators are, therefore, left with the choice of producing a few simple rules which will capture most market risk, or introducing a complex set of rules which captures market risk with more precision. Both approaches require a considerable compromise. Simple rules may not be effective and complex regulation may have the effect of enhancing as opposed to controlling market risk if it is not drawn up properly.

Most risk managers and regulators believe that the only way forward is for banks to implement a risk-measurement system which meets with the approval of the regulators. Banks will, therefore, measure their own risk and calculate capital adequacy accordingly. That said, the main problem is in coming up with guidelines that determine whether a risk-measurement system is adequate. Indeed, there is a strong likelihood that a system like JP Morgan's RiskMetrics will meet with regulators' approval. However, there are some weaknesses with the RiskMetrics approach, which regulators are currently unhappy with. For the moment, regulators multiply VaR figures by an arbitrary factor (currently 3) to overcome possible inadequacies in the various models. RiskMetrics has, unlike other VaR packages, disclosed to the general public its "engine room" and has encouraged experts to offer positive criticism. Many academics have responded to this request. Their feedback is analyzed in Chapter 11. RiskMetrics will, of course, take this on board for future designs and document updates.

2 Portfolio credit risk

The capital adequacy rules do not reward a bank that nets its position. Often, for instance, banks will have no hesitation in entering into an interest rate or currency swap with a customer who already has money on deposit with the bank. To protect themselves, banks will enter into an offsetting arrangement with the counterparty whereby, if the counterparty defaults, the bank can off-set the shortfall against the deposit account. The simplified capital adequacy rules ignore offsetting arrangements and, as a result, overestimate the capital adequacy required from the bank. Where banks are not rewarded for prudent risk measures, they may not bother to look out for them. Also, the approach fails to consider diversification. For instance, a bank which lends 50 percent of its portfolio to, say, American broadcasting and media companies and 50 percent to British energy companies is more diversified than a company that lends 100 percent to British energy companies. The simplified capital adequacy rules developed by the Basle Accord in 1988 are not capable of making this distinction.

Correlation

Example

A bank with assets of $1 000 000 lends 50 percent of its portfolio to British energy companies and 50 percent to American broadcasting companies. Since loans have a weighting of 100 percent, how much capital adequacy should be paid?

	C	D	E	F	G
28		1	2	3	4
29	Value of portfolio	$1 000 000	$1 000 000	$1 000 000	$1 000 000
30	American broadcasting weighting	50%	50%	50%	50%
31	British energy weighting	50%	50%	50%	50%
32	Correlation	1	0.5	0.4	0.1
33					
34	Capital at risk no diversification	$1 000 000	$1 000 000	$1 000 000	$1 000 000
35	Portfolio capital at risk diversification	$1 000 000	$866 025	$836 660	$741 620

Table 2.3 Diversification of credit risk

In theory, the answer should depend on the degree of correlation between the two sectors. Banks can diversify their risks away if they do not over concentrate on one area. Table 2.3 shows that the capital at risk in case one is $1 000 000 when there is no diversification. If the correlation coefficient is equal to 1, then there is no benefit from diversification, and so the diversified capital at risk is the same as the undiversified capital at risk. In the second case, we assume that the correlation coefficient is 0.5. This means that if the British energy sector suffers, there is a small chance that American broadcasting companies will suffer as well. We can see that as the correlation coefficient gets lower, the diversified capital at risk is also lower. Remember that the correlation coefficient in this context measures the relationship between two companies. The above table simply shows that where the correlation coefficient is low, there is little risk of both companies going down together, and so the capital at risk calculation should reflect this.

The Basle 1988 rules ignore correlation and so for each of the cases above, the capital at risk would be $1 000 000. Thus, the Basle rules ignore the benefits and so do not reward banks which control risk through diversification.

Table 2.3 is based on the portfolio calculations discussed in Chapter 1. The spreadsheet formulas behind this table are shown in Table 2.4.

The value of the portfolio $1 000 000 is contained in cell D29 and the weightings and correlations are contained in D30, D31 and D32 respectively. The portfolio capital at risk is based on the formula:

$$\sqrt{w1^2 + w2^2 + 2w1w2\rho}$$

	C	D
28		1
29	Value of portfolio	1000000
30	American broadcasting weighting	0.5
31	British energy weighting	0.5
32	Correlation	1
33		
34	Capital at risk no diversification	=D29
35	Portfolio capital at risk diversification	= (D29^2*D30^2+D29^2*D31^2+2*D29*D30*D29*D31*D32)^0.5

Table 2.4 Spreadsheet formulas for diversification of credit risk

1993 Proposals of the Basle Committee

In 1993, the Basle Committee introduced what has now become known as the "Standard Model." This involves breaking the assets of a bank down into four separate portfolios. The breakdown was based on how the portfolios reacted to different market events. There are four sources of market risk:

1 Interest risk
2 Equity risk
3 Foreign exchange risk
4 Commodity risk.

Assets were grouped together based on their exposure to each of the above, and so four separate portfolios were created. VaR was then calculated on each of these portfolios and then added together.

Interest rate risk

In Chapter 5 we illustrate how VaR is a more precise method of calculating interest rate sensitivity because, unlike the traditional 'modified duration' approach, VaR accommodates shifts as well as changes in the slope of the yield curve. Modified duration measures how exposed an instrument is to a change in interest rates. If interest rates go up, bond prices will fall and vice versa. Bonds with long maturities are more exposed to interest rate risk than bonds with short maturities, and this difference should, of course, be reflected in any risk-measurement system. A bond with a duration of –5, for instance, loses 5 percent of its value if interest rates increase by 1 percent. The higher the duration, the higher the potential loss. To measure interest rate risk, banks calculate the duration of their portfolio of bonds and then estimate how much they could lose if interest rates increase. Table 2.5 illustrates how duration risk operates.

Bond	Duration	Market value	Duration X Market value
Truhand 7.75% Oct 3	5.700	$287 030 000	$1 636 071 000
Bund 8% July 3	5.450	$179 020 000	$975 659 000
		$466 050 000	$2 611 730 000
Portfolio duration		5.604	

Table 2.5 Interest rate risk

The portfolio above comprises two bonds. The individual duration of the bonds are 5.7 and 5.45 respectively. The portfolio duration is simply the weighted average of the two bonds $2 611 730/$466 050 000 = 5.604. The portfolio in this case would fall by 5.604 percent or $26 117 if interest rates went up by 1 percent.

The Basle Committee's approach is not too dissimilar to the calculation shown above. The purpose of the calculation was simply to recognize both the market value of the bond and the sensitivity of the bond's price to a change in interest rates. Once the weighting of the portfolio was known, the 8 percent capital charged applied. The rules also allowed for a reduction in the portfolio to reflect netting positions.

Currency, equity, and commodity risk

The Basle Committee proposed that 8 percent be applied to the balance in the portfolio for currency and equity, and 15 percent for commodities.

Should regulators recognize diversification?

Lack of diversification

Although the 1993 proposals were an improvement on the previous set of proposals, they once again failed to recognize the importance of diversification.

Case profile

Interest Rates and Exchange Rates

The forward exchange rate of any currency is to a large extent influenced by the interest rates. The country with the higher interest rate usually suffers a lower forward exchange rate. Otherwise an arbitrage opportunity situation would arise. If a trader knew that interest rates in the USA were greater than the UK and he also knew that the dollar was going to appreciate in the future, it would make sense now to borrow in sterling, convert to dollars and reconvert when the dollar gets stronger. Such arbitrage opportunities seldom arise. We can conclude therefore that if interest rates are relatively low, the exchange rate will probably appreciate in the long term and if they are high, the opposite will occur. VaR, unlike traditional risk measurement systems, captures this relationship and so gives a more realistic profile. Due to the rules of arbitrage, the probability of a bank losing money both from an interest rate change and an exchange rate movement is often very remote.

Relationship between interest rates and exchange rates

Table 2.6 illustrates the relationship between interest rates and foreign exchange rates. There is a strong correlation between the two. The risk-management system proposed by Basle in 1993 fails to recognize this relationship because it simply sums the VaR of each of the four portfolios. As a result VaR is overstated and although regulators who fail to recognise diversification are being prudent, the ideal risk-management system is one that recognizes the relationship between interest rates and foreign exchange rates. Banks can, for instance, reduce their exposure by going long sterling or going long the dollar in certain instances. Indeed, they may end up reducing their risk through sensible diversification while the bank insists on greater capital adequacy.

Spot rates	1.5
Interest rate UK	10%
Interest rate USA	12%
Forward rate	1.527
Borrow	$1 000 000
Convert to dollars at spot	1 500 000
Invest in US bank account	1 680 000
Convert back to sterling at forward rate	$1 100 000
Repay British loan	–$1 100 000

Table 2.6 The relationship between rates of interest and foreign exchange

Table 2.6 shows that there is a negative relationship between American interest rates and the dollar exchange rate. In the above case, a trader borrows $1 000 000 on January 1 and converts it into dollars. This approach makes sense because the dollar interest rate is higher than sterling, so the trader receives more interest than he pays. However, when he reconverts back to sterling, he loses out because the dollar has depreciated. In short, the trader cannot have it both ways. Either the trader benefits from a stronger dollar or from higher interest rates. If one could have it both ways, an arbitrage profit opportunity would exist. An arbitrage profit opportunity exists where a trader can make a guaranteed profit without taking on any risk. The conclusion to be drawn from the above is that if American interest rates go up, the dollar will depreciate against sterling, and if British interest rates go up the dollar will appreciate against sterling.

Consider a trader whose interest portfolio is long British bonds and whose foreign exchange portfolio is long dollars. If British interest rates go up, the likelihood is that the dollar will appreciate against sterling. Therefore, the British bond will drop in value and the foreign exchange portfolio will increase in value because the trader is long the dollar. Basle Committee's 1993 proposals failed to recognize this with the result that it overcharges VaR.

Correlation and diversification

Generally, if the correlation between assets is quite low, then there are diversification opportunities and a risk-management system should be able to pick this up. To recap, correlations can have a value between 1 and –1. If the correlation is 1, then there are no diversification opportunities and if it is –1 there is plenty of scope for diversification. Regulators, however, are sometimes reluctant to incorporate diversification into their rules for calculating capital adequacy. To some extent their fears are understandable. Consider a situation where there is a severe crash. Correlation across all assets tends to move closer to 1. In other words, when there is a crash, banks and other financial institutions are anxious to sell everything and so all asset prices fall together. A risk system that rewards diversification in such circumstances would have estimated VaR correctly in normal circumstances and underestimated VaR in extreme circumstances. Since risk management is more concerned with extreme as opposed to normal circumstances, the view of the regulators, though overprudent in 99 percent of cases, is understandable.

In fact, most risk managers now tend to calculate two types of VaR, the undiversified and the diversified. The diversified VaR is used to examine resource allocation. Banks naturally want to exploit diversification opportunities as much as possible. Diversified VaR is also used for setting limits. However, undiversified VaR will probably give a more accurate picture of what can happen in extreme circumstances where banks' first priority would be to liquidate assets, regardless of the correlation implications.

Self-regulation

The difficulty facing regulators is that they must introduce a system simple enough to ensure compliance and complex enough to make sure that risk is measured correctly. Their task is not made any easier by the increased use of derivatives such as options, futures swaps, and the even more complex exotic options and instruments. In line with this, banks are becoming more sophisticated in their approach to dealing with risk. Virtually all banks now have a separate risk-management team whose role, in addition to complying with regulator rules, is to make sure that their banks are implementing the appropriate controls to cover market risk, liquidity risk, credit risk and perhaps the most important, market risk. Most banks have now incorporated sophisticated risk-measurement systems to control their risks and, of course, it makes sense if regulators exploit these developments rather than binding banks to a system of rigid rules and regulations.

In 1995, the Basle Committee recommended that banks could utilize their own risk-measurement systems for the purpose of calculating VaR. The role of the regulator is, therefore, confined to developing parameters, which the individual risk systems must comply with, and then to review the model on a regular basis.

The new approach set out how VaR should be computed. To recap, VaR measures the potential loss that a bank can suffer over a given time period and with a certain confidence interval. The Basle Committee has recommended that banks use a 99 percent confidence interval over a ten-day period. The new proposals have also allowed banks to calculate diversified VaR. The system would allow banks to calculate VaR and then the regulators would apply a risk factor. Where a regulator was unhappy with the model he could adjust the risk factor upwards. The minimum risk factor was set at 3 and regulators had discretion to exceed this if the model had flaws or could not be adequately relied upon. This obviously put pressure on banks not only to adopt the best risk practices, that is to avoid risky products unless absolutely necessary, but also to utilize the best risk-measurement system. Otherwise, they were at risk of facing a multiple higher than 3.

Backtesting

Part of the Basle recommendations involves testing a model by comparing forecasts with what has actually happened. This is known as backtesting. The framework which the Committee proposed involves using data from the past 12 months and comparing them with what the model generates. The Committee indicated three possible outcomes: Green Zone, Yellow Zone, and Red Zone.

A model would be awarded the Green Zone label if out of 250 observations, there were fewer than four exceptions. A Yellow Zone label would be awarded if the number of exceptions was between five and nine. Where models fall into the Yellow Zone, bank regulators would increase the multiplication from the minimum of three.

Finally, if there were ten or more exceptions, the bank's model would be considered unreliable. The regulator in these cases would increase the multiplication factor by one and then carry out investigations.

Conclusion

The growth in the complexity of financial instruments has lead to a risk environment which is more sophisticated. In the past, risk measurement was confined to measuring credit exposure. Today, financial regulators must monitor the possibility that a bank will go bankrupt if there are changes in other variables such as interest rates, exchange rates, and equity prices. Regulators face a trade-off. They can implement a simple system that is easy to comply with, but expose themselves to the problem of not measuring risk properly. The alternative is to implement a very complex system that measures risk accurately, but is extremely difficult to comply with. Rather than choose either of these options, an alternative is to allow the banks to measure their own risk and then report this risk to the Bank of England. This alternative has the attraction that the risk-measurement system can be tailored to suit the needs of individual banks and is, therefore, easier to comply with.

To make sure that the risk system is good enough to measure risk accurately, regulators and supervisors will regularly backtest the system. This means comparing estimated results with actual results. If there is a mild deviation, the regulators may apply a scaling factor which effectively penalizes the bank for not implementing a system which is accurate enough.

In terms of diversification, regulators prefer to play safe and assume that no diversification opportunities exist. Diversification opportunities exist when banks can allocate their portfolio in such a way that not all their eggs are in one basket. Some regulators believe that while negative or zero correlation between some assets may exist, in extreme situations such as a market collapse, all assets, whether diversified or not, will lose value and so diversification has no real relevance with extreme events. However, in 99 percent of the cases, ignoring diversification overstates VaR, and if a VaR system fails to reward banks which diversify, there may not be the same incentive to do so.

Portfolio Risk Measurement

A profile of VaR methods

Introduction

Much of the literature written on VaR criticizes various calculation approaches, but for the majority of readers, this criticism goes over their heads simply because they do not fully understand what is being criticized. Many books talk of matrix calculations and refer to variance covariance matrices. Therefore you will need to gain a good understanding of how matrices are applied to VaR calculations. In this interactive chapter, we outline what matrices are and how they can be used to calculate VaR. We also illustrate how the concept of correlation can be incorporated into a multi-asset portfolio. Although the chapter makes reference to spreadsheets and those who study this chapter with an Excel package will benefit, we have deliberately kept the examples simple so that readers without spreadsheets will be able manually to work through the examples. At the end of the chapter, readers will be able to simulate the essential features of JP Morgan's RiskMetrics on spreadsheets. They will also be able to experiment with VaR to see what variables contribute most to Value at Risk. This chapter will also illustrate how we can "decompose" various instruments to be able to analyze in detail the various risks involved. We also show how we can map instruments, such as derivatives, into VaR packages.

Readers will, of course, have already come across the concepts of correlation and volatility. In Chapter 1 we outlined how we could calculate VaR for a portfolio of two assets. We now extend this analysis to show how we can calculate VaR for a multi-asset portfolio using matrices. There is a variety of ways to calculate VaR. At present, the most popular method is the one adopted by JP Morgan's RiskMetrics package, known as the variance covariance approach. This involves using matrices and asset variance models developed by JP Morgan. While the variance covariance approach has many weaknesses, it is reasonably accurate, particularly for non-option instruments.

Traders and portfolio risk managers, anxious to reduce risk, but at the same time to reap the rewards for risk, will benefit from a good understanding of how correlation works in a multi-asset portfolio. Also, risk managers who are undecided between VaR systems will need to know what matrices mean if they intend to read further on VaR. Virtually all the literature and publications on VaR make reference to matrices. This chapter introduces the concept of matrices to VaR calculations. We will first calculate the standard deviation, and hence the volatility of an asset, in the conventional way, and then redo the example using matrices.

Conventional VaR calculations

A portfolio worth $1m is invested in two assets. The risk manager wishes to calculate the standard deviation of the portfolio and hence the VaR at the 95 percent level. The details of the portfolio are set out in Table 3.1.

	B	C	D
2	Value of portfolio	$1 000 000	
3	Confidence level	95%	
4	Time period	1	
5			
6		Asset	Asset
7		One	Two
8	Standard deviation	25%	26%
9	Weighting	30%	70%
10	Correlation coefficient		0.70
11			
12	Variance of portfolio	0.05786	
13	Standard deviation	24.05%	
14	No. of standard deviations	1.644853	
15	Value at Risk %	39.565126%	
16	Value at Risk $	$395,651	

Table 3.1 Portfolio VaR

We use the portfolio standard deviation formula below to calculate the figure 24.05 percent. In this case the first weighting is 30 percent and the first standard deviation is 25 percent. The correlation coefficient P is 0.70. The variance of the portfolio is therefore

$$0.25\wedge2*0.30\wedge2+0.26\wedge2*0.70\wedge2+2*0.25*0.30*0.26*0.70*0.70 = 0.05786$$

and the square root of this figure is 24.05 percent. We then look up how many standard deviations are needed to calculate VaR at the 95 percent level. This is obtained from the normal distribution tables (Appendix 11.2) and gives 1.645. Therefore, we multiply this by 24.05, and then multiply this by the value of the portfolio to get $395 651. This means we are 95 percent confident that our losses will not exceed $395 651. This is the VaR figure. The portfolio standard deviation formula is:

$$\sqrt{w1^2\sigma1^2 + w2^2\sigma2^2 + 2w1w1\sigma1\sigma2\rho}$$

Table 3.2 shows the spreadsheet formulas behind Table 3.1.

	B	C	D
2	Value of portfolio	1 000 000	
3	Confidence level	0.95	
4	Time period	1	
5			
6		Asset	Asset
7		One	Two
8	Standard deviation	0.25	0.26
9	Weighting	0.3	0.7
10	Correlation coefficient		0.7
11			
12	Variance of portfolio	=C8^2*C9^2+D8^2*D9^2+2*C8*C9*D8*D9*D10	
13	Standard deviation	=C12^0.5	
14	No. of standard deviations	=NORMSINV($C$3)	
15	Value at risk %	=C14*C13	
16	Value at risk $	=C15*C2	

Table 3.2 Spreadsheet formulas behind VaR calculation

The value of the portfolio $1 000 000 is contained in cell C2 and the confidence interval is in cell C3. The standard deviations are in cells C8 and D8 respectively.

Matrix calculations

In this section we show how to use matrices to achieve the above result. Readers who are unfamiliar with matrices should first read Appendix 3.1, wherein we give a brief explanation of how to multiply matrices.

Excel function

	B	C	D	E	F	G	H	I
21	Matrix			Matrix			Matrix	
22	one			two			three	
23	1	3		5	7		23	31
24	2	4		6	8		34	46

Table 3.3 Matrix multiplication

Excel provides a function to multiply matrices quickly. In Table 3.3, we wish to multiply Matrix one by Matrix two (to get Matrix three). Matrix one is contained in cells B23:C24 and Matrix two is contained in cells E23:F24. The steps for doing so are as follows:

1 Select the cells where you wish the result to appear. In the above case we have chosen H23:I24 for Matrix three. We know that the result must be a

2x2 matrix and so we must select four cells. (Appendix 3.1 gives an overview on matrix shapes.)

2 Type in the function =mmult(B23:C24,E23:F24)

3 Press Ctrl+Shift+Return (i.e. press all the keys together)

How matrices are used to calculate VaR

In this section we illustrate how we can apply matrix algebra to VaR calculations. This is the method chosen by RiskMetrics.

V		C		VC	
25%	0%	1	0.7	25%	18%
0%	26%	0.7	1	18%	26%
VC		V		VCV	
25%	17.5%	25%	0%	6.25%	4.55%
18.2%	26%	0%	26%	4.55%	6.76%

Table 3.4 Calculation of variance covariance matrix

The first step in a VaR calculation is to calculate a variance covariance matrix. In Table 3.4 we have constructed a "standard deviation" matrix based on the standard deviations contained in Table 3.1. Note that the standard deviations are placed along the horizontal axis of the matrix and the remainder of the matrix is filled with zeros. This requirement is necessary because of the special rules of matrices. The second matrix C is the correlation coefficient matrix. The reason why 1s are placed along the axis is explained below. They simply mean that assets within a portfolio have a correlation of 1 with themselves. Again, the figure 0.7 is obtained from Table 3.1.

Correlation matrix

The correlation matrix is analyzed below.

	Asset One	Asset Two
Asset One	1	0.7
Asset Two	0.7	1

Table 3.5 Correlation matrix: two-asset portfolio

The correlation matrix above simply states that Asset One has a correlation of 1 with itself and 0.70 with Asset Two. When constructing a correlation matrix it is important to maintain the symmetrical relationship along the diagonal. This is why 0.7 appears on both sides of the diagonal. Suppose we had a three-asset portfolio with the following correlations:

Correlation 1,2	0.8
Correlation 1,3	0.7
Correlation 2,3	0.6

We would construct a correlation matrix as follows:

	Asset One	Asset Two	Asset Three
Asset One	1	0.8	0.7
Asset Two	0.8	1	0.6
Asset Three	0.7	0.6	1

Table 3.6 Correlation matrix: three-asset portfolio

Variance covariance matrix

The variance covariance matrix is obtained by taking the standard deviation matrix, and multiplying it by the correlation matrix. This gives the VC matrix. We then multiply the VC matrix by the V matrix to get the VCV matrix.

Table 3.7 gives an intuitive explanation of the variance covariance matrix.

	Asset One	Asset Two
Asset One	6.25%	4.55%
Asset Two	4.55%	6.76%

Table 3.7 VCV matrix

Asset One has a variance of 6.25 percent which is what we would expect since the variance is the square of the standard deviation, that is $25\%^2 = 6.25\%$. Also Asset One has a covariance of 4.55 percent with Asset Two. Remember that the covariance formula is correlation coefficient 1,2 × standard deviation 1 × standard deviation 2. In this case, $0.7 \times 25\% \times 26\% = 4.55\%$. Finally, the figure of 6.76 percent is simply the variance of Asset Two, namely $26\% \times 26\% = 6.76\%$.

Portfolio standard deviation

The final step involves setting up a matrix for the weightings in the portfolio and then multiplying this by the variance covariance matrix. This is shown in Table 3.8.

W		VCV		WVCV	
30%	70%	6.25%	4.55%	5.06%	6.16%
		4.55%	6.76%		
WVCV		W		WVCVW	
5.06%	6.10%	30%			
		70%		5.79%	
		Standard deviation		24.05%	

Table 3.8 Calculation of portfolio standard deviation

The weighting matrix 30 percent and 70 percent was taken from Table 3.1. When using the weighting matrix, we place the figures in horizontal fashion as seen earlier. In other words, we want a one-row two-column matrix. When we multiply the weighting matrix by the covariance (2x2) matrix, we end up with a one-by-two matrix WVCV. Remember a (1x2) matrix multiplied by a (2x2) matrix gives a (1x2) matrix.

Once we know the standard deviation, we multiply this by 1.645 (to get a 95 percent confidence level) and multiply this by the value of the portfolio, that is $24.05\% \times 1.645 \times \$1\,000\,000 = \$395,651$, which represents the VaR, which is the same as Table 3.1.

Summary – variance covariance VaR

When calculating VaR we could adopt the method outlined in Table 3.1 and, although this method is quick and effective for a two-asset portfolio, it is impractical when dealing with a multi-asset portfolio. This section has outlined how we can use matrices to achieve the same result. The benefits of using matrices are that we can simply set up a weighting matrix (with hundreds of assets), a correlation coefficient matrix and a volatility matrix. We then simply multiply the matrices to obtain the standard deviation of the portfolio and the eventual Value at Risk. Readers should, of course, familiarize themselves with the relationship between standard deviation, correlation coefficient, variance, and covariance. Once they can understand this, they are in a position to understand the techniques behind the variance covariance approach and how RiskMetrics calculates VaR.

We now review some of the more important points discussed in this section.

1 The variance covariance approach relies heavily on matrices to calculate the VaR. Under the system, the benefits of diversification are captured because a lower VaR figure is produced. (Readers can see this for themselves if they alter the correlation coefficient and examine how VaR changes. A lower VaR figure is achieved if 0.70 is replaced with –0.80 for instance).

2 The variance covariance matrix is obtained by calculating VCV. This means that we multiply the volatility matrix by the correlation matrix and then multiply the volatility matrix again. The correct order of the matrices is important.

3 When setting up the volatility matrix we put the standard deviations along the diagonal and use zeros for all the other elements. So, if we have a portfolio with four assets, we set up a four-by-four matrix and place the volatilities along the diagonals. We fill the remainder of the matrix with zeros.

4 When setting up the correlation matrix we place 1s along the diagonals and then put the correlation coefficients in the remaining cells. Note that the correlation matrix is a mirror image of itself along the diagonal.

5 Once we have the variance covariance matrix, we then use the weighting matrix to calculate the standard deviation of the portfolio. The weighting matrix will always be one row, and the number of columns depends on the number of assets in the portfolio. If a portfolio has ten assets, we use a (1x10) weighting matrix.

Comparison of the variance covariance approach with other methods, or which VaR method is best?

At this point, we make a comparison between the variance covariance approach and other methods of calculating VaR. We will then return to the variance covariance approach to look at more complex examples.

There are three common methods of computing Value at Risk:

1 variance covariance
2 historical
3 stochastic or Monte Carlo simulation.

The variance covariance method

The easiest method is the variance covariance method. This approach involves using "published" information on volatility and correlation and then constructing an internal weighting matrix. The process is probably the most popular because it is simple to construct. A bank wishing to calculate its VaR must simply construct a weighting matrix, and then obtain the volatility and correlation data from JP Morgan, which publishes and regularly updates its matrices on the Internet. There are a few limitations, however. JP Morgan's approach is not suitable for options. Also, there is the assumption that the relation between assets (i.e. correlation coefficients) are stable. This, of course, may not be true, particularly when there is a major event like a stock market crash. Additionally, JP Morgan's approach places an overreliance on the normal distribution curve. Very occasionally, asset returns are not normal and so JP Morgan's approach may give a biased result. That said, the RiskMetrics approach is intuitively appealing and widely used by risk managers. Rather than go for a state-of-the-art complex system, it sometimes makes sense to go for a model that is intuitively understandable and easy to implement. A slight compromise on precision can often lead to a substantial reduction in operational risk.

The historical method

Like the JP Morgan approach, the historical method is intuitively simple to understand. Risk managers simply keep a historical record of daily profit and losses within the portfolio and then calculate the fifth percentile for 95 percent or 1 percent for 99 percent VaR. As well as being simple, the historical approach is realistic. The same cannot be said for RiskMetrics because the volatilities and correlations are not actual figures, but estimates based on averages over a specified time. In extreme situations, these averages may not hold, so the RiskMetrics approach may not give a realistic result. The historical method is based on actual results and if, during the historical period, major market events happened, these would be picked up accurately by the historical system. A second advantage of the historical method is that it does not require "mapping." When constructing a weighting matrix for RiskMetrics, the instruments may not neatly fit into the model devised by JP Morgan. Therefore, awkward instruments must be broken down and "mapped" onto standard vertices published by RiskMetrics. This process, as we will see later, can be computationally cumbersome, and very often certain assumptions are necessary. With the historical approach, no mapping is necessary and there is no need to make assumptions.

The main weakness of the historical approach is that it is unsuitable if the weightings of the portfolio change, that is to say if the portfolio composition changes over time. To overcome this, the historical approach can be augmented by the historical simulation approach. Here we use the current portfolio composition, but use historical market data. If a current portfolio consists of 70 percent Asset One and 30 percent Asset Two, then we would obtain the share prices of Asset One and Asset Two for, say, the past 1000 days, and for each day calculate the value of the portfolio, keeping the current weightings of 30 percent and 70 percent constant. Obviously, this is more time consuming and, in the case of large portfolios, very demanding of computer resources.

The stochastic or Monte Carlo simulation method

This procedure involves asking a computer to generate a series of share prices using a "random walk" approach. The procedure can be quite complex and, although in terms of precision it is the most effective, it suffers from the fact that it is time consuming and, like historical simulation, demanding of computer resources. Where the portfolio is enormous, we can end up with hardware constraints. Stochastic simulation is probably very appropriate when a portfolio is complex, particularly where it contains many options. Banks writing exotic options would have considerable difficulty in calculating VaR using RiskMetrics and, although the historical approach might prove more accurate, it would be misleading if the historical market prices were unique. In such cases, the historical path would not be representative of all possibilities and, therefore, prices generated from a stochastic system would give a more realistic result.

Variance covariance with a three-asset portfolio

We now extend our analysis to a three-asset portfolio.

Table 3.9 shows a portfolio with a value of $5 000 000 invested in three assets. The correlation between each of the assets is also shown and this time we want to calculate VaR at the 99 percent level. Services like JP Morgan's RiskMetrics will be able to provide details of the volatility and the correlation, and the individual weighting matrix will be constructed by the bank whose VaR we are calculating.

	Weighting	Standard deviation
Asset One	30%	25%
Asset Two	25%	27%
Asset Three	45%	30%
Correlation		
1,2	0.6	
1,3	0.5	
2,3	0.3	
Value of portfolio	$5 000 000	
Confidence level	99%	

Table 3.9 Three-asset portfolio

The first step is to construct the volatility matrix. Up to now we simply took the standard deviation and constructed a volatility matrix by placing the volatilities along the diagonals. To comply with the RiskMetrics approach, we do things a little differently. Before constructing the standard deviation matrix we multiply each standard deviation by the confidence interval factor. Table 3.10 illustrates how this is done.

25%	0	0
0	27%	0
0	0	30%

Number of standard deviations
2.326341928

Volatility matrix

58%	0%	0%
0%	63%	0%
0%	0%	70%

Table 3.10 Volatility matrix

As before, we present the individual standard deviations along the diagonal axis. This time, let's assume that we wish to construct a 99 percent confidence interval, but using the RiskMetrics methodology. We first adjust the standard deviations. From the normal distribution tables (Appendix 11.2), a 99 percent interval is equivalent to 2.326 standard deviations. We then multiply each of the individual standard deviations by 2.326 to obtain the adjusted volatilities. We use this to calculate our variance covariance matrix.

Volatility at 95 percent confidence means – Standard deviation multiplied by 1.645 (this is also known as the "adjusted standard deviation").

Volatility at 99 percent means – Standard deviation multiplied by 2.326 standard deviations (again also known as the "adjusted standard deviation)".

When services like JP Morgan provide statistical information, they do not provide actual standard deviations. Instead, they calculate standard deviations themselves, but multiply them by either 1.645 or 2.326, depending on the level of confidence required.

Volatility matrix		
58.16%	0.00%	0.00%
0.00%	62.81%	0.00%
0.00%	0.00%	69.79%

Correlation matrix		
1	0.6	0.5
0.6	1	0.3
0.5	0.3	1

VC matrix		
58%	35%	29%
38%	63%	19%
35%	21%	70%

Variance covariance matrix		
33.82%	21.92%	20.29%
21.92%	39.45%	13.15%
20.29%	13.15%	48.71%

Table 3.11 Three-asset variance covariance matrix

Table 3.11 shows how the variance covariance matrix is calculated. The VC matrix is simply the volatility matrix multiplied by the correlation matrix and then we multiply the VC matrix by the V matrix to get the variance covariance matrix. The order of multiplying is, of course, very important. To recap: V × C = VC and VC × V = VCV.

Note that the correlation matrix is constructed in such a way that the figures above the diagonal are a mirror image of the figures below the diagonal and, of course, the diagonal contains 1s only. We can check to make sure that the variance covariance matrix is correct. The figure 33.82 percent represents the adjusted variance of Asset One. Therefore, if we square the adjusted standard deviation 58.16 percent, we should get 33.82 percent. Also, the figure 21.92 percent represents the adjusted covariance between Asset One and Asset Two. We can check this because the covariance is the adjusted standard deviation of the first asset multiplied by the correlation between the two assets, multiplied by the adjusted standard deviation of the second asset. Therefore, 58.16%*0.6*62.81% = 21.92%.

Finally, we use the weighting matrix and the VCV matrix to compute the VaR.

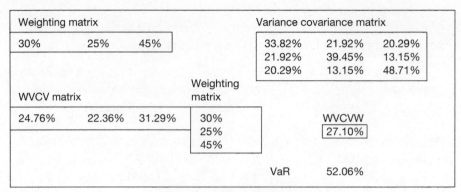

Table 3.12 Three-asset VaR matrix

The first weighting matrix is a (3×1) matrix and the variance covariance matrix is a (3×3) matrix. This gives a (3×1) matrix when multiplied. The WVCV matrix is (3×1). Finally, we rewrite the weighting matrix but this time into a (1×3) matrix. The WVCVW matrix is simply the (1×3) matrix multiplied by the (3×1) matrix to get a (1×1) matrix. The final step is to get the square root and this gives us the VaR in percentage terms, 52 percent.

Value at Risk – shortcut methods

Terminology

Undiversified VaR is VaR calculated on the assumption that the correlation between all assets is equal to 1. Thus, with undiversified VaR, the benefits of correlation are ignored. Many regulators believe that in extreme market situations, such as a crash, all assets will fall in value and so it is more correct to calculate undiversified VaR.

Diversified VaR is VaR calculated on the assumption that the correlation between assets is not always equal to 1. Diversified VaR recognizes the fact that banks which expose their portfolio to a wide range of assets do not suffer the same risk as banks investing all their portfolio in one type of asset. When setting limits, banks use undiversified VaR calculations to make sure that they are exploiting diversification to the full and reducing overall risk.

Now that you intuitively understand the calculation VaR using variances, we can introduce a few shortcuts to arrive at the above result. In this approach, we calculate the undiversified VaR and then use the correlation matrix to adjust the undiversified to the diversified.

Weighting matrix W'				Volatility matrix		
30%	25%	45%		58.16%	0.00%	0.00%
				0.00%	62.81%	0.00%
				0.00%	0.00%	69.79%
Undiversified VaR matrix W'V				Undiversified VaR		
17.448%	15.703%	31.406%		64.556%		

Table 3.13 Calculating undiversified VaR

Table 3.13 shows the weighting matrix and the volatility matrix as before. Since we are calculating undiversified VaR we don't need to concern ourselves with the correlation matrix at this stage. Calculating the undiversified VaR is a simple matter of multiplying the weighting matrix with the volatility matrix. The weighting matrix is (1x3) and the volatility matrix is (3x3). We total the undiversified matrix to arrive at 64.556 percent, which is the undiversified VaR. Since the value of the portfolio is $5m, the undiversified VaR is $3 227 775. Some readers may prefer to work with actual weightings as opposed to percentages, so we represent the above table using nominal as opposed to percentage weightings as shown in Table 3.14.

Weighting matrix W'				Volatility matrix V		
$1 500 000	$1 250 000	$2 250 000		58.16%	0.00%	0.00%
				0.00%	62.81%	0.00%
				0.00%	0.00%	69.79%
Undiversified VaR matrix W'V				Undiversified VaR		
$872 378	$785 140	$1 570 281		$3 227 799		

Table 3.14 Calculating undiversified VaR in sterling

To calculate the diversified VaR we use the correlation matrix. The diversified Var is simply W'VCV'W as before. Table 3.15 shows how this is calculated.

Undiversified matrix U	Undiversified matrix (transpose) U'		
17.448% 15.703% 31.406%	17.448%	15.703%	31.406%
	Correlation matrix C		
	1	0.6	0.5
	0.6	1	0.3
	0.5	0.3	1
	U' × C		
	42.572%	35.593%	44.840%
	U'CU	27.099%	
	Diversified VaR	52.057%	

Table 3.15 Adjusting undiversified to diversified VaR

As before, we need to construct the transpose of the matrix but this time we use the transpose of the undiversified matrix. We multiply U' by C, and then multiply the combined result by U again. As before, we get the square root, to arrive at the VaR. Note that the diversified VaR is, of course, a lot lower than the undiversified VaR, and is probably more realistic. Yet, regulators often prefer the "undiversified" VaR because in extreme situations the correlation of all assets tends to get closer to 1.

Constructing the weighting matrix

In the previous section, we saw that the calculation of non-option instruments is relatively straightforward. We simply construct a weighting matrix of the cash flows, and then use the volatility matrix and the correlation matrix to come up with a VaR. Tables 3.16 and 3.17 show how we can calculate the VaR of a portfolio of bonds. The first step, as before, is to calculate the weighting matrix.

	Bond One	Bond Two
Nominal value	$5 000 000	$7 000 000
Coupon	10%	12%
Years to maturity	4	5

Table 3.16 Bond portfolio

The portfolio above comprises two bonds. Bond One will mature in four years, so the cash flow for years one to three is 10 percent of $5 000 000 = $500 000, and for the final year, when the principal is returned, $5 500 000. For Bond Two, the cash flow for years one to four is $840 000, and for year five $7 840 000.

	Cash flow 1	Cash flow 2	Total value	Current yield	Present value	Price volatility	Undiversified VaR
1	$500 000	$840 000	$1 340 000	7%	$1 252 336	0.80%	$10 019
2	$500 000	$840 000	$1 340 000	8.000%	$1 148 834	0.83%	$9 535
3	$500 000	$840 000	$1 340 000	9.000%	$1 034 726	0.85%	$8 795
4	$5 500 000	$840 000	$6 340 000	9.500%	$4 409 941	0.87%	$38 366
5		$7 840 000	$7 840 000	9.750%	$4 923 721	0.90%	$44 313
							$111 029

Table 3.17 Calculating the undiversified VaR of a bond portfolio

Constructing the weighting matrix is straightforward. However, we must use the present value as opposed to the future value. Intuitively, the present value is the amount of money we must put in the bank today in order to have a certain sum of money in the future. For instance, if we put $1 148 834 in the bank today at 8 percent, we would have $1 340 000 in two years' time. The concept of present value is discussed in more detail in Chapter 4. The weighting matrix is shown under the present value column. Intuitively, we could interpret the weighting column as a portfolio of five bank accounts, that is we have put $1 252 336 on deposit for one year and $1 148 834 on deposit for two years, etc. It is important to realize that in terms of fixed-income products, the weighted average is always based on the present value of a future cash flow.

The final two columns calculate the undiversified VaR. RiskMetrics will, through their Internet site, be able to provide those figures in bond, namely the zero coupon yields and the price volatilities. Calculating the undiversified VaR, therefore, in the above case is quite straightforward.

Diversified VaR

To calculate the diversified VaR we would, of course, need the correlation matrix as well. RiskMetrics provide correlation matrices which show the correlation between, say, one-year rates, and two-year rates, etc. As before, we would multiply the transpose of the weighting matrix by the correlation matrix and then multiply this result by the weighting matrix.

Diversified VaR and duration

One important advantage that diversified VaR has over the traditional calculation of bond risk is that VaR recognizes the possibility that the slope of the yield curve may change. The traditional modified duration calculation involves calculating a sensitivity factor and assuming that this applies all the time. For instance, a bond with a modified duration of 3 means that if interest rates go up by 1 percent, the bond price falls by 3 percent. This is a typical duration application. Unfortunately the modified duration approach is very inaccurate for large changes in interest rates or where there is a significant change in the slope of the yield curve. VaR overcomes these problems.

Mapping

Vertices

VaR services like RiskMetrics do not provide volatility statistics for every day in the year. Instead, they provide volatility estimates for certain periods as follows:

> 1 month, 3 months, 6 months, 1 year, 2 years, 3, 4, 5, 7, 9, 10, 15, 20, and 30 years.

What happens if a bond has a cash flow in, say, five years' time, 1.5 years' time and 2.5 years' time? In an ideal world, RiskMetrics would provide statistical vertices for each day in the year up to, say, 30 years, and provide correlations between each of those days. In computational terms, this would be very difficult, and the amount of data involved would be enormous. To overcome this problem, RiskMetrics publishes data for specific periods and where a cash flow falls between those periods, a mapping procedure is used to allocate to this cash flow the ten vertices or points on either side.

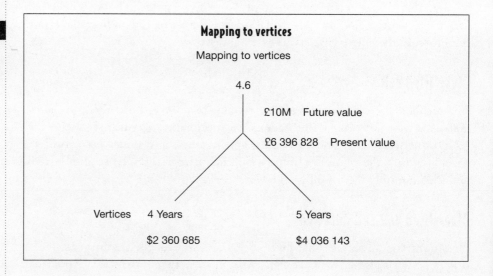

Mapping to vertices

Mapping to vertices

4.6

£10M   Future value

£6 396 828   Present value

Vertices   4 Years   5 Years

$2 360 685 $4 036 143

Figure 3.1 shows a cash flow of \$10m, which is due in 4.6 years' time. In Figure 3.1 we have used an interest rate of 10.2% to obtain the present value of \$6 396 828 to calculate the present value i.e. \$10 000 000 × (1+10.2%) ^ (–4.6)=\$6 396 828. RiskMetrics does not have volatility estimates for 4.6 years, so the cash flow is allocated to the two closest vertices, year 4 and year 5. In this case, most of the money is allocated to year 5 because 4.6 is closer to five than four. Unfortunately, the process of allocating cash between vertices is not straightforward. It would be tempting simply to allocate it evenly or to use a type of weighted average calculation. This would prove inaccurate. Remember that VaR is essentially a measure of volatility, and so when allocating a cash flow that does not fall neatly onto a vertex, we must apportion it in a manner that preserves the volatility characteristic.

Allocation of cash between vertices

There are three objectives used by RiskMetrics when allocating cash between vertices.

1 Market value must be preserved

Suppose a company is due to receive \$10m in 4.6 years, then the allocation to the two vertices must sum to the present value of \$10m.

2 Market risk must be preserved

Allocating to different vertices essentially involves splitting one asset into two separate assets and assigning each asset to the vertices on either side. The volatility of the portfolio of two assets must equate with the volatility of the original cash flow, otherwise the volatility characteristic is lost.

3 Sign must be preserved

To avoid practical calculation problems, we always show positive cash flows on the original vertices. For instance, if we were allocating a cash flow of \$6.83m, we could use a number of approaches which would preserve volatility, that is \$8m and -\$1.17m, or we could use \$3m and \$3.83m. The latter is preferable because both figures are positive.

Portfolio effect

For practical purposes, we use portfolio theory to allocate the cash. To recap, the formula for portfolio variance is:

$$\sqrt{\sigma 1^2\, w1^2 + \sigma 2^2\, w2^2 + 2\sigma 1 w1 \sigma 2 w2 p}$$

Example ## Assigning cash flows to vertices

	B	C
219	FV cash flow	$10 000 000
220	Period to maturity	4.6
221		
222	Yield year 4	**9.00%**
223	Yield year 5	**11.00%**
244	Volatility year 4	**0.533%**
225	Volatility year 5	**0.696%**
226	Correlation coefficient	**0.963**
227		
228	Lower period	4
229	Upper period	5

Table 3.18 Assigning cash flow to vertices

A bank is due to receive $10 000 000 in 4.6 years' time and wishes to calculate the VaR. RiskMetrics only provides statistics for four years forward and five years forward. The bank's risk system must map the present value of $10 000 000 between the vertices for four years and the vertices for five years. The first step is to calculate the present value. In calculating the present value we ask, "How much money should be put aside today to have a future value of $10 000 000 in 4.6 years?" Obviously, we need to known the zero coupon interest rate for 4.6 years, and we follow the approach used by RiskMetrics, namely linear interpolation.

	A	B
234	Alpha	0.4
235	Interpolated yield	10.200%
236	Interpolated volatility	0.6308%

Table 3.19 Linear interpolation

The interpolated yield in Table 3.19 must obviously be between the four-year rate of 9 percent and the five-year rate of 11 percent. Since 4.6 is closer to 5, we would expect the interpolated rate to be closer to 11 percent than to 9 percent. To get this result, we calculate alpha at 0.4, and then use the formulas as shown in the Table 3.20.

In Table 3.20 "alpha" is contained in the cell C234, and is used to calculate the interpolated yield and the interpolated volatility.

	A	B
234	Alpha	=(C229-C220)/(C229-C228)
235	Interpolated yield	=C234*C222+(1-C234)*C223
236	Interpolated volatility	=C234*C224+(1-C234)*C225

Table 3.20 Formulas for Table 3.19

The final part of the calculation involves constructing a portfolio, which achieves the three objectives we discussed earlier:

1 to preserve the present value of the cash flow
2 preserve volatility
3 keep the signs positive.

All of the above is achieved if we allocate a weighting of 0.36904 to vertex 4 and 0.63096 to vertex 5 as Table 3.22 shows.

To recap: a bank is going to receive $10 000 000 in 4.6 years' time. We need to allocate the present value of $6 396 828 between vertices 4 and 5 because no vertex for 4.6 years exists. We allocate $2 360 685 to vertex 4 and $4 036 143 to vertex 5. To confirm that we are correct, we assume that $2 360 685 and $4 036 143 are two separate assets in one portfolio. To calculate the volatility of the portfolio we utilise the portfolio formula below.

$$\sqrt{\sigma 1^2 w 1^2 + \sigma 2^2 w 2^2 + 2\sigma 1 w 1 \sigma 2 w 2 p}$$

where w1 is 0.36904, w2 is 0.63096, the volatilities are 0.533 percent and 0.696 percent respectively, and the correlation coefficient is 0.963. Notice that the portfolio volatility of 0.6308 (or 0.6308 × $10 000 000 = $6 308 000) is equivalent to the linear volatility that we calculated earlier.

		B	C	D
	256	Volatility 4 year yield	0.533%	
	257	Volatility 5 year yield	0.696%	
	258	Correlation (4,5)	0.963	
	259	Future value	$10 000 000	
	260	Yield	10.20%	
	261	Term in years	4.6	
	262	Present value	$6 396 828	
	263			
	264	Weighting vertex 4	0.369040	$2 360 686
	265	Weighting vertex 5	0.63096	$4 036 142
	266	Variance of portfolio	0.0039791%	
	267	Standard deviation	0.6308%	
	268			

Table 3.21 Construction of equivalent portfolio

The final step is to ascertain how the first weightings were calculated. Unfortunately, this can get very mathematical, so is relegated to Appendix 3.2 – Calculation of Mapping Weightings.

	B	C	D
256	Volatility 4 year yield	0.00533	
257	Volatility 5 year yield	0.00696	
258	Correlation (4,5)	0.963	
259	Future value	10000000	
260	Yield	0.102	
261	Terms in years	=4.6	
262	Present value	=C259/(1+C260)^C261	
263			
264	Weighting vertex 4	0.369040037001616	=C264*$C$262
265	Weighting vertex 5	=(1–C264)	=C265*$C$262
266	Variance of portfolio	=(C264^2*C256^2+C265^2*C257^2+2*C256*C257*C258*C264*C265)	
267	Standard deviation	=C266^0.5	
268			

Table 3.22 Formulas behind Table 3.21

Appendix 3.1
MULTIPLICATION OF MATRICES

Many of us will have come across matrices at school and at the time, as with most mathematical concepts, will have wondered how we would ever apply this knowledge in real life. Matrices are used extensively in computer-aided design programs. In the design of cars, for instance, engineers are able to represent prototypes by a series of matrices on computer, and with their knowledge of metal resistance then simulate road tests, check suspensions, and even perform a crash-test on computer. Matrices are also used by social scientists and biologists to simulate population growth, organic growth, etc. Today, teams of VaR designers can simulate market crashes and examine the impact of such crashes on various financial institutions. Value at Risk measures how a financial institution reacts to such crashes and so, like the prototype car design, VaR acts as a simulator using matrix concepts.

A		B		C	
1	3	5	7	23	31
2	4	6	8	34	46

Table A3.1.1 Matrix multiplication

Example

Table A3.1.1 contains three matrices. Each is a two-by-two, meaning that they have two rows and two columns. The first row (or row 1) of matrix A contains the elements 1 and 3, and the second row (row 2) contains 2 and 4. The first column of matrix A contains the elements 1 and 2, and the second column (column 2) contains the figures 3 and 4.

Matrix C is matrix A multiplied by matrix B. There are special rules for multiplying matrices which do not apply to ordinary mathematics. We examine these below. For the moment, the figure 23 in matrix C is in row one and also column one. Therefore, we multiply row one of matrix A by column one of matrix B. In other words, $(1 \times 5) + (3 \times 6) = 23$. The figure 31 is in row one and column two. Therefore, we multiply row one of matrix A by column two of column B. Thus, $(1 \times 7) + (3 \times 8) = 31$.

We obtain the second row of matrix C by using the same procedure. For instance, 34 is contained in both row two and column one. We, therefore, use row two of the first matrix (matrix A) and column one of matrix B $(2 \times 5) + (4 \times 6) = 34$. Finally, 46 is $(2 \times 7) + (4 \times 8)$.

Rules for multiplying matrices

Matrix order

Note that matrices unlike numbers are noncommutative. With numbers, we can change the order and this will not affect the product of the two numbers. For example $3 \times 4 = 4 \times 3$. However, we cannot say the same about matrices. Matrix A $\times$ matrix B in the above example gives matrix C. However, if we multiply matrix B by matrix A, we get an entirely different matrix. Therefore, the order of matrices is important.

Matrix shape

When matrices are of different shapes, there are special rules that we must check before we can multiply them.

A			B		C	
1	2	3	4	7	32	50
			5	8		
			6	9		

Table A3.1.2 Multiplication of different shaped matrices

Table A3.1.2 shows a (1x3) matrix, that is one row and three columns, and a 3x2 matrix (three rows and two columns). To multiply these matrices, we must first make sure that the number of columns in the first matrix equals the number of rows in the second matrix. In the above case, we have three columns in matrix A and three rows in matrix B, so the rule is not broken and we can multiply them. The outcome is a one-by-two matrix. This is because there is one row in the first matrix and two columns in the second. Figure A3.1.1 illustrates this rule. In the above case, $32 = 1x4 + 2x5 + 3x6$ and $50 = 1x7 + 2x8 + 3x9$.

Figure A3.1.1 shows that as long as the two "inside" figures are the same, the shape of the multiplied matrix is the two outside figures. In example 3, the two inside figures differ and so it is not possible to multiply matrix A by matrix B. Example 5 simply shows what readers will already have discovered in Table A3.1.2, namely that a 1x3 matrix multiplied by a 3x2 matrix gives a 1x2 matrix.

Rules for multiplying matrices			**Fig A3.1.1**
		Product of A and B	
	Matrix A	Matrix B	Matrix C
1	(3 x 4)	(4 x 6)	(3 x 6)
2	(2 x 3)	(3 x 4)	(2 x 4)
3	(4 x 5)	(6 x 4)	No solution
4	(1 x 7)	(7 x 7)	(1 x 7)
5	(1 x 3)	(3 x 2)	(1 x 2)

Transpose of a matrix

In Table A3.1.3 we present two matrices. Matrix M has a (3x4) shape and matrix W (the shape of a typical VaR weighting matrix) has a (1x3) shape. The transpose of matrices M and W are also shown. The convention is to call them M' and W'. M' has a 4x3 shape and W' has a (1x3) shape. As mentioned earlier, the shape of a matrix is important for multiplication. The number of columns in the first matrix must equal the number of rows in the second matrix. With VaR calculations this does not always happen, and we may be able to get around this problem by using the transpose of the matrix. So, for example, we cannot multiply a (3x1) matrix and a (3x4) matrix. However, if we get the transpose of the first matrix we may be able to eliminate this problem. Thus, (1x3) × (3x4) satisfies the multiplication rule.

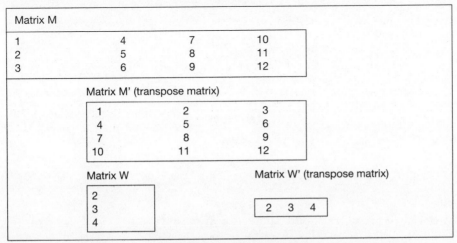

Matrix M

1	4	7	10
2	5	8	11
3	6	9	12

Matrix M' (transpose matrix)

1	2	3
4	5	6
7	8	9
10	11	12

Matrix W

2
3
4

Matrix W' (transpose matrix)

2	3	4

Table A3.1.3 Transpose of a matrix

Appendix 3.2
CALCULATION OF MAPPING WEIGHTINGS

Suppose we wanted to calculate the volatility for a cash flow that a bank will receive in 4.6 years' time. First we use RiskMetrics vertices to obtain the volatilities for the two closest periods. Then, using a linear interpolation technique, we calculate the volatility for 4.6 years, as shown in Figure A3.2.1. Since we know that the volatility of 4.6 is a linear combination of 4 and 6, we can derive a formula for its variance as follows:

Fig A3.2.1

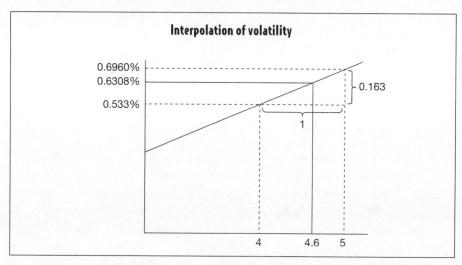

Interpolation of volatility

0.6960%
0.6308%
0.533%

0.163

1

4   4.6   5

Fig A3.2.2

Formula for variance of portfolio

$$\sigma_{xy}^{2} = \alpha^2\sigma_x^2 + (1 - \alpha)^2\sigma_y^2 + 2\alpha(1 - \alpha)\sigma_x\sigma_y\rho_{xy}$$

σ = Volatility α = Weighting $P_{x,y}$ = Correlation coefficient

We can manipulate the above formula so that it becomes a quadratic equation around alpha. We then solve the quadratic equation. Figure A3.2.3 shows how this is achieved and the formulas that are produced.

Fig A3.2.3

Solving for α

$$a\alpha^2 + b\alpha + c$$

$$P = \frac{-b \pm \sqrt{b^2 - 4ac}}{2a}$$

$$a = \sigma_4^2 + \sigma_5^2 - 2P_{4,5}\sigma_4\sigma_5$$
$$b = 2P_{4,5}\sigma_4\sigma_5 - 2\sigma_5^2$$
$$c = \sigma_5^2 - \sigma_{4.6}^2$$

We now present the spreadsheet table that calculates the weightings in the example contained in Table A3.2.1.

	B	C
270	Volatility year 4	0.533%
271	Volatility year 5	0.696%
272	Interpolated volatility	0.6308%
273	Correlation coefficient	0.963
274		
275	Variance lower vertex	0.00284%
276	Variance upper vertex	0.00484%
277	Variance cash flow	3.97909E-05
278		
279	a	5.40206E-06
280	b	-2.543E-05
281	c	0.00087%
282		
283	Weighting 1	0.369040037

Table A3.2.1 Weighting calculation

Finally we look at the formulas behind this in Table A3.2.2.

	B	C
270	Volatility year 4	0.00533
271	Volatility year 5	0.00696
272	Interpolated volatility	0.006308
273	Correlation coefficient	0.963
274		
275	Variance lower vertex	=C270^2
276	Variance upper vertex	=C271^2
277	Variance cash flow	=C272^2
278		
279	a	=C275+C276-2*C273*C270*C271
280	b	=2*C273*C270*C271-2*C276
281	c	=C276-C277
282		
283	Weighting 1	=(-C280-(C280^2-4*C279*C281)^0.5)/(2*C279)

Table A3.2.2 Spreadsheet formulas for the weighting calculation

Note that for the weighting, we have chosen the value that gives a positive sign to both vertices. Readers who are familiar with quadratic equations are, of course, aware that there are two possible solutions to calculating the weighting. Only one, however, is suitable, because we need to have positive values for both vertices.

Fixed Income Products

4

The range of fixed income products

Introduction

The pressures on risk departments have increased considerably because of the growth in new and complex products. One important contribution that VaR has, in relation to fixed income securities is that it can identify natural hedges by measuring risk on a portfolio basis. In this chapter we examine the growth in the complexity of fixed income products and illustrated how VaR can measure their risk.

The growth of derivative products has led to increasing complexity in the requirements and preferences of borrowers and investors. A new "structured finance" industry has evolved to cater for these requirements. Traditionally, investors and borrowers wanted little more than to reduce risk by converting from fixed interest payments to floating payments or vice versa. Now treasurers are more demanding in their financial engineering requirements and, while banks try to respond to these requests, new complications emerge which have risk implications. For instance, issuers of corporate bonds today want as much flexibility as possible in order to appeal to as wide an investor base as possible. The benefit of doing this, of course, is that they can issue notes to suit a wide range of investors, and so increase the demand and the price for the instruments they issue. With interest rates and currency swaps, therefore, an issuer can obtain a loan by issuing fixed and floating notes and, if necessary, foreign bonds, without incurring an interest rate or foreign exchange rate risk.

Option features

Today, options have a very important role to play in financial engineering.

Case profile

Interest rate option US mortgages

In 1981, many American thrift organizations issued mortgages to customers giving them the right, but not the obligation, to pay their interest at a fixed rate. Such an option is valuable if interest rates are high, but if interest rates fall, the customer could exercise the right to repay his or her existing mortgage and obtain a new one at a lower rate of interest. Needless to say, the thrift organization charged the customer for this option. To hedge themselves, these thrift organizations used exchange traded interest rate options, together with swaptions, and issued convertible bonds, which gave the thrift organizations the right to repay a fixed loan from an investor. Banks like Salomon Brothers carried out numerous studies on homeowner mortgage habits and concluded that the customers seldom exercised their options, that is they were collectively not very rational. This meant that Salomon Brothers were able to buy "blocks" of mortgages from thrift organizations, generating substantial profits.

Often, issuers will combine straightforward bonds with option features. They may, for instance, retain the right to redeem a bond in order to finance at a lower rate, should interest rates fall. Alternatively, to make the instrument attractive to investors who want to take a position on interest rates, corporates may issue instruments that give the holder or investor the right to redeem the bond.

In more complex situations, corporates work with swap dealers in order to structure a package which is mutually beneficial to both sides. Swaptions, for instance, give the payor the right, but not the obligation, to enter into an interest rate swap transaction. Often, a swap dealer who is short swaptions in his portfolio will give generous premiums to counterparties who want to write swaptions. Corporates take advantage of this by issuing a callable bond and writing a swaption. Combined, both behave like a fixed bond, but because swap traders give a generous premium, the cost of financing with redeemable bonds and swaptions can be substantially lower than a straightforward fixed bond.

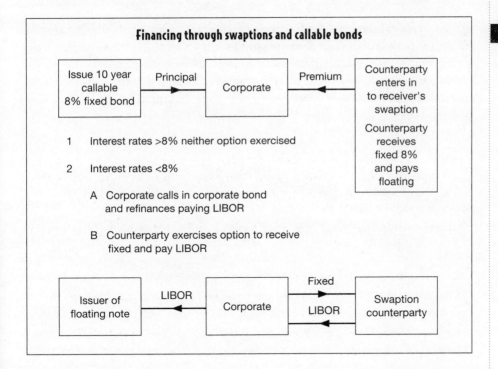

Financing through swaptions and callable bonds

Fig 4.1

Issue 10 year callable 8% fixed bond → Principal → Corporate → Premium ← Counterparty enters in to receiver's swaption

Counterparty receives fixed 8% and pays floating

1   Interest rates >8% neither option exercised

2   Interest rates <8%

   A   Corporate calls in corporate bond and refinances paying LIBOR

   B   Counterparty exercises option to receive fixed and pay LIBOR

Issuer of floating note ← LIBOR ← Corporate — Fixed / LIBOR → Swaption counterparty

Trader writes a receiver's swaption – Trader sells right but not obligation for counterparty to receive fixed payments and pay floating. If interest rates fall, trader must still pay fixed rate to counterparty.

Trader writes a payor's swaption – Trader sells right but not obligation for counterparty to pay fixed interest and receive floating. If interest rates rise, trader must pay floating rate to counterparty.

Trader buys receiver's swaption – Trader buys right but not obligation to receive fixed and pay floating. Loss restricted to the premium paid for the swaption.

Trader buys payor's swaption – Trader buys right but not obligation to pay fixed and receive floating. Loss restricted to the premium paid for the swaption.

The issuer in Figure 4.1 finds that there is a demand for callable bonds among investors, perhaps because these investors want to exploit a view they have on interest rates. At the same time, swap dealers are offering generous premiums to anyone who will write a receiver's swaption. Assume that the investor wants to raise cash by issuing a seven-year fixed coupon note. He has two choices open to him:

1 issue a seven-year note in the conventional way with a fixed coupon (say 8%)
2 issue a seven-year callable note and issue a receiver's swaption. Under this arrangement, the company may exercise its right to redeem the bond. Also, the counterparty to the swaption has the right but not the obligation to receive fixed and pay floating.

If interest rates go down, the counterparty will exercise his right to receive fixed and pay floating

Callable bond – This is a bond where the issuer has the right to buy back the bond it has issued. If interest rates fall, an issuer would normally call back a bond with a fixed coupon and refinance at the lower rate of interest.

Interest rates rise

Suppose the trader goes for choice 1. If interest rates rise, he pays fixed and if interest rates fall he pays fixed. For choice 2, if interest rates rise, the company pays the fixed rate on the callable bond and the counterparty to the swaption will not exercise his or her right.

Interest rates fall

If interest rates fall, then the company exercises its right to call in the bond and refinance by paying at LIBOR (see Glossary). However the counterparty to the receiver's swaption will also exercise his or her right to receive fixed and pay floating. Therefore, the company ends up paying fixed.

Which choice?

The issuer has a straightforward choice in this case. The issuer can compare the principal or cash raised from a straightforward fixed bond with the cash raised plus principal from choice 2. If the total funds from choice 2 are substantially greater than choice 1, then the corporate will go for choice 2, despite the complexities.

In theory, of course, a difference should not arise because all investors are rational and will see the arbitrage opportunities. In reality, the price paid for a callable or fixed bond is based on the laws of supply and demand. If there is a considerable demand for swaptions, they will be overpriced. Therefore, the payoff from option 2 will be greater. Alternatively, the market may be oversupplied with straightforward fixed bonds and so may become underpriced, compared to convertible fixed bonds. In reality, therefore, arbitrage opportunities do arise, not just for banks, but also for sophisticated international corporates. In fact, corporates like Pepsi Cola play the market regularly and are, therefore, demanding on the structured notes which they require from their bankers.

Combinations of credit derivatives and swaps

In the past, corporate bonds issued by Italian companies were grossly underpriced. Traders realized that, in addition to a credit premium, investors also wanted a liquidity premium to compensate for the fact that if they bought these bonds, they would have difficulty in selling them on. The growth of credit derivatives, however, gave some traders the opportunity to make arbitrage profits as Figure 4.2 shows.

In Figure 4.2 a trader has bought an Italian corporate bond very cheaply. By entering into a *total return swap* (TRS), the trader was able to enhance the value of the bond. Under the TRS, the trader pays to the counterparty a premium. In return, the counterparty offers credit protection in the event of default. The counterparty would obviously have an AAA rating, otherwise the TRS would not be worthwhile. The trader also entered into an Italian interest rate swap converting from fixed coupon to floating coupon and finally entered into a currency swap whereby he converted Italian lire to dollars. The result of all this is that the trader converted a risky fixed lira bond into a (close to) risk free floating dollar bond. The bond is now, of course, worth a lot more because any potential buyer knows that it is both risk free and very liquid. The trader, therefore, has created value by introducing greater liquidity. He would, naturally, have had to pay a premium to remove the credit risk, but pays nothing (or very little) to remove the liquidity risk.

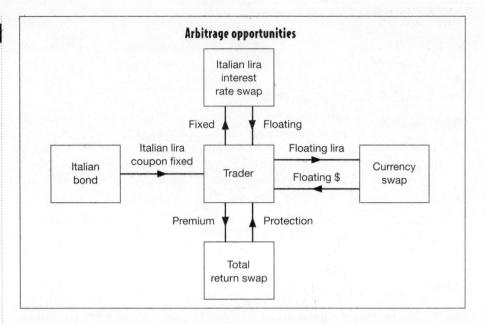

Fig 4.2

Arbitrage opportunities

Differential swaps

One important development of structured finance is the differential swap. This involves switching cash flow streams between two parties. Although the currency is the same for both payments, they are calculated by reference to different yield curves. For instance, a company in Britain might be worried about the Bank of England's monetary policy and expect an upward slope in the sterling yield curve. That company might prefer to have its interest charge calculated by reference to the short-term floating interest rates in, say, the USA, where interest rates are expected to come down The company could achieve this through a straightforward currency swap. In doing so, however, the company exposes itself to an exchange-rate risk. The solution to this problem is to engage in a differential swap. Under this arrangement, a UK company could exchange sterling interest payments, calculated by reference to American floating rates, for sterling, calculated by reference to British floating rates (LIBOR). The result of this is that the company is using a sterling loan but the interest charge is calculated by reference to American as opposed to sterling interest rates. A British company might do this if it felt that the UK yield curve did not fully reflect the fact that interest rates were about to rise. Figure 4.3 illustrates how this works.

While differential swaps are popular, they are very difficult to hedge and so cause liquidity risk, operational risk and market risk problems for risk managers and traders. Indeed, most of the popular hedges involve using interest rate swaps in the two currencies (in this case dollars and sterling), along with exchange rate put options and call options. Such a hedge is not only complex, it is also not guaranteed to work. This is why the profit spread on differential swaps is so high and offered only by a relatively small number of banks.

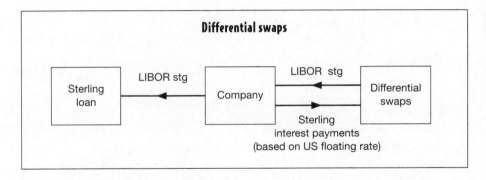

Fig 4.3

Differential swaps

Role of VaR in structured finance

Value at Risk can get around the complex hedging problems of structured finance by identifying natural hedges from other trades within the bank. For differential swaps, VaR involves decomposing complex swap transactions into their bare parts and then identifying the inherent risk of each. Differential swaps are, of course, exposed to interest rate risks and currency risks and VaR can identify these. Rather than hedge differential swaps individually, therefore, a trader could look instead at a portfolio of swaps and then hedge each of the individual exposures such as duration risk, or convexity risk and exchange rate risk. By operating on a portfolio basis, which VaR encourages, risk managers can hedge more efficiently and probably with more accuracy, as long as VaR can pick up all the inherent risks. In the next section, we look at how we can decompose complex instruments with a view to hedging more effectively, and we show basic interest rate conventions, and then look at the decomposition of complex instruments.

Interest rate conventions

Simple vs compound interest

There are two types of interest calculation used in finance: simple interest, compound interest. When interest is paid once per annum and for periods of one year or less, we tend to use the simple interest convention. This convention assumes that no interest is earned on interest earned. Compound interest, on the other hand, calculates interest not only on the principal but also on interest previously earned. As a general guideline, money market instruments tend to use the simple interest convention (because it relates to periods of less than one year), while instruments of greater than one year tend to use the compound interest convention.

Principal	Interest	Term	Lump sum at maturity
$100 000	10%	2	$120 000 (simple interest)
$100 000	10%	2	$121 000 (compound interest)

Table 4.1 Simple vs compound interest rate convention

In Table 4.1, $100 000 is placed on deposit for two years at 10 percent. Under the simple interest convention interest is not earned on previous interest paid, so the amount of money at maturity is simply $100 000 + (10% of $100 000 × 2) = $120 000. The formula for the simple interest convention is P*(1+nr).

We deal with compound interest calculation later.

Forward rate agreement (FRA)

An FRA is an agreement to fix an interest rate that will apply at some period in the future. Banks normally offer FRAs to customers who are worried about their exposure to movements in interest rates. A company that is due to receive money in, say, nine months' time would find the task of budgeting cash flows a lot easier if it could lock into an interest rate today rather than risk an adverse movement in interest rates in the future. When the bank buys an FRA, it is equivalent to offering a deposit at a fixed rate. However, in reality the bank will simply pay the difference if the floating rate turns out to be below the agreed rate and receives a payment if the floating rate remains above the fixed rate.

Example

A company expects to receive $1 000 000 in six months' time and wishes to place this on deposit with a bank for three months. What rate should the bank offer if the company wants to lock into an interest rate today? Assume that six-month interest rates are 8 percent and nine-month interest rates are 9 percent.

	B	C	D	E	F
11				Six month rate	8%
12				Nine month rate	9%
13			Company	Borrow for	Place on
14		Number of	cash	six months	deposit for
15		days	flow		nine months
16	01-Jan-98			$962 045	-$962 045
17	30-Jun-98	180	$1 000 000	$1 000,000	
18	30-Sep-98	272	-$1 026,568		$1 026 568
19					
20					
21		Implied interest for period		2.657%	
22		Number of days		92.00	
23		Annual adjustment		10.54%	

Table 4.2 Forward rate calculation

The bank will calculate a "break-even" forward rate which is 10.54 percent as shown in Table 4.2. To intuitively understand this, we assume that the bank borrows $962 045 (the present value of $1m) for six months, and places this on deposit for nine months. Apart from credit risk, there is no major risk to the bank and so 10.54 percent represents the break-even forward rate. Here the bank uses the money market rates and the convention is to apply the simple interest convention. The formulas behind the above calculations are:

	B	C	D	E	F
11				Six months rate	0.08
12				Nine month rate	0.09
13			Company	Borrow for	Place on
14		Number of	cash	six mnths	deposit for
15		days	flow		nine months
16	35796			=D17/(1+C17/365*F11)	=-E16
17	35976	=B17-$B$16	1000000	=E16*(1+F11*C17/365)	
18	36068	=B18-$B$16	=-F18		=-F16*(1+C18/365*F12)
19					
20					
21		Implied interest for period		=D18/-D17-1	
22		Number of days		=(C18-C17)	
23		Annual adjustment		=365/E22*E21	

Table 4.3 Spreadsheet formulas behind Table 4.2

(NB We assume that American interest rates are adjusted for 365-day convention)

In Table 4.2, the interest rates are contained in F11 and F12 and the dates are in cells B16, B17 and B18. The principal $1 000 000 is contained in cell D17.

A buyer of an FRA agrees to accept money at some stage in the future (in this case six months) and then pay out the principal plus interest at a later date (in this case nine months). This is the equivalent to being short a nine-month fixed bond and long six-month floating bond. (i.e. a liability and an asset). In the above case we calculated the FRA rate to be 10.54 percent. This is the break-even rate which is fair to both sides. In reality, of course, the bank will pay a lower rate in order to cover its administration costs and profit margin. However, for the purpose of these illustrations we will assume that the bank has entered into an FRA that is "fair" to both sides, that is at the break-even rate of 10.54 percent. Given the zero rates, 10.54 percent represents the forward rate for three months beginning in six months.

Settling a forward rate agreement

To settle an FRA, we take the difference between the fixed rate and the floating rate and multiply this by the principal after adjusting it for the fraction of a year (in this case three months). This amount is strictly speaking payable at the end of the FRA period. However, the convention is to pay a discounted amount early, in order to take the swap off the books. A few examples will reveal how this works.

Example

	B	C	D	E
26	Date	30-Jun-98		
27	Principal	$1 000 000		
28	Duration of FRA	0.252054795		
29	Fixed rate	10.54%		
30		Actual		
31	Example	interest	Future	Present
32		rates	value	value
33	1	8%	–$6 404	–$6 277
34	2	9%	–$3 883	–$3 797
35	3	11%	$1 158	$1 127
36	4	12%	$3 678	$3 570

Table 4.4 FRA payments

In the above case, the bank has agreed to guarantee a rate of 10.54 percent. If the actual rate of interest turns out to be less than 8 percent, the bank pays the difference. In the first two examples, the figures are negative because the FRA represents a liability to the bank. In the second two cases, the figures are positive because the bank will receive the excess over 10.54 percent. Strictly speaking, the future amounts are payable at the end of the FRA period (in this case September 30, 1998). In reality, banks will pay a discounted amount early. Therefore, the $6277 represents the fact that the settlement amount is paid three months earlier. In other words, if $6277 was placed in the bank at 8 percent for three months (92 days), we would get $6404.

The table to construct the above is:

	B	C	D	E
26	Date	35976		
27	Principal	1000000		
28	Duration of FRA	=(C18-C17)/365		
29	Fixed rate	=E23		
30		Actual	Future	Present
31	Example	interest	value	value
32		rates		
33	1	0.08	=$C$27*$C$28*(C33-$C$29)	=D33/(1+$C$28*C33)
34	2	0.09	=$C$27*$C$28*(C34-$C$29)	=D34/(1+$C$28*C34)
35	3	0.11	=$C$27*$C$28*(C35-$C$29)	=D35/(1+$C$28*C35)
36	4	0.12	=$C$27*$C$28*(C36-$C$29)	=D36/(1+$C$28*C36)

Table 4.5 Spreadsheet formulas for Table 4.4

The date is contained in cell C26 The duration of the FRA is in cell C27 and the fixed rate in cell C28. The individual interest rates of 8 percent, 9 percent, 11 percent, and 12 percent are in cells C33:C36.

Valuing an forward rate agreement

To value an FRA, we decompose it into its asset and liability. In the above case the bank has an asset of a six-month zero coupon bond and a liability of a nine-month bond with a principal of $1 026 568. To value the FRA we simply take the present value of both.

Value	Term	Interest	Present value
-$1 000 000	0.4932	9%	$957 503
-$1 026 568	0.7452	10%	-$955 373
			$2 129

Table 4.6 Value of forward rate agreement

In Table 4.6 we assume that six-month interest rates have moved to 9 percent and nine-month interest rates to 10 percent. Remember that the original present values were $962 045 (see Table 4.2) when interest rates were 8 percent and 9 percent. The increase in interest rates has reduced the present values in both cases. However, the liability has decreased at a faster rate than the asset and so the overall NPV is positive. In other words, it has gone in the bank's favor.

Compound interest

In the case of compound interest, we assume that interest is earned on interest. So, at the end of year one, the deposit account will be worth $100 000 + (10% × $100 000) = $110 000 and then interest is calculated on this amount for year two, namely $110 000 + (10% × $110 000) = $121 000. The formula for compound interest is: $S = P*(1+r)^n$, where

P = present value
n = time period (years) and
r = interest rate

A company is due to receive $100 000 in two years' time and wishes to place this on deposit for one year. Assume that the company wants to place the money on deposit for one year, what rate of interest should the bank quote today if two-year zero coupon rates are 10 percent and three-year rates are 11 percent?

Example

Year 1	Company cash flow	Two-year rate 10% Three-year rate 11% Borrow for six months	Place on deposit for nine months
1		$82 645	–$82 645
2	$100 000	$100 000	
3	-$113 027		$113 027
	Implied interest for period		13.027%

Table 4.7 Calculating forward rates (compound interest)

Since we are now dealing with periods of greater than one year, the convention is to use the compound interest formula. The company is going to give the bank $100 000 in two years' time, and the bank will place this on deposit for a year. Today, the bank will borrow the present value of $100 000, assuming that interest rates are 10 percent and n = 2 years. This comes to $82 645. At the same time, the bank will put this on deposit for three years (n=3) at 11 percent, giving $113 027. This money will then be returned to the company, so the implied rate of interest for one year is 13.027 percent.

Hedging in reality

Tables 4.3 and 4.7 simply illustrate how a bank can use the cash market to hedge a forward rate agreement. In reality, they will use the above procedure to simply calculate the forward rate, but will not necessarily hedge using the cash market. An alternative is to use the futures market or to hedge all forward rate agreements collectively. In the event that they decide to adopt the portfolio approach, Value at Risk can help because services like RiskMetrics can provide details of zero yield rates and volatilities, with the result that VaR can be calculated on a portfolio basis. The only question is how we should map forward rate agreements. This is dealt with in the next section.

Weighting matrix for fixed income instruments

When valuing a portfolio of bonds, we treat them as a series of forward rate agreements. In the example that follows, we have three bonds in a single portfolio and we wish to calculate (a) the value of the portfolio and (b) the undiversified and diversified VaR.

	Bond one	Bond two	Bond three
Nominal value	$1 000,000	$1 500 000	$2 000 000
Coupon	10%	12%	15%
Term	4	3	5

Table 4.8 Bond portfolio

To arrive at an individual value for each of the bonds in Table 4.8 we break down the cash flows into each of the years, and then calculate the present value from the relevant zero coupon interest rate. This is shown in Table 4.9.

Term	Future cash flow One	Two	Three	Zero curve rates One	Present values Two	Present cash flows Three		
1	$100 000	$180 000	$300 000	7.00%	0.93458	$93 458	$168 224	$280 374
2	$100 000	$180 000	$300 000	8.00%	0.85734	$85 734	$154 321	$257 202
3	$100 000	$1 680 000	$300 000	8.50%	0.78291	$78 291	$1 315 286	$234 872
4	$1 100 000		$300 000	8.75%	0.71496	$786 458	$0	$214 489
5			$2 300 000	9.00%	0.64993	$0	$0	$1 494 842
						$1 043 941	$1 637 831	$2 481 779
					Total		$5 163 550	

Table 4.9 Valuation of bond portfolio

The zero curves are the equivalent of traditional deposit rates. So, if a person put $85 734 on deposit at 8 percent for two years, he or she would get $100 000 at the end of two years. The interest is compounded because we are dealing with periods of greater than one year. No coupon is paid until maturity. Table 4.10 shows how we calculate VaR on the above.

Term	Future cash flow	Present values	Volatilities	Undiversified VaR
1	$580 000	$542 056	0.480%	**$2 602**
2	$580 000	$497 257	0.501%	**$2 491**
3	$580 000	$454 087	0.522%	**$2 370**
4	$400 000	$285 985	0.533%	**$1 524**
5	$300 000	$194 979	0.554%	**$1 080**
				$10 068

Table 4.10 Undiversified VaR for a portfolio

To calculate the undiversified VaR, we use the correlation coefficient matrix for short-term/long-term interest rates. The procedure as before is to take the undiversified matrix (shown in bold in Table 4.10) and then calculate U'CU where U is the undiversified matrix and C is the correlation matrix.

VaR on forward rate agreements

Undiversified VaR

We now calculate the VaR on the FRA used in Table 4.2.

Example

Cash flow	Term		Price volatilities	Present value	Undiversified VaR
$1 000 000	0.4932	8.00%	0.21%	$962 045	$2 020
-$1 026 568	0.7452	9.00%	0.48%	-$962 045	$4 618

Table 4.11 Undiversified VaR for FRA

The first step is to calculate the undiversified VaR. Where a bank has bought an FRA, it is the equivalent of granting deposit facilities at the FRA (or fixed) rate of interest. In this case, the bank has agreed to accept $1 000 000 in six months' time (n = 180/365 = 0.4932) and pay out $1 026 568 in nine months' time when n = 272/365 = 0.7452. The agreed FRA rate is 10.54 percent and covers 92 days. Therefore, the figure of $1 026 568 represents $1 000 000*(1+92/365*10.54%). The risk facing the bank is, of course, that the asset of $1 000 000 may decrease in value (if the six-month interest rates increase), and that the liability may increase in value (if nine-month interest rates decrease). Our first step is to calculate the present value of the asset and the liability. In the case of $1 000 000, we divided this by (1+0.4932 *8%) to get $962 045. Similarly, if we discounted $1 026 568 at 9 percent for nine months, we would also get $962 045. The present value of the asset and liability are the same. This stands to reason because in Table 4.2 we calculated the break-even forward rate and then used this to calculate $1 026 568 above.

Once we know the weighting matrix and the volatility matrix (0.21% and 0.48%) were obtained from RiskMetrics, we can calculate the undiversified VaR. For the asset of $1 000 000 it is $2020 (0.21% × $962 045). If interest rates went up the present value would fall and this is effectively what VaR measures. For the liability of $1 026 568, we calculate a positive VaR since if interest rates go down, the present value of our liability increases. The total undiversified VaR is therefore $2020 + $4618 = $6618. This undiversified figure is, of course, grossly misleading and overstates VaR. The figure would be correct if there were high chance that six-month interest rates would increase and nine-month interest rates would decrease simultaneously. The possibility of that happening is very remote since there is a high correlation between six-month and nine-month interest rates. To be more realistic, therefore, we must recognize this correlation and be aware that we are dealing with an asset and a liability.

Diversified VaR

When calculating diversified VaR we recognize that there is a negative correlation between the asset and the liability, and so adjust the undiversified VaR matrix. This is achieved by placing a negative sign before the $4618 to reflect the fact that the VaR is based on a liability.

The calculation of diversified VaR then follows the usual ritual. We obtain the

	Correlation coefficient C	
	1	0.7
	0.7	1
Undiversified	Undiversified VaR W'V'	
VaR VW		
	$2020	-$4618
$2020		
–$4618	W'V'C	
	–1212.177122	–3203.610965
	W'V'CVW	12344735.49
	VaR	$3514

Table 4.12 Diversified VaR for a FRA

correlation matrix from RiskMetrics. Here the correlation is 0.7 and this is intuitively what we would expect. If six-month interest rates are going to go up, then nine-month interest rates are likely to go up by close to the same amount. A more realistic figure for VaR, therefore, is $3514. For non-Excel users, the figure –1212 is $(1 \times 2\,020) + (0.7 \times -4\,618)$ and $12\,344\,735 = (2\,020 \times -1\,212) + (-4\,618 \times -3\,203)$. Alternatively, $(2\,020.30)^2 + (-4\,617.82)^2 + 2 \times 2\,020.30 \times (-4\,617.82) \times .70 = 12\,344\,735$.

How swaps work

Up to now we have looked at companies which may wish to fix a single interest receipt or payment through a forward rate agreement. A company that takes out a long-term loan may wish to fix the interest payments throughout the entire period of the loan. By entering into an interest rate swap, the company can make an agreement with its bank to pay a fixed interest charge throughout the entire period of the loan. Of course, by agreeing to this, the bank automatically takes on an interest rate exposure and, as for the FRA, the bank must hedge itself. Choices open to the bank include the cash market, the futures market, or to simply "warehouse" the swap until an opposing swap agreement is reached with a counterparty.

As with FRAs, most banks will include the swap in their interest rate portfolio and then hedge the entire portfolio using either futures or bonds. Before hedging the portfolio, the risk manager must firstly decompose a swap. In the case of an interest rate swap, this is quite easily achieved, as Figure 4.4 shows.

Fig 4.4

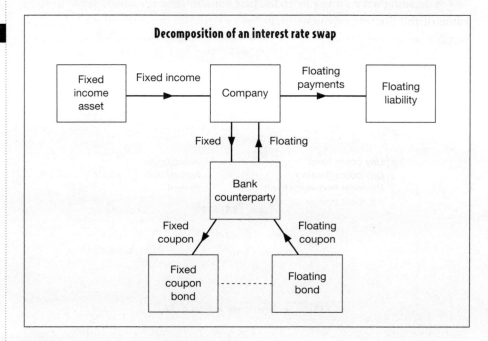

Decomposition of an interest rate swap

In Figure 4.4, assume that the company derives most of its income from renting property at a fixed rate. The risk facing this company is that it is receiving a fixed income, but has floating liabilities. In other words, if interest rates go up, the company is in trouble. To eliminate this uncertainty and make budgeting easier, the company could enter into an interest rate swap whereby it pays fixed and receives floating. The length of the swap should, of course, match the length of the loan. The company is effectively passing the interest rate risk to the bank.

For the bank, being the fixed rate receiver is the equivalent of buying a fixed bond and selling or shorting a floating bond. If interest rates go up, the value of the fixed bond will go down but the floating bond (which is the equivalent to borrowing the principal) will remain unchanged. In such a case, the bank will lose money. To reduce this risk, the bank could consider "reversing the position," in other words, buying a floating bond and selling or shorting a fixed bond. Although this type of hedge works in theory, it is unattractive for a number of reasons, and so unlikely to be used in practice. The chief problem is that it may be impossible to sell a fixed bond whose coupon and period to maturity exactly matches the bond. Second, bonds tend to tie up cash reserves, and thus cause capital adequacy problems. A more convenient way to hedge a swap, therefore, is to take an opposing swap position or use interest rate futures or a combination of both.

Setting the swap fixed rate

When deciding what swap rate to use, the bank must make sure that the present value of the floating payments matches exactly the present value of the fixed income received. The bank must, therefore, estimate the future floating rates and then calculate their present value (Table 4.14 illustrates how this is achieved).

Description	Interest rate swap
Principal	$5 000 000
Fixed rate	12.5156%
Fixed payment	$625 782
Day count fixed	Actual/365
Day count floating	Actual/365
Payment frequency fixed	Annual
Payment frequency floating	Annual
Trade date	Nov-01-01
Effective date	Nov-04-01
Termination date	Nov-04-06

Table 4.13 Term sheet for an interest rate swap

Table 4.13 illustrates a typical interest rate swap agreement. This swap will last for five years and the fixed rate payer (the company) has agreed to pay 12.516 percent per year or $625 782 per year. The day convention is actual 365. This assumes that for the purpose of interest-rate calculations, there are 365 days in the year.

To calculate the "break-even" swap rate, the bank predicts what payments it must make over the next five years and then makes sure that the present value of its floating commitment is equivalent to the present value of the fixed commitment. If these are not equal, then the swap is an "unbalanced swap." Table 4.14 illustrates how a balanced swap is constructed.

	Zero coupon rates	Discount factors	Forward rates	Floating payments	Present value floating payments	Present value fixed payments
1	9%	0.91743	9.000%	$450 000	$412 844	$574 112
2	10%	0.82645	11.009%	$550 459	$454 925	$517 176
3	11%	0.73119	13.027%	$651 368	$476 274	$457 567
4	12%	0.63552	15.054%	$752 719	$478 367	$397 696
5	13%	0.54276	17.090%	$854 504	$463 791	$339 650
		3.65335			$2 286 200	$2 286 200

Table 4.14 Calculation of fixed rate

Forward rates

The zero coupon rates are simple deposit rates. They are "zero coupon" because if a customer put money on deposit for, say, five years at 13 percent, no coupon is paid until maturity. In fact, the first payment occurs at maturity when the principal, together with interest, is returned. In the "discount factors" column, we calculate the discount factor in the conventional way using the formula $1/(1+r)^n$. To calculate 0.73199, for instance, we let r =11% and n = 3. Next we try to predict the forward rates. The first forward rate 9 percent and the one-year spot rate will, of course, be the same. In year two, the forward rate is 11.009 percent, which is the predicted (one-year) spot rate for year two. This means that if a customer were to put, say, $100 000 on deposit in one year's time, for a year, he would get $111 009 at the end of the year (or the end of the second year). To calculate 11.009 percent, we divide the previous discount factor by the current discount factor and subtract 1. For instance, 0.91743/0.82645-1 = 11.009%. To obtain the forward rate for year three, we divide 0.82645/0.73119 and subtract 1 to get 13.027 percent. If a company expected to receive, say, $1 000 000 in two years and wanted to place this on deposit for a year, then the bank would quote a break-even forward rate of 13.027 percent (subject to any adjustment for a profit margin). The forward rate is the same as the one we used in Table 4.7. This is because the zero coupon rates for years two and three are the same, namely 10 percent and 11 percent.

Once we know the floating rate, the next step is to calculate actual floating payments that the bank expects to make. This is simply the floating rate multiplied by the principal. In practice, only the net difference between the fixed and floating rate is payable. However, we will assume for the sake of simplifying the analysis that at the end of each year, the bank makes a floating payment and the company makes a fixed payment. In year one, the bank would expect to make a floating payment of $450 000 and in year two, $550 459, etc. Once this is decided, we need to calculate how much the bank needs to set aside today in order to meet these floating payments. The answer is $2 286 200. We multiply each of the individual future floating payments by the relevant discount factor to get the present value and then sum them. In theory, what this means is that if the bank puts $2 286 200 into an account today, it would be able to write cheques for $450 000 at the end of year one, and $550 459 at the end of year two, etc. Therefore, this is the amount of money it must recover from the fixed side of the swap.

The figure of $2 286 200 is the equivalent of buying a floating bond today and then stripping the principal due at maturity away. Table 4.15 illustrates this.

Nominal value Term in years	$5,000,000 5		
	Floating payments	Discount factor	Present value
1	$450 000	0.91743	$412 844
2	$550 459	0.82645	$454 925
3	$651 368	0.73119	$476 274
4	$752 719	0.63552	$478 367
5	$854 504	0.54276	$463 791
5	**$5 000 000**	**0.54276**	**$2 713 800**
			$5 000 000

Table 4.15 Floating coupon bond

As stated earlier, a floating bond is the equivalent of an ordinary bank account. Such an account pays interest per annum based on the floating rate of interest. The present value of a standard bank account is simply the principal invested. The same is true of a floating bond. Its present value is simply the principal and this present value does not change. It follows that there is no risk with holding a standard floating bond and so the VaR will be very close to zero.

We can calculate present value of the floating payments on a swap very simply by splitting a floating bond between floating payments for years one to five, and a zero coupon bond for year five. Figure 4.5 reveals this.

Example

Fig 4.5

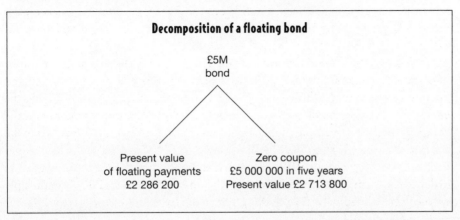

Decomposition of a floating bond

£5M
bond

Present value
of floating payments
£2 286 200

Zero coupon
£5 000 000 in five years
Present value £2 713 800

Therefore, to calculate the present value of the floating payments the formula is simply P(1-Dfn) where Dfn represents the zero discount factor for the last year of the swap. In this case, the last year is 5 so n = 5 and r represents the zero coupon rate for year five, 13 percent. Therefore, $1/(1+0.13)^5 = 0.5428$.

To calculate the present value of the fixed side, we simply use the formula P × Cfn × F, where P is the principal, Cfn is the cumulative discount factors, which is the sum total of all the individual discount factors 3.653, and F is the fixed rate.

Given that the fixed side must equal the floating side, we can use a little algebra to show that F= (1-Dfn)/Cfn. Alternatively, (1-0.5428)/3.653 = 12.516%. This is the break-even fixed rate in the swap.

VaR Swap						Undiversified
Term	Fixed	Floating	Discount factors	Present value	Price volatility	VaR WC
0		−£5 000 000				
1	−£625 782		0.91743	−£574 112	0.03%	−£155
2	−£625 782		0.82645	−£517 176	0.07%	−£347
3	−£625 782		0.73119	−£457 567	0.11%	−£512
4	−£625 782		0.63552	−£397 696	0.15%	−£593
5	−£5 625 782		0.54276	−£3 053 449	0.19%	−£5 802
						−£7 408

Table 4.16 VaR on a swap transaction

Table 4.16 calculates the undiversified VaR for the five-year swap. The main difficulty here is in establishing the weighting matrix to represent the cash flows. In this case, the bank is paying fixed and this is why all the fixed figures appear as negative figures. The bank is also receiving floating and this is the equivalent of receiving $5 000 000 today and paying it back at the end of five years.

As before, when calculating the undiversified VaR we ignore the signs of the weightings, but when calculating the diversified VaR we keep the original signs in the matrix and combine these with the correlation matrix as shown in Table 4.17.

	W'V' matrix				
WV matrix	−£155	−£347	−£512	−£593	−£5 802

WV matrix	C Matrix				
−£155	1.000	0.940	0.932	0.921	0.910
−£347	0.940	1.000	0.981	0.976	0.961
−£512	0.932	0.981	1.000	0.987	0.982
−£593	0.921	0.976	0.987	1.000	0.986
−£5 802	0.910	0.961	0.982	0.986	1.000

W'C'V Matrix

−6 784	−7 149	−7 279	−7 300	−7 363

W'V'CVW matrix	54 301 916
Matrix	
VaR matrix	£7 369

Table 4.17 Diversified VaR for a swap

Conclusion

In this chapter we have concentrated on fixed income instruments. One important benefit that VaR has in measuring interest rate risk is that, unlike the duration approach, VaR identifies not only shifts in the yield curve, but also changes in the slope of the yield curve. This is achieved by recognizing that the correlation between short-term rates and long-term rates is not always 1 (which is what duration and convexity assume). VaR models, therefore, are able to indicate to us how exposed we are to short-term and long-term interest rate movements.

The area of fixed income portfolio has become extremely complex in the last few years as treasurers become more demanding on their financial engineering requirements. Banks have tried to respond to this, but by doing so they have had to deal with complex products, and this has important risk implications. Obviously, with complex products, natural hedges can emerge and risk managers must, therefore, implement a system where natural hedges can be exploited. Value at Risk models can help in achieving this. By decomposing complex instruments into their base components (i.e. bonds), risk measurement becomes more "standardized," therefore reducing the risk of operational errors.

Measuring the Risk of Complex Derivative Products

Interest rate sensitivity

In previous chapters, we looked at how we could map various instruments into "vertices" in order to calculate the VaR for a portfolio. In this chapter, we look at products whose risk profile is complex and thus difficult to model, particularly using the basic procedures introduced in previous chapters. We first make a distinction between linear and nonlinear instruments. We then look at alternative methods of measuring these risks. Lastly, we introduce a concept known as the "delta gamma" method, which is designed to overcome weaknesses when measuring the risk of complex derivative products.

Linear and nonlinear products

Terminology

Linear – a linear relationship exists where there is a straight line between movements in the underlying and the profit and loss account (i.e. a foreign exchange forward). Risk measurement for these products is usually straightforward.

Nonlinear curvature – this is where the relationship between the profit and loss and the underlying asset can be represented by a curved line. There is a convexity risk with such relationships. VaR is capable of measuring such convexity with a reasonable degree of accuracy.

Nonlinear option – the relationship between the underlying asset and the profit and loss is represented by a "kinked or broken" line. These can be extremely difficult to measure and usually require Monte Carlo simulation techniques.

In Chapter 3 we dealt with risk analysis for linear products. The variance covariance method can capture such risks with relative ease. For nonlinear curvature, risk measurement is a little more difficult. To capture this risk we use what is known as a delta gamma approach. The phrase *delta and gamma* is to options what *duration and convexity* is to bonds. In this chapter, we concentrate on noninear curvature. RiskMetrics has devised a procedure to cope with nonlinear curvature which we examine in this chapter. In the first section, we introduce the reader to duration and convexity and then illustrate how the variance covariance approach deals with this area. Although the variance covariance approach is capable of dealing with delta and gamma, options, because of their nonlinear "kinked" relationship structure, are even more complex. While RiskMetrics has made attempts at incorporating options, it has had to make many simplifying assumptions and this, of course, can defeat the original purpose. In the next chapter, we will look at nonlinear options in more detail, and later in the book we will see how Monte Carlo simulation can deal with such issues.

Duration – this measures how a bond price changes when the underlying interest rate changes. When interest rates go up, bond prices go down and vice versa. A bond with a high duration (such as a long maturity bond) is very sensitive to changes in interest rates.

Convexity – duration gives only an approximation of the change in the bond price. The approximation is due to the fact that a curved line represents the relationship between bond prices and interest rates. Duration assumes that there is a linear relationship (i.e. a straight line). Convexity corrects this error.

Delta – the delta measures how an option price changes when there is a change in the underlying asset. In mathematical terms, the delta is to options what the duration is to bonds (the first differential with respect to an underlying variable).

Gamma – the delta gives only an approximation of the call options price when the underlying share price changes. In reality, like the duration, the delta itself changes and the speed of this change is known as the "gamma." For more precision on how the option price changes when the underling asset price changes, risk managers calculate the gamma of the option and make the appropriate adjustment.

Fig 5.1

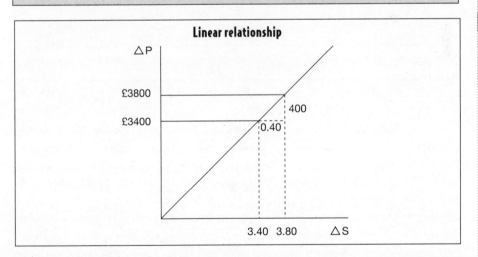

Linear relationship

Figure 5.1 illustrates a linear instrument, one that has a one-to-one relationship with the underlying asset. Note that the line is straight and, therefore, not too complex to deal with. Consider a portfolio consisting of 1000 shares in Company X. If the value of the shares in Company X moves from $3.40 to $3.80, the value of the portfolio will increase from $3400 to $3800. The line therefore, has a slope of $400/0.40 = 1000$. We can assume that this relationship will always hold, so we can calculate the value of the portfolio almost instantly, when we know the share price. The matrix procedures that we saw in the previous chapter can, therefore, calculate the value of this portfolio with relative ease.

Nonlinear structure of bonds

Next we look at the nonlinear situation of a bond, with respect to interest rates. Figure 5.2 shows how a bond price changes when interest rates change. Note the curve in the line. This simply illustrates that the change is not constant, and so it is more difficult to deal with in our VaR calculations. The slope changes (it gets flatter) as interest rates increase, and gets steeper as interest rates decrease.

Fig 5.2

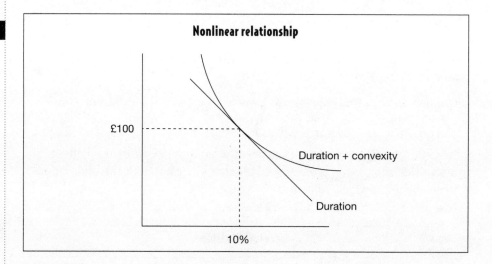

	A	B	C	D	E	F	G
2			8%	9%	10%	11%	12%
3		Cash flow	Present	Present	Present	Present	Present
4			value	value	value	value	value
5	1	$10	$9.26	$9.17	$9.09	$9.01	$8.93
6	2	$10	$8.57	$8.42	$8.26	$8.12	$7.97
7	3	$10	$7.94	$7.72	$7.51	$7.31	$7.12
8	4	$10	$7.35	$7.08	$6.83	$6.59	$6.36
9	5	$110	$74.86	$71.49	$68.30	$65.28	$62.42
10							
11		Value	$107.99	$103.89	$100.00	$96.30	$92.79
12		Difference		$4.10	$3.89	$3.70	$3.51

Table 5.1 Changes in the value of a bond as interest rates change

The difference gets smaller and smaller as interest rates increase by the same absolute amount 1 percent. We cannot assume, therefore, that there is a constant relationship between interest rates and the value of a bond. In practice, most risk managers get around this problem by realizing that although the bond price does not fall by a constant amount, we can simplify matters considerably by assuming that it does. The practice, therefore, among most managers is simply to calculate the modified duration. This tells us the percentage drop in a bond's price as a result of an increase in interest rates. In the last case, for instance, the modified duration is -3.79 (we show the calculation below). This means that if interest rates drop by 1 percent, then the bond's price will increase by 3.79 percent. Alternatively, if interest rates increase by 1 percent then the bond's price will fall by about 3.79 percent.

For Excel users, Table 5.1 can be set up as shown in Table 5.2

	A	B	C	D	E	F	G
2			0.08	0.09	0.1	0.11	0.12
3		Cash flow	Present	Present	Present	Present	Present
4		value	value	value	value	value	Value
5	1	10	=$B5/(1+C$2)^$A5	=$B5/(1+D$2)^$A5	=$B5/(1+E$2)^$A5	=$B5/(1+F$2)^$A5	=$B5/(1+G$2)^$A5
6	2	10	=$B6/(1+C$2)^$A6	=$B6/(1+D$2)^$A6	=$B6/(1+E$2)^$A6	=$B6/(1+F$2)^$A6	=$B6/(1+G$2)^$A6
7	3	10	=$B7/(1+C$2)^$A7	=$B7/(1+D$2)^$A7	=$B7/(1+E$2)^$A7	=$B7/(1+F$2)^$A7	=$B7/(1+G$2)^$A7
8	4	10	=$B8/(1+C$2)^$A8	=$B8/(1+D$2)^$A8	=$B8/(1+E$2)^$A8	=$B8/(1+F$2)^$A8	=$B8/(1+G$2)^$A8
9	5	110	=$B9/(1+C$2)^$A9	=$B9/(1+D$2)^$A9	=$B9/(1+E$2)^$A9	=$B9/(1+F$2)^$A9	=$B9/(1+G$2)^$A9
10							
11		Value	=SUM(C5:C10)	=SUM(D5:D10)	=SUM(E5:E10)	=SUM(F5:F10)	=SUM(G5:G10)
12		Difference		=C11-D11	=D11-E11	=E11-F11	=F11-G11

Table 5.2 Spreadsheet formulas to calculate the market value of a bond

The cash flow figures $10–$110 are contained in cells B5 to B9 and the interest rates are contained in C2 to G2.

Calculating duration and convexity

Bond sensitivity

A bond's duration shows how sensitive the bond is to interest rates. A bond with, say, 20 years might have a duration of about 17. This means that if interest rates go up by 2 percent, the bond's value will fall by about 34 percent and if interest rates fall by 1 percent, the bond's value will rise by about 17 percent. There is always an inverse relationship between bond prices and interest rates.

> **Bond VaR**
>
> A bond portfolio has a value of $10m. Interest rates are currently 10 percent and an external VaR provider believes that there is a 5 percent chance that interest rates will go above 11.2 percent at the end of the year. What would the VaR be for the portfolio at 95 percent? If interest rates do go to 11.2 percent at a time when the duration is 3.79, then the portfolio will fall in value by: $10m × -3.79 × 1.2% = – $454 800. This is the VaR.

The duration is calculated as follows:

	A	B	C	D
14		Interest	10%	Weighted
15				time
16	1	$10	$9.09	9.09
17	2	$10	$8.26	16.53
18	3	$10	$7.51	22.54
19	4	$10	$6.83	27.32
20	5	$110	$68.30	341.51
21				
22		Market value	$100.00	
23			Total	416.987
24			Duration	4.170
25			Modified duration	3.791

Table 5.3 Duration calculation

The figures of $9.09 and $8.26 represent the present value of the coupon $10 using a discount rate of 10 percent. For instance, $9.09 placed on deposit for one year at 10 percent will give $10, and $8.26 placed on deposit for two years at 10 percent will give $10, etc. To obtain the weighted time, we multiply $9.09 by 1 to get $9.09 and $8.26 × 2 to give $16.23, etc. The figure 416.99 is simply the addition of the weighted time column and to obtain the duration we simply divide 416.987 by the market value of the bond $100 = 4.17. Finally, we multiply this figure by $1/(1+0.10)$ to give the modified duration at 3.79.

The formula for duration (which summarises the above) is simply:

$$Md = \frac{\Sigma\ (PV\ C\ (f))}{MV\ (1 + r)}$$

The duration calculation that is shown by the above formula is simply the sum of the present values of the future cash flows divided by the market value multiplied by $(1+r)$. The duration can be calculated on spreadsheet as follows:

	A	B	C	D
14		Interest	0.1	Weighted
15				time
16	1	10	=B16/(1+$C$14)^A16	=A16*C16
17	2	10	=B17/(1+$C$14)^A17	=A17*C17
18	3	10	=B18/(1+$C$14)^A18	=A18*C18
19	4	10	=B19/(1+$C$14)^A19	=A19*C19
20	5	110	=B20/(1+$C$14)^A20	=A20*C20
21				
22		Market value	=SUM(C16:C20)	
23			Total	=SUM(D16:D22)
24			Duration	=D23/C22
25			Modified duration	=D24/(1+C14)

Table 5.4 Spreadsheet calculation for duration

The cash flow is contained in cells B16 to B20 and the interest rate of 10 percent is contained in cell C14.

Convexity

Unfortunately, we cannot assume that the slope or the relationship between interest rates and changes in the bond price is constant. The duration calculation, therefore, only gives a reasonable approximation for the bond's value once interest rates change. For a very small change in interest rates the error is quite small, but for large changes the error can be substantial. We can obtain better precision if we use a convexity adjustment along with duration when calculating how interest rates affect the bond price. The procedure for calculating convexity is as follows:

	A	B	C	D	E
27			Interest	10%	
28	Years	Cash	present	Convexity	Convexity
29		flow	value	column 1	column 2
30					
31	1	$10	$9.09	2	18.18
32	2	$10	$8.26	6	49.59
33	3	$10	$7.51	12	90.16
34	4	$10	$6.83	20	136.60
35	5	$110	$68.30	30	2049.04
36		Market value	$100.00		
37					2343.57
38				Convexity	23.44
39				Modified convexity	19.37

Table 5.5 Convexity calculation

Table 5.5 is calculated based on the formula:

$$\frac{\Sigma\, C\,(f) * n\,(n + 1)}{MV\,(1 + r)^2}$$

The present values of the cash flows are calculated as before. Column 1 is simply n(n+1) where n is the number of years. In year five, for instance, 30 is 5(5+1), and in year four, 20 is 4(4+1). The final column is the present value multiplied by the convexity factor. So, in year five 2049 = $68.30 multiplied by 30. The sum of the convexity column is 2.343 and like the duration, this figure is divided by the market value of the bond, to get 23.44. This time, when we convert to the modified duration we multiply by $1/(1+10\%)^\wedge 2$ to get 19.37. As before, we illustrate the formulas behind the spreadsheet for readers who want to set this up on computer.

	A	B	C	D	E
27			Interest	0.1	
28	Years	Cash	present	Convexity	Convexity
29		Flow	value	column 1	column 2
30					
31	1	10	=B31/(1+$D$27)^A31	=A31*(1+A31)	=C31*D31
32	2	10	=B32/(1+$D$27)^A32	=A32*(1+A32)	=C32*D32
33	3	10	=B33/(1+$D$27)^A33	=A33*(1+A33)	=C33*D33
34	4	10	=B34/(1+$D$27)^A34	=A34*(1+A34)	=C34*D34
35	5	110	=B35/(1+$D$27)^A35	=A35*(1+A35)	=C35*D35
36		Market value	=SUM(C31:C35)		
37					=SUM(E31:E36)
38				Convexity	=E37/C36
39				Modified convexity	=E38/(1+D27)^2

Table 5.6 Spreadsheet formula for calculating convexity

The cash flow is contained in cells B31 to B35 and the interest rate is in cell D27. The years (numbers 1 to 5) are contained in cells A31 to A35.

We will conclude this section by illustrating how more precision can be obtained when we use both duration and convexity to estimate the new price of a bond (Table 5.12). First, however, we illustrate a shortcut way of valuing a bond.

Bond valuation: shortcut method

In this section we develop a shortcut technique for valuing bonds and then compare an actual price change with a price change estimated from duration and convexity calculations. We have seen above that the value of a bond can be obtained by taking the present value of all the cash flows. A more compact way of achieving the above is to break down a bond between its zero coupon component and its annuity. For instance, consider a bond that pays a coupon of $10 per annum and is due to mature in five years' time. We can strip this bond down between its coupon component (the annuity) and its zero coupon component which is the $100 payable at maturity. This concept is known as bond stripping.

Bond stripping

When bonds were first traded actively, traders had difficulty selling coupon bonds because most of the players in the bond markets preferred zero coupon bonds (those bonds that only paid a lump sum at maturity). Coupon bonds, therefore, contained a liquidity premium. Bond traders could overcome this by splitting the bond down between an annuity (which comprised the coupons) and the zero coupon part. Both were sold separately. The annuity was sold to pension companies and the zero coupon parts were sold to bond traders who preferred the extra liquidity.

Provided the yield curve is flat (i.e. short-term interest rates are the same as long-term rates) the annuity part of a bond can be valued as (1-Dfn)/r × coupon. The zero coupon part can be valued as $100 × Dfn, where $100 represents the nominal value. Table 5.7 illustrates this.

Example

	B	C	D
43	Interest	10%	12%
44	Coupon	$10	$10
45	Years to maturity	5	5
46			
47			
48	Discount factor	0.62	0.57
49	Annuity factor	3.79	3.60
50			
51	Zero coupon	$62.09	$56.74
52	Annuity	$37.91	$36.05
53	Value of bond	$100.00	$92.79

Table 5.7 Valuation of a bond

Table 5.7 shows how a bond with a coupon of $10 per annum and five years to maturity is valued. In the first case we would intuitively expect a value of $100 since the yield to maturity 10 percent is equal to the coupon on the bond $10/$100 = 10%. In the second case, interest rates (or the yield to maturity) at 12 percent is above the coupon and so the value is slightly less than $100. The discount factor in both cases is $1/(1+r)^n$, where n =5 and r = 10% in the first case, and 12% in the second case. The zero coupon value of the bond is $62.09 when interest rates are 10 percent. In theory, this means that if we placed $62.09 on deposit at 10 percent for five years, we would have $100 at maturity. The annuity factor of 3.79 is calculated as follows: 3.79 = (1-0.62)/0.10 and for the second bond, when interest rates are 12% (1- 0.57)/0.12 = 3.60. We use these factors to calculate the values of the annuities. For instance, $10 × 3.79 = $37.90. Intuitively, this means that if we placed $37.90 on deposit today for five years when interest rates are 10 percent, we would be able to withdraw $10 a year for the next five years, after which, the balance in the account would be zero. The value of a coupon bond is, therefore, the sum of the zero coupon bond and the value of the annuity. In this first case, this is $62.09 and in the second case, $37.91. The spreadsheet setup used to obtain the above table is set out in Table 5.8.

	B	C	D
43	Interest	0.1	0.12
44	Coupon	10	10
45	Years to maturity	5	5
46			
47			
48	Discount factor	=1/(1+C43)^C45	=1/(1+D43)^D45
49	Annuity factor	=(1-C48)/C43	=(1-D48)/D43
50			
51	Zero coupon	=100*C48	=100*D48
52	Annuity	=C44*C49	=D44*D49
53	Value of bond	=C51+C52	=D51+D52

Table 5.8 Spreadsheet formulas for bond valuations

The above table is self-explanatory. In the case of the first bond, the interest rate, coupon, and years to maturity are contained in cells C43, C44 and C45 respectively. The bond has a nominal value of $100 in each case.

Application of duration and convexity

For VaR calculations, it would be both tedious and time consuming to value a bond for each interest rate. To overcome this, risk managers use the duration procedure outlined earlier and where greater precision is required, convexity. We show how these can be applied in this section and then conclude the chapter by showing how VaR methodologies incorporate bond risk in fixed income portfolios.

Consider a five-year coupon bond which pays a coupon of $10 a year and a lump sum of $100 at maturity. We show how the value of the bond changes when interest rates move from 10 percent to 11 percent and from 10 percent to 15 percent.

Example

Interest	10%	11%	15%
Coupon	$10	$10	$10
Years to maturity	5	5	5
Discount factor	0.62	0.59	0.50
Annuity factor	3.79	3.70	3.35
Zero coupon	$62.09	$59.35	$49.72
Annuity	$37.91	$36.96	$33.52
Value of bond	$100.00	$96.30	$83.24

Table 5.9 Valuation of a five-year bond when interest rates increase

When interest rates move from 10 percent to 11 percent, the value of the bond drops from $100 to $96.30, and when interest rates move from 10 percent to 15 percent, the value of the bond moves from $100 to $83.24. For the sake of simplicity, assume that the yield curve is flat and that the increase in interest rates represents a parallel shift in the yield curve. A parallel shift in the curve simply means that both short-term and long-term interest rates change in the same direction and by the same absolute amount.

We now see how effectively the duration of a bond can estimate the bond's price change and later we will try to improve that estimation by considering convexity as well. Assume that the duration of the bond is –3.791 which means that if interest rates increase by 1 percent the value of the bond decreases by 3.791 percent.

Table 5.10 shows how the value of the bond is estimated when interest rates change from 10 percent to 11 percent, and from 10 percent to 15 percent.

	C	D	E
73	Value of bond		
74	Change in interest rate	1%	5%
75	Duration	- 3.791	- 3.791
76	Duration estimation	-3.79%	-18.96%
77	New value of bond	96.21	81.05

Table 5.10 Duration estimate

An increase of 1 percent in interest rates leads to a 3.79 percent decrease in the bond's value from $100 to $96.21. The correct price is (from Table 5.9) $96.30 giving an error of 9p. There are two points to observe from this table:

1 the duration calculation is relatively accurate for small changes in interest rates
2 the duration calculation overestimates the fall in the bond's price.

In fact, the duration calculation always overestimates a fall in the bond's price, but as we shall see later, it underestimates a rise in the bond's price when interest rates fall. Also, the accuracy of the duration estimate becomes weaker when the change in interest rates is quite large. When interest rates rise by 5 percent, the duration calculation shows an estimated bond value of $81.05, when the correct value is $83.24.

The formulas behind the above calculations are:

	C	D	E
73	Value of bond		
74	Change in interest rate	0.01	0.05
75	Duration	-3.791	-3.791
76	Duration estimation	=D75*D74	=E75*E74
77	New value of bond	=100*(1+D76)	=100*(1+E76)

Table 5.11 Formulas for Table 5.10

Since we are dealing with the same bond, the duration is –3.791 in both cases. To see how much the bond price should fall when interest rates increase, we multiply –3.791 by the change in interest rates 1%, i.e. D75*D74. We then reduce the initial bond price $100 by this percentage.

Characteristics of duration

1 Duration is a measure of how sensitive a bond's price is to changes in interest rates, and is simply the weighted average (measured in time) of the cash flows.

2 Duration will always underestimate a price rise when interest rates fall, but overestimate a price fall when interest rates rise.

3 Duration estimations will be very accurate when there is a small change in interest rates, but the estimation is quite weak when there is a large change in interest rates in either direction.

Convexity adjustment

Convexity formula

Convexity represents the second term of the Taylor expansion (the equation is explained in Appendix 5.1). So, when we need to make a convexity adjustment, we use the following formula:

$$1/2 \times \text{Gamma Value} \times (\text{Change in interest rate})^2$$

Regardless of the change in interest rates, the gamma adjustment will always be positive. Therefore, it reduces the impact of the duration when interest rates rise, and increases the impact of duration when interest rates fall.

We now try to gain better precision by using the convexity adjustment. In very simple terms, the convexity adjustment is required to cope with the non-linearity of bond prices in relation to interest rates. There is a special formula that we use to calculate the convexity adjustment. It is:

$$1/2 \; x \; Convexity \; \times \; (\Delta r)^2$$

We will now see how this formula is used

Assume that we calculate the convexity of the bond to be 19.37.

Example

	C	D	E
74	Change in interest rates	1%	5%
75	Duration	−3.791	−3.791
76	Duration estimation	−3.79%	−18.95%
77	New value of bond	96.21	81.05
78			
79	Convexity	19.37	19.37
80	Convexity adjustment	0.097%	2.421%
81	Duration and convexity	−3.69%	−16.53%
82	New value of bond	96.31	83.47

Table 5.12 Duration and convexity calculation

The convexity estimation of 0.097% is obtained as follows: $0.5 \times 19.37 \times (0.01)^2 *100\% = 0.097\%$. The convexity adjustment will always be a positive figure. To obtain the estimated reduction in the bond price, we add −3.79% +0.097% to give 3.69 percent. Therefore, the new value of the bond drops by 3.69 percent to give a more accurate 96.31. Remember that the figure we are trying to reach is 96.30 (from Table 5.9). For a 5 percent change in interest rates, we calculate the convexity adjustment as follows $0.5 \times 19.37 \times (0.05)^2 = 2.421\%$. The duration estimation on its own is −18.95% (−3.791 $\times$ 5%). We add the convexity adjustment to this figure giving −16.53 percent, and so the fall in the bond's value is 83.47. The correct figure from Table 5.9 is 83.24. The duration convexity adjustment is therefore a considerable improvement on the duration estimation 81.05.

The spreadsheet formulas necessary to construct Table 5.12 are set out in Table 5.13.

The interest rate changes of 1 percent and 5 percent are contained in cells D74 and E74 and the convexity 19.74 is contained in D79 and repeated in E79.

	C	D	E
74	Change in interest rate	0.01	0.05
75	Duration	-3.791	-3.791
76	Duration estimation	=D75*D74	=E75*E74
77	New value of bond	=100*(1+D76)	=100*(1+E76)
78			
79	Convexity	19.37	19.37
80	Convexity adjustment	=0.5*D79*D74^2	=0.5*E79*E74^2
81	Duration and convexity	=D76+D80	=E76+E80
82	New value of bond	=$C$70*(1+D81)	=$C$70*(1+E81)

Table 5.13 Spreadsheet formulas for duration and convexity

Impact of an increase in interest rates

For the sake of completeness, we now look at what happens when interest rates fall. Remember that the duration calculation always underestimates a rise in the bond price when interest rates fall. Table 5.14 illustrates this.

Interest	10%	9%	6%
Coupon	$10	$10	$10
Years to maturity	5	5	5
Discount factor	0.62	0.65	0.75
Annuity factor	3.79	3.89	4.21
Zero coupon	$62.09	$64.99	$74.73
Annuity	$37.91	$38.90	$42.12
Value of bond	$100.00	$103.89	$116.85

Table 5.14 Bond valuations when interest rates decrease

Table 5.14 simply reveals what we would intuitively expect: the price of the bond has increased with a reduction in interest rates. If we were to use the duration and convexity estimates, we would come up with the following:

Notice how the duration estimate on its own underestimates the increase in the bond's price, and that the duration and convexity adjustment give a more precise result. For a 1 percent change, the estimated price equals the real price of $103.89, while for a 4 percent decrease, the estimated price of $ 116.71 is not too far off the target figure of $116.85.

Value of bond		
Change in interest rate	-1%	-4%
Duration	- 3.791	- 3.791
Duration estimation	3.79%	15.16%
New value of bond	103.79	115.16
Convexity	19.37	19.37
Convexity adjustment	0.097%	1.550%
Duration and convexity	3.89%	16.71%
New value of bond	103.89	116.71

Table 5.15 Duration and convexity

The unique risk characteristics of convexity

Definition

Convexity measures the curvature between the bond price and interest rates. Gamma does the same for options.

In mathematical terms, as we will see shortly, there is no difference between these two terms. Both represent the second derivative or, more intuitively, a measure of curvature. If a risk system fails to measure this curvature the system may have serious problems, particularly if the institution is heavily dependent on options or bonds which demonstrate very high convexity. Consider a situation where a trader is long a high convexity bond. A bond may be regarded as highly convex if the line showing the relationship between interest rates and bond prices has a very high curve. Figure 5.3 shows the difference between a high convex bond, i.e. C and a low convex bond, i.e. A.

Fig 5.3

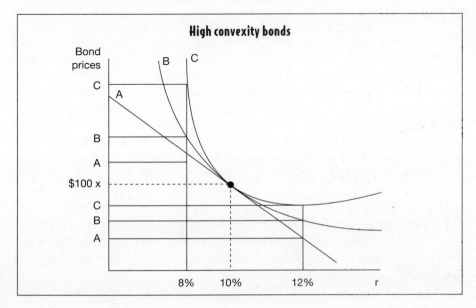

High convexity bonds

Suppose that interest rates are currently at 10 percent and increase to 12 percent. Bond A will suffer the most because it will suffer the greatest price fall. Bond C, which has the highest curvature and so the highest convexity, will suffer the least. Also, if interest rates fall, bond A will show the smallest increase, and bond C (the high convex bond) will enjoy the greatest increase. It follows, therefore, that a high convex bond is always worth a lot more than the low convex bond, in spite of the fact that the present values of the cash flows will be the same.

Now consider a situation where a bondholder is short a high convex bond. Such a position may be regarded as very dangerous because, as Figure 5.4 illustrates, a small drop in interest rates can lead to a substantial increase in a trader's liability.

Assume that a trader has shorted a future on a five-year bond. The trader is obviously hoping that interest rates will rise. If they fall, then the trader's liability has increased, and if the bond he has shorted has high convexity, then the trader will have suffered a huge increase in his liability.

Fig 5.4

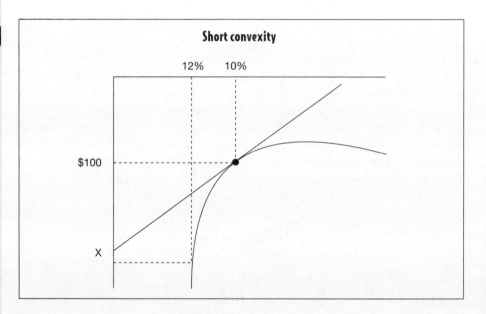

Short gamma

Definition

> A writer of an option, whether it is a call or a put, is effectively short gamma. Intuitively, this is the equivalent of being short convexity. Therefore, the underlying asset moves in an adverse manner and the writer who is short a lot of gamma, would experience a substantial increase in his liability. Often, novice traders are overwhelmed with the amount of losses that they can make when they are short options. Indeed, many firms place very strict gamma limits on new traders.

Most VaR packages cannot measure this gamma correctly. This is because if a product has high convexity or high gamma, the relationship is nonlinear. VaR is, at the moment, best suited to linear products. However, attempts are being made to overcome this with a new VaR technique that is known as the "delta gamma approximation." This method recognizes that certain instruments behave in a nonlinear fashion. Even where firms adapt this delta gamma approach, they are still not guaranteed 100 percent accuracy. Where there is a substantial change in the price of the underlying asset, an option can behave in a very unpredictable manner. Fortunately, bonds are not so unpredictable and so the delta gamma approach would work. The delta gamma method can be quite cumbersome, and for nonmathematicians is often fairly daunting.

Loosely speaking, the delta gamma approach is equivalent to the duration convexity approach that we have applied in this section. Sometimes, it may be reasonable to assume that options behave in a linear fashion, particularly where the gamma value is not high. However, for the majority of options, the delta gamma approach is very necessary, even though it may involve more complex calculations. Readers who have understood the duration convexity approach, outlined above, will get an intuitive feel for the way in which the delta gamma approach applies to options.

VaR is capable of dealing with convexity but not gamma. Readers may find this statement inconsistent since mathematically both mean the same thing (the second derivative). The reason for the inconsistency is that bonds are essentially a series of zero coupon bonds and when services like RiskMetrics publish information on zero coupon yields, they can quite easily adjust their volatilities to reflect convexity. Options are, however, more difficult to deal with because the gamma behaves in a very irrational way as the option approaches maturity. Indeed, experienced option traders recognize that in the days prior to maturity, an at-the-money option can have violent swings in gamma and from a risk modeling viewpoint, capturing this risk is close to impossible. Nevertheless, in the hope of extending the variance covariance matrix method to capture option risk, risk modelers have devised the delta gamma approach, perhaps as a stepping stone toward developing a variance covariance approach to the measurement of option risk. This is looked at next.

The role of delta gamma in VaR measurement

The following example illustrates how delta gamma is incorporated into VaR calculations.

Example

Assume that a trader has gone long a French franc zero coupon bond with a nominal value of the equivalent of £1 500 000 in sterling. The bond will mature in three years. The yield to maturity on this bond is 7.5 percent. This gives the bond a present value in sterling terms of £1 207 441. Assume also that the trader has purchased a put option to convert French francs to sterling on a notional sum of £1 207 441. Although strictly speaking the zero coupon bond is nonlinear, the conventional variance covariance approach can pick up the convexity error with reasonable accuracy. For the option, however, such an approach would be misleading because the second derivative, or the gamma, is quite high and its behavior is irrational (particularly as the option approaches maturity). Hence, for more precision, we use the delta gamma approach.

The details of the portfolio are contained in Table 5.16.

Zero coupon bond	1 500 000
Years to maturity	3
Yield	7.500%
Nominal value of option	1 207 441
Delta of option	0.44
Gamma of option	3.1

Table 5.16 Portfolio details

We start by assuming that the portfolio is delta normal, in other words, we ignore both convexity and gamma and concentrate simply on duration and delta.

	Value	Volatility	Correlation	
Zero bond	1 207 441	1.30%	1	−0.291
FX option	1 207 441	5.40%	−0.291	1

Table 5.17 Relevant VaR matrices

The first step is to calculate the weighting matrix. In the case of the zero coupon bond, we convert the future value to the present value by multiplying £1 500 000 by the discount factor 0.8050 where n =3 and the yield to maturity (obtainable from RiskMetrics) is 7.5 percent. This discount factor, when multiplied by £1 500 000, gives £1 207 441. The volatility matrix is available from RiskMetrics, as is the correlation matrix. The figure of 1.3 percent represents the volatility of the three-year zero curve interest rate for the French bond. The second figure 5.4 percent represents the volatility of the exchange rate between Britain and France. To calculate the undiversified VaR, we simply multiply the weighting matrix by the volatility matrix. However, in the case of the option we must make an adjustment for the delta. We therefore revise the option weighting by multiplying it by the delta. Since the modified duration of the bond is equivalent to the modified duration of the three-year interest rate, no duration adjustment is required for the bond. We therefore have an undiversified VaR as shown in Figure 5.18.

The VaR for the zero bond is simply £1 207 441 × 1.3 percent, while for the FX option the figure of £28 688 is £1 207 441 × 0.44 × 5.4%.

Zero bond	15 696.73
FX option	28 688.79
VaR	44 385.53

Table 5.18 Undiversified VaR

The delta adjustment is necessary because, in the above case, when the underlying asset (in this case the foreign exchange forward) loses, say, £10 000 in value then the option (with a delta of 0.44) loses only £4400 in value. Obviously, there is a negative correlation between the French/UK exchange rate and the French interest rate. The interest rate parity theory states that the country with the highest interest rate is the one whose currency will depreciate in the future. If French interest rates go up, the value of the French bond falls in value, but the French currency will also depreciate and so the value of the put option increases. We can conclude from this that it makes sense to calculate the diversified VaR which will be a lot lower than the undiversified VaR. There are two ways in which we can achieve this. We can use matrix algebra, or (given that we are only using two assets) we can use the formula to calculate the variance of a portfolio. This is:

$$Variance(p) = w1^2\sigma2^2 + w2^2\sigma^2 + 2w1, w2, \sigma1, \sigma2p$$

Table 5.19 shows how the variance and the standard deviation of the portfolio is calculated in this case.

First term	246 387 367
Second term	823 046 941
Last term	–262 086 412
Variance	807 347 896
Standard deviation or VaR	28 413.87

Table 5.19 Diversified VaR

The first term is simply 15 697 squared since 15 697 equals the volatility 1.3 percent × the weighting matrix £1 207 441. The second term is the delta adjusted weighting £1 207 407 × 0.44 × 5.4%, to give 28 689. When we square this, we get the second term of 823 046 941. The third term is simply 2 × –0.291 × 15 697 × 28 689. Finally, we get the square root of the total to get the standard deviation, or the diversified VaR.

Delta gamma approximation

We now calculate VaR using more precision, that is, we take into account the gamma of the option. Once again, we must return to the Taylor expansion to achieve this.

	VaR %	VaR value
Delta approximation	−2.3760%	−$28 689
Gamma approximation	0.4520%*	
Delta gamma approximation	−1.9240%	−$23 231

*0.4520% =1/2 × 3.1 × (5.4%)^2

Table 5.20 Delta gamma approximation

Remember that the present value in this case is $1 207 749. The undiversified VaR of the option was based on the first term of the Taylor expansion, that is we took the volatility 5.4 percent and modified it by the delta to get 2.376 percent. We now take into account the gamma and replace −2.376% with −1.9240 percent. As before, we multiply this by the weighting to get a new VaR figure of $23 231. This is then captured in Table 5.21 by adjusting the weighting as follows: $23 231/0.054 = $430 204.

	Weighting	Volatility	Undiversified VaR
Zero bond	1 207 441	1.22%	14 730.78
FX position	430 204	5.40%	23 231.40
			37 962.18

Table 5.21 Undiversified VaR for portfolio

The diversified VaR is calculated using the same methodology as in Table 5.19, giving 23 612.

Conclusion

Nonlinear curvature is a very important risk concept and risk managers or traders who fail to appreciate its importance may find that they are unknowingly taking on too much risk. A trader who is long a bond is automatically long convexity and this benefits him in two ways. When interest rates rise, the price of a highly convex bond does not fall by as much as a low convex bond. Second, when interest rates fall, the rise in the price of a high convex bond is a lot greater than the rise in the price of a low convex bond. These benefits turn into problems when a trader, instead of being long a bond is short one. Being short convexity could mean that a trader suffers losses a lot quicker than he or she originally expected. Gamma has the same characteristics. A trader who is long an option (whether a call or a put) is automatically long gamma and obviously the converse is also true. Being short too much gamma can prove to be highly risky.

Capturing convexity in the variance covariance approach is quite straightforward, but capturing gamma is a bit more troublesome. This is chiefly due to the fact that as an option approaches maturity, gamma tends to swing violently, particularly if that option is at-the-money. However, some models do attempt to capture the gamma effect by adjusting the weighting matrix. Finally, for those with mathematical training, we illustrate how gamma and convexity are derived from the Taylor expansion. Nonmathematicians could save themselves a lot of stress by moving on to Chapter 6, which illustrates the unique risk characteristics of options.

Appendix 5.1
TAYLOR'S EXPANSION

In this section, we illustrate how the duration and convexity formulas were derived. The Taylor expansion is an important equation, underpinning a lot of areas in financial engineering. It was from Taylor's expansion that Macaulay developed modified duration and convexity. The equation was also used by Black and Scholes when developing their famous option pricing model, and more recently the Taylor expansion has been used to develop the delta gamma approximation to enable risk managers to calculate the VaR on portfolios containing options and other complex instruments. The formula appears like this:

$$\Delta G = \frac{dG}{dx} \Delta x + \frac{1}{2} \frac{d^2 G}{dx^2} \Delta x^2 + \frac{1}{6} \frac{d^3 G}{dx^3} + \dots$$

The first term represents the first derivative and is equivalent to the duration in bond pricing terms. The second term is the second derivative and is equivalent to the "convexity" term. The third term is usually considered to be too small and is, therefore, ignored in financial markets.

Taylor's expansion was developed hundreds of years ago to perform approximations to complex calculations at a time when calculators or spreadsheets were not available. To illustrate how Taylor's expansion operates, we will use it to calculate 9^7. Doing this manually could take forever. Taylor's approach would be to let x equal to a convenient figure (10), then calculate $x^7 = 10\,000\,000$ and then use the expansion formula to approximate the value, assuming that x changed by -1, that is from 10 to 9. We will apply Taylor's expansion for the first three terms, allowing G to equal 10 000 000 and Δx to equal -1. Our task therefore is to calculate ΔG. The first derivative is $7x^6$, the second derivative is $42 x^5$ and the third derivative is $210 x^4$. Table A5.1.1 shows how Taylor's expansion is applied.

	B	C	D	E	F
126	X =	10		9^7 =	**4 782 969**
127	Delta X =	−1		10^7	10 000 000
128					
129	First term	−7 000 000			
130	Second term	2 100 000			
131	Third term	− 350 000			
132					
133	Delta G	−5 250 000			
134	Estimated value	4 750 000			

Table A5.1.1 Taylor's expansion

The bold figure represents the true value of 9^7, that is 4 782 969.

We can obtain a first approximation by considering the first term of the Taylor expansion. This is simply the first derivative of x^7, which is $7x^6$ This comes to –7,000,000 when $x = 10$. If we relied on the first term of the Taylor expansion (which is also known as the duration or the delta term), it would suggest that 9^7 = 10 000 000–7 000 000 = 3 000 000. This is a reasonable approximation, but not very accurate. More precision can be obtained if we consider the second term as well.

The second term is simply half of the second derivative, and so 2 100 000 is obtained as follows: $42/2 \times 10^5 \times (-1)^2$ = 2 100 000. This gives a value for delta G of –7 000 000 + 2 100 000 = –4 900 000 giving a value for 9^7 as 10 000 000–4 900 000 = 5 100 000. Remember the correct figure is 4 782 969. The figure of 5 100 000 is a better approximation than 3 000 000 but not close enough.

We can obtain better precision if we take the third term of the Taylor expansion, namely $1/6 \times 210 \times 10^4 \times (-1)^3$ to give –350 000. This gives a value for delta G of –5 250 000 giving an approximate value for 9^7 of 4 750 000. This is reasonably close to our target of 4 782 969. The conclusion we can draw from all of this is that the more terms in the Taylor expansion we use, the more precise our result will be.

Assume that a bond represents the present values of future cash flows. We can write the formula for a bond as follows:

	B	C	D	E	F
126	X =	10		9^7 =	=9^7
127	Delta X	=1		10^7	10000000
128					
129	First term	=7*C126^6*C127			
130	Second term	=0.5*42*C126^5*C127^2			
131	Third term	=210*C126^4*C127^3/6			
132					
133	Delta G	=SUM(C129:C132)			
134	Estimated value	=F127+C133			

Table A5.1.2 Spreadsheet formulas for Taylor's expansion

The value of 10 is contained in cell C126, while the value –1 is contained in cell C127.

We can now see how the formulas for the duration and the convexity were derived. The duration is simply the first term of the Taylor expansion. The value of a bond is simply the present value of the future cash flows:

$$\Sigma Cf * (1 + r)^{-n}$$

When we get the first differential of this we obtain the absolute change in the bond's price and when we divided this by the bond's price we get the relative or percentage change. This is in effect the duration of the bond. We can derive the convexity of the bond by getting the second differential and dividing it once again by the bond's price. Note that the second term in the Taylor expansion contains the coefficient of 1/2. For this reason, we must divide the convexity by 2 to obtain the convexity adjustment. Options are treated in the same way. The first term of the Taylor expansion is the equivalent of the delta and the second term the gamma.

For option traders, the formulas for delta and Gamma are simply the first and second derivative of the Black and Scholes formula for option pricing. Should readers wish to prove this, they should keep in mind that:

$$SN'(d1) + Xe^{-rt} N'(d2) = 0$$

In the above case, $N'(d1)$ represents the first differential of $N(d1)$, and $N'(d2)$ is the first differential of $N(d2)$.

The Greeks

The risk sensitivities of options

Introduction

Risk managers and regulators face an important choice when implementing a VaR system. On the one hand, as we have emphasized continuously, they may choose a system which is state-of-the-art and very accurate, but a "black box" when it comes to understanding it, because of its complexity. The alternative is a system which is full of flaws, but whose "engineering" is well understood by managers. Most experienced risk managers would prefer to have a system they understand, despite its limitations, rather than a state-of-the-art system. Most banks today trade options in some shape or form and so, in appraising VaR systems, a good understanding of the inherent risks in options is crucial when deciding on a system. In this chapter, we look at option risks and how option prices respond to changes in certain variables such as volatility and gamma. In the previous chapter, we introduced gamma; we now examine it in more detail, and illustrate how traders exploit weaknesses in models to make money.

In Chapter 5 we distinguished between two types of nonlinearity – curved nonlinearity and "kinked" or broken nonlinearity. Here we concentrate on "kinked" nonlinearity. As Figure 6.1 illustrates, options do not have a linear relationship all the time. For instance, a call option is only linear with the underlying asset as long as the share price exceeds the exercise price and for a put, a negative linear relationship exists as long as the exercise price is above the share price. The bend or break in the line causes particular problems for VaR models.

Fig 6.1

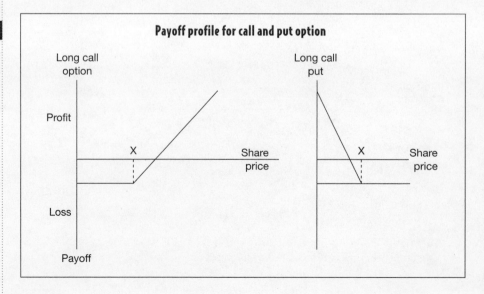

Payoff profile for call and put option

Apart from the nonlinearity, there are other factors that affect the value of an option. These include changes in interest rates, time to maturity, and volatility. In this section we look at the important sensitivities and examine their risk implications. Most of the sensitivities that we are going to look at are derived from the Black and Scholes model, so we start by looking at this model.

The Black and Scholes model

The Black and Scholes pricing formula

When the Black and Scholes model was originally introduced in 1973 it was criticized and rejected by the academic press as being inadequate and full of flaws. Yet, 25 years later, one of its authors Myron Scholes won a Nobel Prize for his work on option pricing. His partner in the original model, Fischer Black, died in 1995 before the award was granted. Today, the Black and Scholes model remains the benchmark for pricing European options. Its simplicity is appealing, despite the fact that its pricing system is not precise.

Fischer Black was Professor of Finance at the University of Chicago's Graduate School of Business, and later joined the MIT's Sloan School of Management. Myron Scholes co-founded the firm of Long-Term Capital Management, which specializes in the development of sophisticated financial software.

If history is to repeat itself, the architects behind RiskMetrics may welcome the criticism that the academic writers have lavished on their VaR package. Indeed, if they can survive another 25 years, an award might be forthcoming.

The Black and Scholes formula is:

$$c = SN(d1) - e^{-r\Delta t} XN(d2)$$

where

$$d1 = \frac{\ln(S/X) + (r + \sigma^2/2)(\Delta t)}{\sigma \sqrt{\Delta t}}$$

$$d2 = \frac{\ln(S/X) + (r - \sigma^2/2)(\Delta t)}{\sigma \sqrt{\Delta t}}$$

where $\sigma =$ sigma
   S   the share price
   X   the option's exercise price
   t   the amount of time remaining to expiration
   sigma the volatility of the underlying contract
   r   the risk free interest rate over the life of the option
   N(.)   represents a draw from the normal distribution curve.

Example We will now illustrate how the Black and Scholes formula works for the following call option.

	B	C
5	Present share price	£100
6	Volatility	20.00%
7	Time to maturity	0.2
8	Exercise price	£98.00
9	Interest rate	10%

Table 6.1 Call option parameters

The first column in Table 6.1 contains cell references, which we will deal with later. Notice that this call is almost at-the-money. There is a slight intrinsic value of £2.00 but, because of the high volatility, the option will have a time value as well. Table 6.2 shows how d2 is calculated.

	B	C
11	ln (S/X)	0.02020
12	Adjusted return	0.01600
13	Time adjusted volatility	0.08944
14	d2=	0.40476
15	N(d2) =	0.65717

Table 6.2 Calculation of N(d2)

N(d2) represents the probability that the option will be exercised. Notice that the figure is about 65 percent. Intuitively, we would expect the figure to be above 50 percent particularly because the option is in-the-money. Table 6.3 shows the formulas behind the above.

	B	C
11	ln (S/X)	=LN(C5/C8)
12	Adjusted return	=(C9-C6^2/2)*C7
13	Time adjusted volatility	=C6*C7^0.5
14	d2=	=(C11+C12)/C13
15	N(d2) =	=NORMSDIST(C14)

Table 6.3 Spreadsheet formulas to calculate N(d2) in Table 6.2

The first two figures represent the top part of the d2 formula. We then divide this by the third cell to get d2. Finally, the N(.) operator simply means that we look up the function in the normal distribution tables (Appendix 11.2).

Algebraically, it is easy to see that:

$$d1 = d2 + \sigma\sqrt{\Delta t}$$

We therefore use this relationship to calculate N(d1), shown in Table 6.4.

	B	C
16	d1=	0.49420
17	N(d1) =	0.68942
18	Discount factor	0.98020
19		
20	Call	£5.81

Table 6.4 Black and Scholes calculation of call premium

Once we know S, N(d1), the discount factor, the exercise price, and N(d2), we can value the call option. This is shown in cell C20. The formulas behind these cells are shown in Table 6.5.

	B	C
16	d1=	=C14+C13
17	N(d1) =	=NORMSDIST(C16)
18	Discount factor	=EXP(-C7*C9)
19		
20	Call	=C5*C17-C8*C15*C18

Table 6.5 Black and Scholes Excel formulas for Table 6.4

Delta and gamma

The delta of an option is simply N(d1). It is closely related to but not equal to the probability that the option will be exercised. From a risk-management perspective, the delta of an option is important particularly for creating a risk neutral portfolio. In the case of the above option, the delta is 0.689. If a trader writes 1000 calls, he can create a delta neutral portfolio by buying 689 of the underlying shares. This means that if the share price goes up in value from, say, £100 to £101, the value of the shares in the portfolio will increase by £689. This will offset the loss on the underlying options contract, which would be 1000 × 0.689 × £1.

The delta measures how much the option's price changes when there is a change in the underlying asset price. In the above case, if the share price moved up by £1, the price of the underlying contract would move up by £0.689p. In more formal terms, the delta measures the change in the option price as a result of a change in the price of the underlying asset.

Delta and VaR

As long as the delta remains relatively constant, then most VaR methods are capable of picking up the inherent risks in options. For instance, if a trader is long 1000 options at a time when the delta is 0.689 and the share price is £100, this is the equivalent of being long £100 × 1000 × 0.689 shares = £68 900. This is the figure that would appear in the weighting matrix for the variance covariance method of calculating VaR, as used in RiskMetrics.

VaR should be able to pick up situations when a trader is delta hedging and when a trader writes uncovered or naked calls or puts. A naked call is simply an unhedged written call. Sometimes traders will write uncovered calls because they want to take a position. If they do this, the VaR calculation should pick it up. On the other hand, if they hedge their position, then the weighting matrix will consist of two weights. First, the weighting of the option portfolio which is £100 × 1000 × 0.689 and also the weighting of delta times the underlying share i.e. 689 × £100 000. Both figures come to £68 900. Obviously, there will be a negative correlation between the option position and the hedged position and so the VaR will be zero.

Gamma measurements and VaR

Where VaR falls down in practice is that many of the systems fail to recognize that a position can be delta neutral, but not gamma neutral or vega neutral. We will look at gamma and vega separately later. In terms of delta, however, there are two weaknesses of most VaR systems which are worth mentioning here.

1 Sensitivity of the portfolio to changes in the market rate

A simplified VaR system fails to capture how an option price will change when there is a change in the underlying asset. The principal reason for this is that simple models assume that delta will remain constant. In reality, of course, the delta of the option changes when the underlying asset changes.

2 Joint probability distribution of changes

Most VaR systems work on the assumption that the underlying asset follows a normal distribution. In reality, the normal distribution does not deal correctly with extreme situations because it underestimates the probability that an extreme event will occur. Given that risk measurement is to a large extent concerned with extreme movements, this weakness needs to be addressed by most risk managers. It can also have implications for the valuation of options, as we will see later.

Values of delta

The chief headache with options as far as VaR model designers are concerned is that the delta changes as the underlying asset changes. Assuming that delta remains constant can lead to a considerable amount of inaccuracy. Figure 6.2 shows how delta behaves when the underlying asset price changes. The curved line represents an option which has some time left to maturity. If the strike price is £100 and the current share price is £80, then although the call option is out-of-the-money, it still has some chance of being exercised.

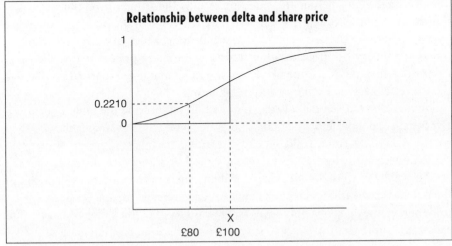

Fig 6.2

Figure 6.2 was constructed from the bold columns in Table 6.6.

Present share price	£80	£80	£80	£80	£80
Volatility	20.00%	20.00%	20.00%	20.00%	20.00%
Time to maturity	0.0001	0.25	0.5	0.75	1
Exercise price	£100.00	£100.00	£100.00	£100.00	£100.00
Interest rate	10%	10%	10%	10%	10%
ln (S/X)	−0.2231	−0.2231	−0.2231	−0.2231	−0.2231
Adjusted return	0.0000	0.0200	0.0400	0.0600	0.0800
Time adjusted volatility	0.0020	0.1000	0.1414	0.1732	0.2000
d2=	−111.5678	−2.0314	−1.2950	−0.9419	−0.7157
N(d2) =	0.0000	0.0211	0.0977	0.1731	0.2371
d1=	−111.5658	−1.9314	−1.1536	−0.7687	−0.5157
N(d1) =	0.0000	0.0267	0.1243	0.2210	0.3030

Table 6.6 Relationship between delta and time to maturity

Since the share price £80 is below the exercise price £100, the option has a small chance of being exercised. If there is only 0.0001 of a year left to maturity, the option is almost certain not to be exercised and so the delta is close to zero. On the other hand, if the option has 0.75 of a year left to maturity (represented by the curved line in Figure 6.2), there is still some probability that the option will be exercised. In this case, the probability is 17.31 percent (this equals

N(d2)) and the delta (N(d1)), which is always higher than the probability is 22.10 percent. The other columns in the table are there to reveal how the probability increases as the time to maturity increases.

Deltas of puts

Generally, puts have the same characteristics as call options, and like call options are easy to map using VaR techniques, provided the delta remains relatively constant. Since the delta has a negative relationship with the underlying asset, the delta of a put will have a value between zero and –1. If a put has a delta of, say, –0.6, then as the share price falls the value of the put increases. For instance, if the share price fell by £1.50, the value of the put would increase by 90p when the delta is –0.60. As the put approaches maturity, we tend to move to a binary position, in other words, if the share price is below the exercise price, the put has a value of –1 or close to –1 and if the share price is above the exercise price, the put has a value of zero.

A writer of a put can delta hedge his position by shorting the underlying asset. For instance, if a put has a delta of –0.6 and is based on a share worth £35, then a trader who has written 1000 puts must short 600 shares to remain delta neutral. If the underlying share falls in value, then there is a greater probability that the option will be exercised. Once the probability increases, so too does the delta of the put and so the trader must rebalance his or her hedge. If, as a result of a share price falling, the delta of a put moves from –0.60 to –0.65 then the writer of 1.000 calls will short (or sell) an extra 50 shares to bring his total position to –650 shares.

As with calls, even the simplest of VaR systems are capable of coping with delta hedging. A writer of a put who is not delta hedged is taking on huge risks, and the lack of a delta hedge will show up because the trader will have a bigger VaR figure on his or her portfolio. If the trader is perfectly delta hedged and the delta remains fixed, the short position on the shares will have a negative correlation with the long position on selling a put. This would result in a close to zero VaR figure.

The problem with calls and puts is that delta jumps up and down with the share price. The delta also changes when there is a change in the expected volatility of the underlying asset. To overcome this problem, risk managers use the technique we introduced in the previous chapter – the delta gamma approach – as opposed to the delta normal approach. This simply means that the weighting matrix is adjusted to reflect not only the delta but also the gamma. Loosely speaking, the gamma measures the rate of change in the delta. In mathematical terms, it is the second derivative of the option with respect to the underlying asset price. Although this leads to more precision, it is by no means 100 percent accurate. The main reason for this is that option prices are affected by other variables such as volatility and time decay. For small changes in the share price, the delta gamma approach is reasonably accurate, but problems arise for large changes or extreme movements in the underlying asset. Again, this is a major flaw in simple VaR methods. JP Morgan, the architects behind RiskMetrics, emphasize that their variance covariance approach is not suitable for options. VaR systems that rely on the more laborious Monte Carlo simulation approach (discussed in Chapter 8) are capable of achieving greater accuracy when dealing with options.

Gamma

Gamma measures the rate at which delta changes. Some options have very high gamma which means that a small change in the underlying asset's price can lead to a significant change in delta. Gamma can be a headache for risk managers because they must delta hedge their portfolio on a regular basis. This can often involve considerable transaction costs. There are other practical problems with a high gamma. Very often, when exchanges close on a Friday evening, they reopen on the following Monday with a very different delta. This is due mainly to off-market or weekend trading. The result is that risk managers go home on Friday with the illusion that they are delta hedged, only to return to nasty surprises on Monday. The higher the gamma, the greater the risk that the delta will change by a large amount, leaving the risk manager exposed to a lot of market risk. Clearly, VaR has its limitations because it cannot deal with these complications.

The gamma of a portfolio is simply:

$$\Gamma = \frac{N'(d1)}{S\sigma\sqrt{t}}$$

Table 6.7 illustrates how gamma is calculated.

	B	C
112	Present share price	$100
113	Volatility	20.00%
114	Time to maturity	0.2
115	Exercise price	$98.00
116	Interest rate	10%
117		
118	ln (S/X)	0.02020
119	Adjusted return	0.01600
120	Time adjusted volatility	0.08944
121	d2=	0.40476
122	N(d2) =	0.65717
123	d1=	0.49420
124		
125	Coefficient	0.39894
126	(d1^2/2)=	0.12212
127	Exp-(d1^2/2)=	0.88504
128	N'(d1)=	0.35308
129		
130	Gamma	0.0395

Table 6.7 Calculation of gamma

The figure of 0.0395 can be interpreted as follows:

If the share price increases by £1 (in this case from £100 to £101) the delta will increase by approximately 0.0395.

As usual, we present the formulas behind Table 6.7:

	B	C
112	Present share price	100
113	Volatility	0.2
114	Time to maturity	0.2
115	Exercise price	98
116	Interest rate	0.1
117		
118	ln (S/X)	=LN(C112/C115)
119	Adjusted return	=(C116-C113^2/2)*C114
120	Time adjusted volatility	=C113*C114^0.5
121	d2=	=(C118+C119)/C120
122	N(d2) =	=NORMSDIST(C121)
123	d1=	=C121+C120
124		
125	Coefficient	=(2*3.1416)^-0.5
126	(d1^2/2)=	=C123^2/2
127	Exp-(d1^2/2)=	=EXP(-C126)
128	N'(d1) =	=C125*C127
129		
130	Gamma	=C128/(C112*C120)

Table 6.8 Excel formulas to calculate gamma for Table 6.7

The gamma of an option is highest when the option is at-the-money and reduces as the share price goes up or down, pushing the option either in-the-money or out-of-the-money. Risk managers should be aware that the writer of an option is always negative gamma, whether that option is a call or a put. The holder or buyer of an option is, therefore, positive gamma. For traders who are negative gamma, the only way to reduce this gamma exposure is to go long other options.

The important point to remember about gamma is that being short gamma is the equivalent of being short convexity in a bond. Negative gamma, like negative convexity, is dangerous because an adverse movement in the underlying asset can lead to a substantial loss while a favorable movement leads to only a minor profit. A problem with VaR is that it cannot measure accurate high convexity. Even the delta gamma approach is only an approximation. The delta represents the first derivative, the gamma is the second and, where gamma is high, traders and risk managers must even measure the change in the gamma. This is the equivalent of the third derivative, and it is where the mathematics can get complex and confusing, leading to operational risk problems.

Reducing the risk of option portfolios

From a risk point of view, market makers – those who are obliged to quote two-way option prices at all times – can suffer from gamma risk. This risk is imposed by their obligations as market makers. In a turbulent market environment, market makers may be called upon to write options. They are obliged to offer a two-way price, and although they have the facility to charge a high price to write options, it still does not guarantee them immunity from gamma exposure.

Very few market makers will allow their portfolios to build up too much negative gamma without hedging against it. For market makers, a practical hedge would be to overprice options. This encourages more writers than sellers and quickly reduces negative gamma. Another approach is to go long options in order to reduce the gamma.

Gamma hedging

Example

Suppose a number of traders, worried about a potential market correction, have bought puts on the FTSE index as insurance against possible losses arising from such a fall. Assume that these puts have an exercise price of 5300. In other words, if the FTSE 100 falls below 5300, the purchaser of the put exercises his option. Despite charging prices over the theoretical value, the market maker has failed to deter purchasers, and so he is left with a portfolio which is short gamma and long delta as follows:

Nominal value of portfolio		£10 000 000
Delta	0.5	£5 000 000
Gamma	–0.018	–£180 000

Note that the delta on the portfolio is positive because, being short puts, the market maker is hoping for an upward movement to avoid counterparties exercising the options. Since he is in a net short position, he is automatically long gamma.

The only way that he can hedge the gamma is by going long options. The question is should he go long a call or a put. Remember that he has a net positive delta and must counteract this with a negative delta. Since puts have negative deltas (for the buyer), he will simply go long a put. As he is hedging the FTSE index, the most appropriate put is the FTSE 100 5300 index at-the-money puts. The details of these puts are as follows:

Nominal value of option		£53 000.00
Delta	–0.32	–£16 960.00
Gamma	0.026	£1 378.00

The index is currently 5300 and each point movement represents £10, so the total nominal value is £53 000. The overall delta and gamma for the option contract size are self-explanatory. To cancel the gamma, therefore, we must buy £180 000/ 1 378 to get 130.62 (rounded to 131) contracts, as follows:

Number of options	131.00
Nominal value of hedge	£6 943 000
Gamma	£180 518
Delta	–£2 221 760

The positive gamma of £180 518 (131 × –£16 960) cancels out the negative gamma of the portfolio £180 000. We have also introduced negative delta of £2 221 760 (131 × –£16 960) to get a net positive delta of £5 000 000 – £2 221 760) = £2 779 240.

Rather than use options to hedge the remaining delta, we would instead use futures, simply because there is no gamma in a future and, of course, no premium is thus payable.

Nominal value of futures	£53 570
Number of futures	–52
Delta	–£2 785 640

The future we choose is the FTSE 100 which has a tick size of £10. Given that the futures index is currently 5357 and the tick size is £10, the nominal value of each futures contract is 5357 × £10 = £53 570. Since the delta is clearly 1, we simply need £2 779 240/£53 570 = –52 rounded.

Theta

Theta measures the time decay in an option. A person who is long an option (whether a call or a put) suffers from time decay because as the option approaches maturity its value gets closer and closer to its intrinsic value (which may be zero if the option ends up out-of-the-money). For the option holder, as each day passes, then, all other things being equal, the time value of the option falls, which means that his liability is reduced. There is a relationship between theta and gamma. Remember that gamma measures the rate of change in the delta of an option. When gamma is high, theta is also high, which means that the option loses value more quickly as it approaches maturity. From a risk point of view, a high theta option might be good news for a party who is short, and bad news for the trader who is long. However, there is also high gamma and the party short the high theta option is effectively holding a very risky option. Most traders are familiar with the phrase "theta pays for gamma." This means that if you benefit from theta, you are suffering from high gamma. A trader cannot have it both ways. He cannot benefit from theta and gamma on the same option.

Theta is also important for certain types of option strategies. Many traders, for instance, sell a near-dated option (one that will expire, say, in April) and purchase a far-dated option on the same share and with the same exercise price, but which expires at a later stage, say August. Such traders play on the theta of the option. If the time value of the far-dated option is expected to decay at a slower rate than the near-dated option, the trade will make money. Time spread strategies are considered in more detail in the next chapter.

Unfortunately, the formula necessary to calculate theta is very cumbersome. If, however, we assume that interest rates are zero, the formula slims down to a version which is intuitively easier to work with. The slimmed down version of theta is:

$$\Theta = \frac{-SN'(d1)\sigma}{2\sqrt{t}}$$

The term N'(d1) is the equation for the normal distribution curve, which is:

$$N(x) = \frac{1}{\sqrt{2\Pi}}e^{-x2/2}$$

In the example which follows, we assume that pi equals 3.1416, and the interest rate is zero. We also assume that no dividend is payable on the share. The option whose theta we are going to calculate is the same as the one we used in Table 6.1 but this time, for the sake of considerable simplicity, we assume that interest rates are zero.

		B	C
31	Present share price		£100
32	Volatility		20.00%
33	Time to maturity		0.2
34	Exercise price		£98.00
35	Interest rate		0%
36	d1=		0.27059
37			
38	Coefficient		0.39894
39	(d1^2/2)=		0.03661
40	Exp-(d1^2/2)=		0.96405
41	N'(d1) =		0.38460
42			
43	Theta		−8.60

Table 6.9 Theta of an option

The theta can be interpreted as follows. For every one-hundredth of a year that passes (approximately three days), the option premium falls by £0.086. That works out at about 3p a day. The formulas behind Table 6.9 are as shown in Table 6.10.

	B	C
31	Present share price	100
32	Volatility	0.2
33	Time to maturity	0.2
34	Exercise price	98
35	Interest rate	0
36	d1=	0.27059
37		
38	Coefficient	=(2*3.1416)^-0.5
39	(d1^2/2)=	=C36^2/2
40	Exp-(d1^2/2)=	=EXP(-C39)
41	N'(d1) =	=C38*C40
42		
43	Theta	=−C31*C41*C32/(2*C33^0.5)

Table 6.10 Excel formulas to derive theta in Table 6.9

The coefficient is that part of the formula which appears before the letter e in the last equation. Here, we take pi to be 3.1416. We use the exponential function in cell C40 which represents the letter e.

When is theta highest?

Table 6.11 shows how the theta changes when the underlying share price changes.

Theta	− 8.09	− 8.42	− 8.63	− 8.73	− 8.72	− 8.60	− 8.38
Share price	£95	£96	£97	£98	£99	£100	£101

Table 6.11 Relationship between theta and share price

Notice that the theta is at a minimum (i.e. it is most effective) when the share price equals the exercise price. The gamma is also highest at this point as well. Figure 6.3 illustrates the relationship between theta and the share price.

Very often traders try to make money by exploiting the time spreads between options. For instance, assume that today is January 1 and a trader sells a £4.60 BskyB March option and buys a £4.60 BskyB June option. The trader would, of course, pay more for the June option than he would receive for the March option, and so is a net premium payer. However, if the gap widens between the prices, the trader will, of course, make money, and if it narrows he loses money. Both options will have the same intrinsic value, so the difference in premium is represented by the time value only. When the short contract expires in March, the value of the near-dated option reduces to its intrinsic value since the time value disappears at maturity. The June option, on the other hand, still maintains its time value.

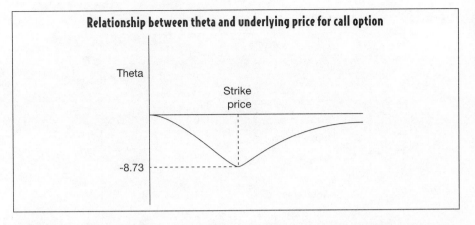

Fig 6.3

Such a trade will prove profitable as long as the far-dated option is at-the-money or close to it. This happens to be the point where the rate of theta decay is at the highest and so an option trader could realize his profit by closing out the June position in March.

Vega

Vega measures the sensitivity of an option to a change in the volatility of the underlying asset. A trader who is absolutely sure that volatility is going to increase would try to construct his or her portfolio so that it has a very high vega. The vega for a European call option is given in Table 6.12.

		B	C
80	Present share price	£100
81	Volatility	20.00%
82	Time to maturity	0.2
83	Exercise price	£98.00
84	Interest rate	0%
85	d1=	0.27059
86		
87	Coefficient	0.39894
88	(d1^2/2)=	0.03661
89	Exp-(d1^2/2)=	0.96405
90	N'(d1) =	0.38460
91		
92	Vega	17.20

Table 6.12 Vega of an option

Vega $= S \sqrt{\Delta t}\, N'(d1)$. The N'(d1) calculation is exactly the same as for theta. The figure 17.20 is simply $100 \times 0.4472 \times 0.38460 = 17.20$. 0.4472, is, of course, the square root of 0.20.

For Excel users the relevant formulas are shown in Table 6.13.

	B	C
80	Present share price	100
81	Volatility	0.2
82	Time to maturity	0.2
83	Exercise price	98
84	Interest rate	0
85	d1=	0.27059
86		
87	Coefficient	=(2*3.1416)^-0.5
88	(d1^2/2)=	=C85^2/2
89	Exp-(d1^2/2)=	=EXP(-C88)
90	N'(d1) =	=C87*C89
91		
92	Vega	=C80*C82^0.5*C90

Table 6.13 Spreadsheet formulas for vega of an option

As with theta, the option is most sensitive when it is at-the-money. Figure 6.3 shows the relationship. Obviously, vega is positive when we are long both calls and put options. An increase in volatility makes the option more valuable. The vega calculation of 17.20 can be interpreted as follows: a one percent increase in volatility will lead to an increase in the option premium of 0.1720.

Vega calculations are very important for volatility trading. Very often traders with a sound intuitive knowledge of the markets can tell when an option has too much or too little implied volatility. Often, they will construct their portfolios so that they are long volatility. Generally, there are several strategies that a trader can choose from. These include butterflies, straddles, and strangles, which are discussed in Chapter 7. A trader in such cases will simply calculate the implied volatility inherent in an option's price, for example, by working backwards through the Black and Scholes formula and then compare this with his own estimate of volatility. If he feels that the implied volatility in the options is too high, he could sell both a call and a put and then buy them back at the cheaper price, when volatility calms down.

Exploiting volatility smiles profitably

The implied volatility for deeply in-the-money or deeply out-of-the-money options is normally a lot greater than those options which are at-the-money. This is illustrated in Figure 6.4 where the term "volatility smile" is self-explanatory. Risk managers and traders should be aware of the fact that option pricing models and risk-measurement systems which overrely on the normal distribution curves can underestimate the level of risk, and therefore the price of some options. For instance, a trader may write a deeply out-of-the-money put option on, say, BskyB shares. The normal distribution curve might produce a probability of, say, 2.5 percent, which means that there is a 2.5 percent chance that the option will be exercised. The reality is that the normal distribution curve underestimates the probability, and so underestimates the price and risk of the option. Loosely speaking, the reason for this is that the markets are not completely rational and suffer from the "herd instinct." This means that if a share price starts to fall, traders are worried about holding long positions and so, like all other traders, they will sell. For an out-of-the-money option, this type of activity pushes the share price very quickly, close to or even below the exercise option. The real probability that the option is exercised is, therefore, much higher than that shown by the normal distribution curve.

Weakness of the Black and Scholes model

The Black and Scholes model assumes a constant volatility and, because it is mathematically based, fails to pick up on the panic that the market sometimes creates when a share price falls. The result is that it underprices out-of-the-money calls and puts. Traders valuing options overcome this weakness in a very practical way. They simply push up the price of any deeply in-the-money or out-of-the-money options they write. If Black and Scholes comes up with a value of, say, £2.30 for a put option that is deeply out-of-the-money, a trader will add some arbitrary figure, say, 15p to compensate for the fact that the Black and Scholes model underestimates the risk that the put will be exercised.

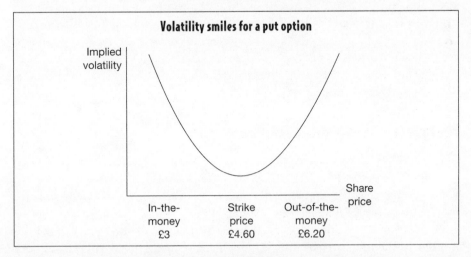

Volatility smiles for a put option

Implied volatility

| In-the-money £3 | Strike price £4.60 | Out-of-the-money £6.20 | Share price |

Fig 6.4

Figure 6.4 illustrates the volatility smile effect. The put option has an exercise price of £4.60. If the put is at-the-money, volatility will be at its lowest. If the share price is at £3, a trader will realize that the probability of the option being exercised is a lot greater than what Black and Scholes suggests, and so he will "twig" the price. By increasing the price, the trader automatically increases the implied volatility.

Exploiting the volatility smile

Straddles and strangles react differently to the volatility smile. To recap, a short straddle is the combined sale of a call and put option at-the-money and a short strangle is a combined sale of a call and a put but this time, they are both out-of-the-money. In relative terms, a short strangle is safer than a short straddle because the underlying asset needs to move some distance before the trader suffers a loss. The disadvantage of a strangle over a straddle, however, is that the premiums received are a lot lower. Obviously, the premium received on an out-of-the-money option is a lot lower than one which is at-the-money. Straddles use at-the-money (ATM) options and so the premium is higher than strangles which use out-of-the-money (OTM) options. Straddles and Strangles are examined in more detail in Chapter 7.

The impact of the volatility smile on straddles

Very often traders buy straddles and hedge them by shorting strangles. Although the hedge may not be perfect, such a strategy will allow the trader to capture the increase in implied volatility arising from the volatility smile, particularly if there is a large movement in the price of the underlying asset. When a trader buys a straddle, he is long volatility and so benefits if there is an increase in implied volatility. For instance, a trader may buy straddle with a strike of £4.60 on BskyB shares. Since these options are at-the-money, the price of the underlying share must be £4.60. Now consider what happens to volatility if there is a major upward movement in the share price. Both the call and the put will become deeply in-the-money and deeply out-of-the-money respectively. The result is that implied volatility will increase and since the trader is long volatility, the trader profits from this.

The impact of the volatility smile on strangles

The position is very different with a strangle. Suppose the trader writes a strangle using a £4 put and a £5.20 call. Both options are initially out-of-the-money, which means that the implied volatility is relatively high. If the share price moves up, to say £5.20 then the call ends up in-the-money and so the implied volatility drops. The put, of course, will go further out-of-the-money, but since it is out-of-the-money to begin with, the increase in volatility will only be very slight. If a trader is short a strangle, he is short volatility and so benefits from a major upward movement in the share price. Overall volatility on a strangle will fall when the share price increases.

We can conclude, therefore, that a volatility trader benefits if he goes long a straddle and uses a short strangle to hedge, as long as there is a major movement in the underlying asset. Where there is no such movement, the trader loses the difference in the premium between the straddle and the strangle.

Conclusion

This chapter has outlined the complex nature of options and the inadequacies of most of the VaR methods in dealing with the risk implications. Essentially, there are two ways to estimate the market risk of options. The first is to break options down and examine the underlying factors that affect these prices. The second approach involves generating a large number of scenarios and then taking, say, the lowest value portfolio, at the 5 percent level (for a 95 percent) VaR figure.

Ideally, we would like to pick a method that keeps computations intuitively simple and easy to understand. At the same time we want accuracy, particularly in extreme situations. Using equations to estimate the potential loss of an option works for small changes, but when the changes get too large, the losses are almost unpredictable, hence breaking the options down into their various components is inadequate. In the next chapter, we look at option strategies that traders adopt. An analysis of these strategies will give the risk manager an insight into how options are used and the risk complications that can arise from such strategies.

Option Strategies

Which option strategies work?

Introduction

In Chapter 6 we identified some of the risk characteristics of options. Nevertheless, despite their complex risk, they are still very popular and banks are becoming increasingly dependent on them. In this chapter, we illustrate how traders can achieve precision in some of the trades they implement. Such precision is not normally available with ordinary cash products. In each of the strategies we examine what risks a VaR system is capable of picking up and those that VaR fails to measure.

Call and put options

> Options can be broken down between calls and puts. Calls give the holder a right, but not an obligation, to buy a particular asset at an agreed exercise price. Puts give the holder the right, but not the obligation, to sell a particular asset at an exercise price. Options are available in shares, foreign exchange, commodities, and bonds.

There are various benefits in buying options on a share as opposed to the share itself. First, a trader can take a position both ways. If he feels that the share price is about to drop, he can either long a put option or short a call. Shorting, therefore, is a facility by which traders can profit if the share price drops. Without options, many traders would have difficulty shorting. A second advantage of options is that the initial cash outlay is close to zero. A trader can take a position on, say, 10 000 BskyB shares going up or down, simply by providing a premium to go long either the call or the put, depending on how he feels the share price is going to go. A third advantage is that a trader can exploit any profit potential but limit his loss exposure. Going long a call option on, say, BskyB shares means that the trader benefits from any upward movement in the share price, but does not suffer if the share price falls. In fact, the most that a trader who is long options loses is his premium. Finally, a trader who speculates with options will suffer a lower bid offer spread than a trader who speculates with the underlying cash product.

For many traders, however, the advantage of options over ordinary cash instruments is that traders can take views on volatility that would not normally be available in the underlying cash market. For instance, a trader may believe that attempts toward trying to achieve a common currency may end up going disastrously wrong, creating a panic in the market. Some currencies may benefit while others may suffer. A foreign exchange trader in these circumstances might predict wild fluctuations in the exchange rate, but be unsure of its direction. In these cases, he will simply take a position on volatility either increasing or decreasing. A trader who, for instance, takes a position that is long volatility will benefit if volatility subsequently increases and, of course, lose money if his predictions are wrong and volatility falls. In this chapter we look at various option strategies and, more importantly, their risk implications. Some of these risks can be picked up by VaR techniques. Others will fall outside the VaR net. For each of the strategies, we highlight the various risk factors and identify how a risk manager might be able to hedge against them.

The advantages of using options over the cash market are summarized below.

Advantages of options over cash instruments

1 The trader is able to take a short position on any asset even if he does not own it in the first place.

2 Initial outlay of cash in many cases is restricted to the premiums paid.

3 Traders can arrange positions so that they benefit from any favorable movement in the share price, and at the same time place restrictions on losses.

4 Transaction and custody charges are relatively low for options.

5 Traders who are unsure about the direction of an underlying asset can take a position on volatility.

Bull call spreads

These strategies are designed to restrict the potential losses that a trader will make and also to put a ceiling on potential profits. A trader would use a bull call spread if he felt that a particular asset was likely to increase in value but by a small amount only. Such a trader would normally take out a call option, but the benefit of a bull call spread is that the trader can reduce the premium normally payable on a call option by selling off the right to receive profits over a certain amount. Figure 7.1 illustrates how this is achieved.

Fig 7.1

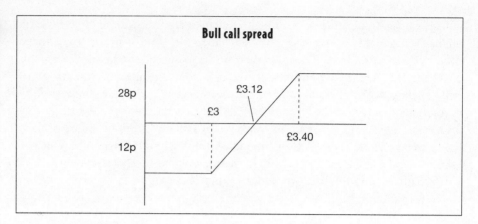

Bull call spread

28p

£3

£3.12

£3.40

12p

Example

A trader buys a call option with an exercise price of £3 for 18p and sells a call option on the same share, with an exercise price of £3.40 receiving a premium of 6p. Naturally, we would expect the premium on the call sold (with a high strike price) to be a lot less than the one for the call purchased. The net premium payable is 12p and the maximum profit that can be achieved is when the underlying asset price hits the highest strike price £3.40. In this case, only the option purchased will be exercised, producing an intrinsic value of 40p less the premium paid 12p giving a profit of 28p. The break-even price for this trade is £3.12 which means that the trader can only make a profit as long as, at the date of expiration, the share price is £3.12 or above. For the sake of simplicity, we assume that we are dealing with European options. Small administrative problems may arise if we use American options because the party short the option may exercise early, creating a temporary cash flow problem.

Decision to exercise an option

Given the nonlinear nature of the payoff profile, such trades, where they are part of a portfolio are very difficult to deal with. Remember that there are three methods to measure VaR: the historical, the variance covariance, and Monte Carlo simulation. Each of these were examined in Chapter 3. The trouble with an option is that the holder may be forced to make a choice and of the three, only the Monte Carlo simulation approach can incorporate this decision-making process with precision. Monte Carlo simulation involves generating random share prices and calculating the potential losses that can be made, say, 95 percent of the time. If the simulation was run, say, 10 000 times, using 10 000 different share values, we would calculate the maximum losses that could be made and take the five-hundredth worst case. This would be our 95 percent VaR. The problem with Monte Carlo is that it is time consuming and can exhaust computer resources. A mildly less accurate but more convenient approach is to use the delta gamma method. This involves calculating the delta and the change in the delta (i.e. the gamma) and then using this to calculate the

VaR. This method is quicker and easier and is relatively accurate for very small changes in the underlying asset price. However, for substantial share price movements, the delta gamma approach may produce very inaccurate results. This is simply due to the nonlinear nature of the bull call spread. The payoff profile, as shown in Figure 7.1 is not a straight line. This is where the chief difficulty lies as far as risk measurement is concerned.

Bull put spreads

This is similar to a bull call spread but the trader uses puts instead of calls. A trader would use such a position if he anticipates a small rise in the underlying share price. In this case, a trader buys and sells a put. The strike price of the put purchased is lower than the strike price of the put sold. The maximum profit that the trader makes is the net premium received and the maximum loss is the difference between the exercise prices less the net premium received.

Example

A trader believes that BskyB shares are likely to increase slightly and so uses put options to take a position which, although placing a cap on potential profits, also places a restriction on the maximum loss that the portfolio can make. He buys one £4 put and sells a £4.40 put. The premium on the put purchased is 8p, while the premium on the put sold is 21p. Figure 7.2 shows the payoff profile. When the share price is below £4, say, £3.80, both options will be exercised and the maximum intrinsic value will be 40p. However, we deduct the net premium receivable, to produce a net loss of 27p. If the share price ends above £4.40, neither option will be exercised, and so the trader makes a profit of 13p. The break-even point is £4.27.

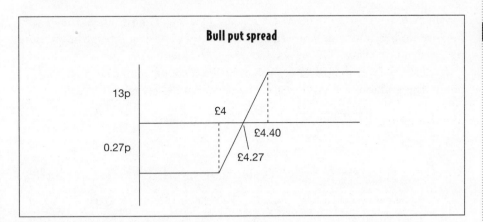

Fig 7.2

As before, the VaR measurement which is most appropriate for a bull put spread is the Monte Carlo approach.

Bear call and bear put spreads

A trader may have a view that a share price is about to fall, but not too dramatically. He, therefore, has a bearish view and in the circumstances would probably adopt a bear call or bear put strategy. With a bear call strategy he would buy a call and sell another on the same share. The exercise price of the call purchased would be greater than the exercise price of the call sold. In Figure 7.3 the trader has purchased a call with a strike price of £3.60 for 10p and sold a call with a strike price of £3 for 30p. His net premium receivable is 20p. If the share price is below £3, neither call is exercised, so the trader makes a profit of the net premium receivable 20p. On the other hand, if the share price at maturity is, say, £4, then both calls are exercisable and the trader loses a net intrinsic value of the difference between the strike price 60p. From this, we must deduct the net premium receivable 20p, producing an overall loss of 40p.

Fig 7.3

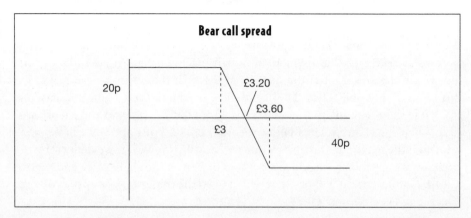

Bear call spread

Example

Finally, we demonstrate with a spreadsheet (Table 7.1) how a bear put spread operates. A bear put is similar to a bear call, but we construct the position using puts instead of calls.

A trader believes that the BskyB share price is about to fall. He buys a £3.30 put at 16p and sells a £3 put at 6p. The net premium receivable is 10p.

	B	C	D	E	F	G
4	Share price	£2.70	£3.00	£3.24	£3.30	£3.60
5						
6	Intrinsic liability put £3	−£0.30	£0.00	£0.00	£0.00	£0.00
7	Intrinsic value put £3.30	£0.60	£0.30	£0.06	£0.00	£0.00
8	Premium put £3	£0.06	£0.06	£0.06	£0.06	£0.06
9	Premium put £3.30	−£0.16	−£0.16	−£0.16	−£0.16	−£0.16
10						
11	Overall profit	£0.20	£0.20	−£0.04	−£0.10	−£0.10

Table 7.1 Bear put spread

The formulas necessary to compute the above table are set out in Table 7.2.

	B	C	D
4	Share price	2.7	3
5			
6	Intrinsic liability put £3	=MIN(C4-3,0)	=MIN(D4-3,0)
7	Intrinsic value put £3.30	=MAX(3.3-C4,0)	=MAX(3.3-D4,0)
8	Premium put £3	0.06	0.06
9	Premium put £3.30	–0.16	–0.16
10			
11	Overall profit	=SUM(C6:C10)	=SUM(D6:D10)

Table 7.2 Spreadsheet formulas for bear put spread in Table 7.1

The MAX function shows the greater of the intrinsic value of the option or zero. Given that we are dealing with a put, the intrinsic value is the difference between the exercise price £3.30 and the share price £2.70, contained in cell C4 and D4. Obviously, if we are long the option, we will simply abandon it if the intrinsic value turns negative. In the case of the £3 put, we are short this option which means that our liability is represented by the intrinsic value of the option. If the option is not exercised, the value of our intrinsic liability is zero and if it is in-the-money then our liability is simply –1 times the intrinsic value. The MIN calculation, therefore, gives us either the negative intrinsic liability or, if greater, zero. The MAX and MIN functions are used quite extensively for Monte Carlo simulation models. Such models generate share prices and then use the MAX or MIN functions to calculate the intrinsic liabilities of the options. These values are then used as part of the VaR calculations. In Chapter 8, we look in more detail at how the Monte Carlo approach is adopted.

Summary

Traders use combination strategies like those shown above to take positions without taking on too much risk. In each of the above strategies the trader has sacrificed the chance of making huge profits in order to minimize the potential losses that he can make. From a risk point of view, such strategies make sense. The problem, however, is trying to incorporate such volatilities into a VaR calculation. The straightforward delta normal VaR calculation cannot deal with nonlinear situations and the delta gamma approach, while it may give a more accurate result, is still deficient in a number of respects. In fact, probably the only way to capture the above trades is to use Monte Carlo simulation. For Excel users, the Monte Carlo simulation is quite easy to apply. Because of the nonlinearity of options, the MAX and MIN Excel functions are quite useful.

Volatility trading: straddles, strangles, butterflies, and ratio spreads

Two types of trading

There are two types of trading: *position trading* and *volatility trading*. Traders engage in position trading when they have views on the future price of the underlying asset. Bull call and bull put spreads may be used where a trader feels that the underlying price is about to increase. The benefit of such trades is that traders can tailor the risk profile to suit their limits and the confidence the traders have in their views. Similarly, bear call and bear put spreads are also a form of close to risk free trading when the shareholder has a view that the underlying price is about to fall.

The other type of trading, known as "volatility" trading, is used by traders who feel that the volatility of the underlying asset is about to increase or decline. A trader who wants exposure to volatility only, and not to the underlying position, can choose from a number of strategies including straddles and strangles. All of these trades essentially involve setting up portfolios which are "delta neutral" or at least close to delta neutral. A trader who has a view that volatility is going to increase can go long either a straddle or strangle, or short a butterfly. Alternatively, if a trader feels that volatility is about to fall, he or she can short a straddle or strangle, or long a butterfly.

Straddles

Figure 7.4 illustrates how a straddle operates.

Fig 7.4

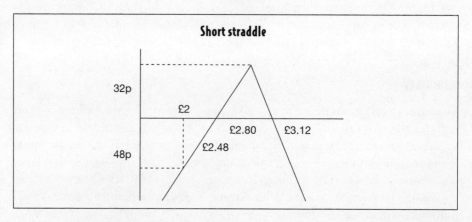

The trader in the above case has shorted a call and a put on the same share, with the same strike price £2.80. The premium for the call was 22p and for the put 10p total 32p. If, at maturity, the share price ends up at £2.80, the trader has maximized his profits at 32p. However, if the share price steers too far away from the strike price of £2.80, the trader could make a loss. The break-even points are £2.48 and £3.12. If the share price ends up outside this range, the trader makes a loss. For instance, if the share price ends up at £2, the put will be exercised producing a loss of 80p, and when this is netted against the premium received, 32p, the overall loss is 48p. A bank might sell a straddle to a company if, say, the company's treasurer was committed to hedging the company against interest rate, foreign exchange, and commodity fluctuations. The share price would, therefore, remain relatively stable.

The opposite to a short straddle is a long straddle. Here a trader believes that volatility in the share price of a particular company is about to increase.

A trader would take such a position if he expected a major change in the price (i.e. high volatility), but was unsure which way the share price was going to go. The policy might be appropriate if, say, a tobacco company was awaiting the outcome of litigation by a group of cancer sufferers. The court's decision will cause the share price to go either up or down. The trader is unsure of direction, but he is very sure of the potential increase in volatility. In such a case, the trader would simply long a put and long a call and the diagram would be the mirror image of Figure 7.4.

From a risk point of view, the main problem with straddles is their ability to make unlimited losses. A substantial increase in volatility can lead to substantial losses and so such strategies, if they are unhedged, can prove very dangerous. An important point to bear in mind also is that while such trades are delta hedged, they are not gamma hedged. This has caused considerable problems for novice traders in the past.

Case profile

Barings Bank and COMEX Gold Exchange

Traders who short straddles expose themselves to huge gamma risk. This means that if the underlying asset changes by a small amount, the straddle can lose substantial amounts of money. Nick Leeson was able to generate a lot of premium income by shorting straddles on the Nikkei index. He obviously didn't anticipate the Kobe earthquake which created considerable volatility in the market, contributing to Barings' huge losses. In 1985, COMEX traders used a combination of straddles and strangles to speculate on the volatility of gold. They believed that the relatively calm volatility of the past on gold prices would prevail in the future. They were wrong and volatility increased. So large was their gamma exposure, that they caused a number of companies to collapse. Indeed, the exchange itself was very close to closure.

Barings regularly produced "delta normal" VaR reports, which outlined only the delta exposure on option trades. Traders could, therefore, in theory, take short gamma positions such as short straddles. Since the delta on the short call (–) offset the delta on the short put (+), VaR would have incorrectly assumed that there was no risk. A "delta gamma" VaR system would, however, have identified that the short straddle is also short gamma, and so would have issued warning signals to senior management.

Straddles and high gamma

It is important to appreciate that although a short straddle is delta neutral, it is certainly not gamma neutral. A person who is long a high convexity bond is long gamma. This means that when interest rates rise, the fall in the bond price is relatively small, whereas when interest rates fall, the rise in the bond price can be substantial. The situation is more risky for a person who is short gamma. In these cases, the increase in a trader's liability for even a very small change in the underlying asset can be substantial. This can be a considerable nightmare for a risk manager.

In terms of VaR measurement, straddles, like bear calls and bear spreads, are very nonlinear. Therefore, the delta normal method (which assumes that the slope between the underlying asset and the value of the straddle remains constant) would be very misleading. The delta gamma method, on the other hand, is more precise but not 100 percent accurate for large changes in the value of the underlying. As with bear call and bear spread strategies, the time consuming Monte Carlo method is capable of picking up both volatility and gamma risk.

Strangles

For the sake of completeness, we show how strangle strategies are constructed. Essentially, strangles are equivalent to straddles, but rather than use at-the-money options, a trader will use out-of-the money options. Although the premiums on out-of-the-money options are lower, the trader is at least given a bit of leeway before he or she starts to make losses when volatility increases.

Example

A share price is currently trading at £3.50. A trader sells a call with a strike of £3.30 and a put with a strike price of £3.50. The respective premiums are 20p and 17p. The highest profit that the trader can make is the sum of the premiums received, 37p. This profit is attainable as long as the share price remains between the two strike prices £3.30 and £3.50. Once it moves outside these bands, the trader starts to lose money; the break-even bands are £2.93 and £3.87 respectively. This is illustrated in Figure 7.5.

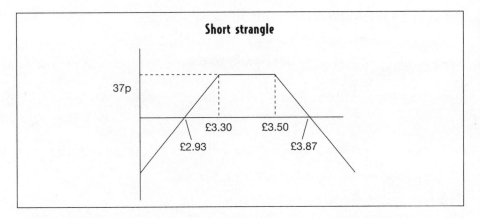

A long strangle is, in diagram form, a mirror image of the short strangle, and could be set up by buying an out-of-the-money call and put option.

Butterflies

One problem we outlined with straddles and strangles is that the possibility of making losses is unlimited. A trading strategy known as the "short or long butterfly" allows traders to trade volatility and, like a bull call spread, place a cap on the maximum losses that they can make.

Long butterfly

A trader buys one call for 100, sells two for 105 and buys one for 110. The premiums payable are £4.40, £1.20, and £0.30 respectively. The total cash outlay is, therefore, −£4.40 + 2*£1.20 − £0.30 = −£2.30. The payoff profile is as shown in Table 7.3.

Underlying price	95.0	100.0	102.3	105.0	107.7	110.0	115.0
Payoff 1	0	0	2.3	5	7.7	10	15
Payoff 2	0	0	0	0	−5.4	−10	−20
Payoff 3	0	0	0	0	0	0	5
Premium	−2.3	−2.3	−2.3	−2.3	−2.3	−2.3	−2.3
Total profit	−2.3	−2.3	0	2.7	0	−2.3	−2.3

Table 7.3 Long butterfly payoff profile

Figure 7.6 below shows the payoff profile.

Fig 7.6

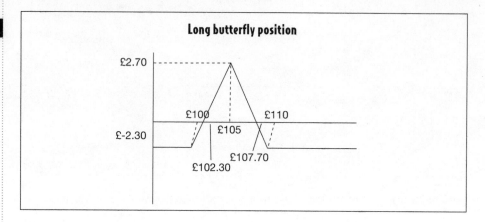

Long butterfly position

£2.70

£100 £110

£-2.30 £105

£107.70

£102.30

We refer to this type of trade as a "long" butterfly even though, intuitively, the diagram looks like a short position. The reason that it is a long butterfly is simply because like most long positions, the trader pays out the net premium rather than receives a net premium, which is characteristic of a short position. The profit at £105 is not the net premium received, but the difference between the intrinsic value of all the options and the premiums payable, that is £5 −£2.30 = £2.70. From a risk point of view, the main difference between a long butterfly and a short straddle is that there are no limits to potential losses with a short straddle, while, with a long butterfly, the losses are restricted to the premiums payable. To go short a butterfly, we could sell a call at the lower exercise price, buy two calls at the middle exercise price and sell a call at the higher exercise price. This would give a payoff profile as shown in Figure 7.7. Again losses are restricted and so too are profits.

Fig 7.7

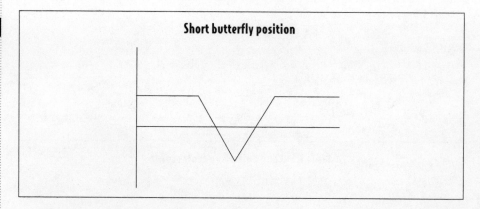

Short butterfly position

Once again, the diagram appears confusing since a short butterfly looks like a long straddle. However, in a long straddle, the premium is negative, in other words, the trader has to pay out a net premium. For a short butterfly, the premium is positive because the trader is receiving more premium than he is paying out. The peak on the butterfly, therefore, is not the net premium paid but the intrinsic value of the option (which is a liability in this case) less the premium receivable.

From a VaR point of view, long butterflies are generally difficult to deal with. In the majority of cases, share prices will step outside the range and so the potential loss is limited and known in advance. However, again, because of the nonlinear payoff profile, butterflies are difficult to deal with as part of an overall portfolio. Nevertheless, risk managers prefer butterflies to straddles and strangles because losses are limited.

Ratio spreads

Where traders have views on volatility and market direction, they tend to use ratio spreads. A ratio spread is like a short straddle except that the potential losses from a downward movement in the share price are restricted. This strategy might be used by trader a trader who wants to earn money from an expected reduction in volatility and believes that the share price is likely to move downward instead of upward. The payoff profile is shown in Figure 7.8.

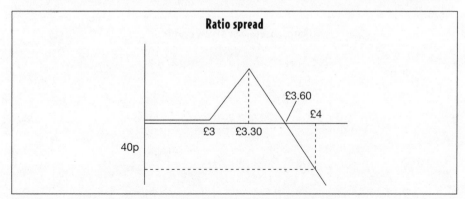

Ratio spread

Fig 7.8

In Figure 7.8, the trader has bought one call option for £3, and sold two call options for £3.30. The premium for the call purchased is 18p, and for the two calls sold 9p each. If the share price is £3 or below, neither call is exercised. Also, since the premiums received exactly equal the premiums paid, there is no profit or loss on the strategy. If the share price is £3.60, then the two calls sold will be exercised, creating an intrinsic liability of 30p each. However, this must be offset against the intrinsic value of the long option (£3.60 – £3) = 60p. This represents the second break-even point (£3 is the first break-even point). If the share price rises above £3.60, the trader makes a loss and so such a trade is not advisable unless the trader feels that the share price is going to drop. For instance, when the share price is £4, the call option is exercised producing an intrinsic value of £1, and the two short positions will also be exercised producing an intrinsic liability of £1.40. The overall loss is, therefore, 40p. Finally, the peak in the payoff diagram represents the point where profits are maximized. If the share price is £3.30, the trader's long call position has an intrinsic value of 30p while the short call positions, because they are at-the-money at £3.30, will not be exercised. The maximum profit, therefore, is 30p.

A ratio backspread is the mirror image of a ratio spread. The advantage of such a trade is that there is unlimited profit potential and losses are limited. There is also downside protection. A trader might use such a strategy if he felt that the share price volatility implied in the option was too high and also felt that if the share price was going to move, it would move upward. To set up the trade featured in Figure 7.9, a trader would go long two calls with a strike of £2.90 for 8p each and sell one call with a strike of £2.50 with a premium of 18p. Here, the net premium receivable is 2p. The break-even points are £2.52 and £3.28. If the share price ended at £3.28, the trader would earn 76p intrinsic value on the two long £2.90 calls and also earn 2p on the net premium receivable. The trader would, however, have to pay 78p on the short call position (£3.28 − £2.50). The trader produces the greatest loss when the share price is £2.90. Here, the trader loses 40p on the short call, but gains 2p on the net premium. The total loss is, therefore, 38p.

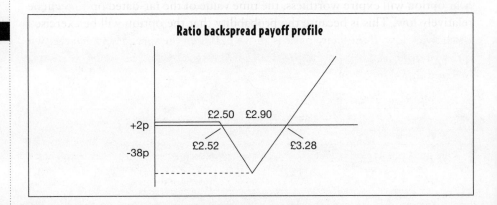

Fig 7.9

Ratio backspread payoff profile

£2.50   £2.90

+2p

-38p

£2.52

£3.28

Time spread strategies

Types of time or calendar spreads

An option premium can be broken down between the time value and the intrinsic value. An at-the-money option with a long time to maturity, for instance, will have zero intrinsic value, but there is still a good chance that the option will be exercised and so it will have a relatively high time value. As the option approaches maturity, the time value erodes. The rate of time decay is known as theta. There is a trade-off between theta, which measures the rate of time erosion, and gamma, which measures the rate of change in delta. If an option has a long time to maturity, then the rate of decay will be relatively slow and if the option is very close to maturity, the rate of decay tends to be faster. Option traders can exploit this by engaging in a calendar spread. This involves selling an option which is close to maturity and buying an equivalent option, but with a later maturity date. If the time erosion on the near-month option is quite rapid in comparison to the time erosion on the far month, the trader stands to make a lot of money.

Example

Today is the March 28. A trader sells a call on HSBC shares with a strike of £20. The option is due to expire in April. At the same time, he goes long a similar type option on the same share with the same strike but this particular contract expires in July. Obviously, the long-dated option will have a higher premium because it has a longer time to maturity. Assume that the premium on the near option is 2.60 and the premium on the far option is £3.20. Since both options have the same intrinsic value, the difference in the premium is simply the difference in the time value.

The best outcome that the trader could hope for, when the first option expires in April, is that the far-dated option will be at-the-money. The time value for this option is highest when it is at-the-money. It will also have three months' time value remaining. If the share price is below £20 then although the near option will expire worthless, the time value of the far-dated option will be relatively low. This is because the probability that the option will be exercised is relatively low. If the share price is above £20 then the spread between the two series of options narrows and the trader will lose money. The situation is summarized in Table 7.4.

Share price below exercise price	The near call expires worthless but the far option will have a reduced time value.
Share price equals exercise price	Maximum profits are achieved. The near option has zero intrinsic value and so expires worthless. The far-dated option is at-the-money and so has a high time value.
Share price above exercise price	The near-dated and far-dated option both have intrinsic value and one will offset the other. The time value of the far option is likely to be very low, perhaps creating a loss for the trader.

Table 7.4 Outcome of long calendar spread

Long time spread

In this case, a trader expects the time value between a near-dated option and a far-dated option to increase. He will, therefore, go long a far-dated option and short a near-dated option.

Short time spread

A trader would adopt this strategy if he felt that the time value differential was about to narrow. In such cases, he would purchase a near-dated option and go short (or sell) a far-dated option. The far-dated option would have a higher premium and would, therefore, have a higher time value. If volatility in the market increased, then the time value of the long-dated option would fall and so the trader would make money from the narrowing of the spread. This is illustrated in Figure 7.10.

Fig 7.10

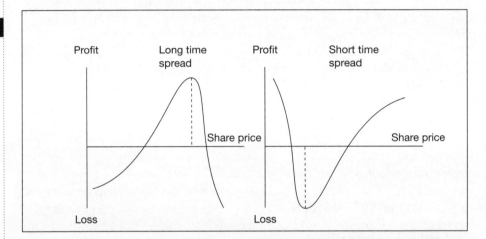

In the first case, the trader is long the time spread. If the far-dated option remains at-the-money then the difference in time value of both options will increase and so the trader will make money. In the second case, the trader is hoping that the time spread will narrow since he is short the time spread. If, when the near-dated option expires, the far-dated option is deeply out-of-the-money, the trader stands to benefit.

Increase in implied volatility

Who benefits if there is an increase in implied volatility: the trader who is long the time spread or the trader who is short the time spread?

The trader who is long the time spread benefits from such an increase. An increase in implied volatility makes an option more valuable. An option with a long time to maturity will benefit more than an option with a short time period to maturity. Therefore, the difference in the premium widens and, since the intrinsic value remains the same, the time gap widens. We can conclude, therefore, that there is a positive relationship between implied volatility and the time spread. Table 7.5 makes a distinction between a swift movement in the value of the underlying asset and an increase in implied volatility.

	Long time spread	Short time spread
Swift movement of underlying asset in either direction	Trader makes loss	Trader makes profit
Increase in implied volatility	Trader makes profit	Trader makes loss

Table 7.5 Relationship between implied volatility and time spread

A trader engaging in time spread strategies is effectively taking a position on two factors. He is attempting to forecast potential movements in the underlying markets, and is also attempting to forecast implied volatility. There appears to be an anomaly here. On the one hand, the trader who is long a time spread is hoping for no movement in the underlying price, and at the same time he is hoping for an increase in volatility. Is it possible to achieve these two objectives? Surprisingly, the answer is yes. Consider a situation where a court is about to hand down a decision on whether tobacco companies should be liable for damage to cancer sufferers. No one knows which way the decision will go, and so swift movements in the underlying asset are not expected in the lead up to the court case. However, traders will anticipate an increase in volatility, so we have a situation where there is no swift movement in the share price, but there is an increase in the implied volatility. A trader anticipating such a situation would go long a time spread.

Real and implied volatilities

Traders need to distinguish between real and implied volatilities. In fact, this is what distinguishes a time spread trade from an ordinary straddle or strangle. A short straddle, or short strangle, or long butterfly all have one factor in common: an increase in realized volatility can cause considerable losses, and a reduction in realised volatility can lead to profits. A risk manager must, however recognize that with a time spread, implied volatilities and realized volatilities will have opposite effects.

Risk-reduction strategies

A risk manager in charge of a busy operations desk needs to be aware of the various factors that will influence or drive profits. We have seen that where traders rely on volatility trading, monitoring the movement in volatility is more important than monitoring the movement in the underlying asset price. Where traders use time spread strategies, then implied volatility and realized volatility must be measured separately in order to measure the impact that they will have on the portfolio. A distinction must also be made between vega, which shows how a trader's profits are influenced by a change in volatility, and gamma, where the trader's profits are influenced by a change in delta. Many VaR systems adopt a "delta gamma" approach, which recognizes the gamma effect of options. However, the vega is just as important and in some cases, even more important. Even the delta gamma approach, although an improvement on the delta normal approach, needs to be refined if it is to be heavily relied upon.

High gamma and zero vega

Traders and risk managers can influence the profile of their options portfolio by carefully segregating options according to their risk profiles. For instance, a trader who requires a high gamma but low vega exposure could buy short maturity at-the-money options. A risk manager who feels that his overall portfolio is long gamma and is worried about the constant changes in the delta would simply short at-the-money options (particularly those whose maturity date is very close). At the moment, most VaR systems are not at an advanced enough stage to pick up on these little intricacies.

Similarly, if a trader requires high vega and little or no gamma he could purchase long maturity at-the-money options. Such options are very sensitive to changes in volatility but the gamma effect is minimal because they are too far away from maturity. Such positions should, of course, be rebalanced daily.

Conclusion

The above strategies are used widely in derivative trading and their sheer complexity can create a lot of problems for the risk manager. Most VaR systems (with the exception of those that are based on Monte Carlo simulation) are simply incapable of making subtle distinctions such as for implied and realized volatilities. Nor are they designed to deal with the nonlinear relationships discussed above. Most experienced risk managers believe that VaR systems, no matter how complex, are incapable of giving a realistic figure for options risk. This is a setback for the risk industry because it is options and complex derivatives that have been responsible for most of the losses setbacks in the past.

One possible solution is to make VaR more complex so that it can deal with nonlinear situations more effectively. There are two choices open to the designers. They can use a Monte Carlo approach or a parametric approach. Monte Carlo simulation, as discussed earlier, involves generating a number of scenarios and examining the impact they will have on a portfolio of option strategies. While this is capable of giving a theoretically correct figure, it must be very complex to deal with situations like implied volatility, realized volatility, theta, and so forth. There is the danger that in making the risk-measurement system more and more complex, risk managers will simply create opportunities for operational risk problems. They may have the most up to date and accurate model available, but if they don't understand it, relying on its output may prove dangerous.

The other alternative is to rely on a parametric approach. Loosely speaking, this involves setting up a complex series of mathematical equations which will incorporate the various risks associated with options. While this may be quicker and more efficient than the Monte Carlo simulation approach, accuracy is sacrificed for convenience and the problem of complexity remains. Most risk managers willingly admit that they don't fully understand the complex risk systems that they use. Indeed, given the choice of having a 100 percent accurate but complex system and an inexperienced risk team or a team of experienced risk professionals and a not too accurate system, most risk managers would choose the latter.

Monte Carlo Simulation

Monte Carlo simulation and its applications

Generating the share prices

Applying Monte Carlo simulation to VaR

Conclusion

Monte Carlo simulation and its applications

Introduction

Up to now we have looked at how VaR principles apply to straightforward products like bonds, forwards, and swaps. In relation to nonlinear products, we made a distinction between nonlinear owing to curvature, and nonlinear owing to a "break" or "kink" in the line. Most VaR models can cope with linear instruments and nonlinear instruments owing to curvature. We now deal with the unique nonlinear (broken line) risk that is associated with options. Consider an option that is close to at-the-money. One small movement in the underlying asset, in the days prior to maturity, could have a significant impact on its value. This erratic nature of options makes risk measurement a little difficult. A possible solution to this problem is to use Monte Carlo simulation techniques. In simple terms, Monte Carlo simulation (named after the famous roulette wheel) involves generating a series of prices for the underlying asset and then seeing how the derivative, in this case an option, behaves. In this chapter we look at how Monte Carlo simulation techniques apply.

VaR

Many critics of VaR believe that it is very unsuited to those derivatives with an implied option. With options there are too many parameters, and the interplay of these parameters makes risk modeling of options particularly difficult. Bonds, swaps, and forwards are relatively simple in comparison. The previous chapter revealed the unique characteristics of options. We now show how these unique characteristics are captured in the more accurate, but intensively time consuming, Monte Carlo approach.

Terminology

We saw in Chapter four (page 75) that there were two ways to calculate interest rates, simple and compound. For option pricing there is a third convention called **continuous compounding** (also known as the **exponential interest rate**). This convention assumes that interest is compounded literally every second. The more often interest is compounded the greater is the effective rate. For instance $e^{0.10} = 1.10518$. This simply means that if £1 was invested in an account for one year for 10% using the continuous compound convention, the actual interest paid would be 10.518p. The discount value under the same convention, for 10% is 0.9048. Option modelers prefer to use the continuous compound convention when pricing options. Since it is based on the natural logarithm it is easier to manipulate in formula terms and also allows a consistent basis for calculating interest rates. The simple and discrete compound conventions are not as effective for this purpose.

Valuing an option using Monte Carlo

In Table 8.1 we set out details of a call option that we wish to value using a Monte Carlo approach. The call is European, which means that, unlike an American option that is exercisable at any time up to maturity, the European option is exercisable at maturity only. The option is based on a share whose current value of £100 and has an exercise price of £95. It is clear to see that the option is currently in-the-money, meaning that it is worth something (in this case £5) if exercised now.

	A	B
193	Current share price	£100
194	Volatility	20%
195	Drift	10%
196	Time to maturity	1
197	Exercise price	£95

Table 8.1 Option details

We present a very simplified Monte Carlo type simulation in Table 8.2.

	A	B	C	D	E	F
199		First	Second	Third	Fourth	Fifth
200		trial	trial	trial	trial	trial
201	Generated share price	£126.48	£110.52	£93.40	£85.53	£135.97
202	Intrinsic value of option	£31.48	£15.52	£0.00	£0.00	£40.97
203	Discount factor	0.9048	0.9048	0.9048	0.9048	0.9048
204	Present value of option	28.48	14.04	0.00	0.00	37.07

Table 8.2 Option values

Imagine a (Monte Carlo) roulette wheel containing possible share prices. At the first trial we throw the ball and it lands on £126.48. This means that the option will be exercised and, at maturity, its value will be the difference between the share price and the exercise price of £126.48 – £95 = £31.48. This money is payable in the future and as we wish to obtain the call's current value, we discount the future amount back to the present. Therefore, the first trial suggests that the option is worth £28.48. Note that the discount factor assumes that the interest rate is a "continuous compound." We, therefore, use the exponential function "e" to get the present value.

In the second case, the roulette wheel produces a share price of £110.52, and a similar procedure applies. The intrinsic value, which is the future value of the option this time, is £15.52 and, as before, we convert to present value. In the third and fourth cases, the future share price comes to £93.40 and £85.53 respectively. Since both of these figures are below £95, the option will not be exercised and so it is worth zero. In the fifth case we get £37.07.

The above shows that with each possible simulation we get values ranging from £37 to 0. The final step of Monte Carlo simulation is simply to obtain an average and this represents our option value. We can also estimate the probability that the option will be exercised by counting the number of times the intrinsic value has a positive value. In this case, the average of the five present values is 15.92. In theory this is what we should pay for the option. Second, the probability that the option will be exercised is 0.60 since three out of the five simulations produced a positive intrinsic value. Readers who are familiar with Black and Scholes will recognize that 0.60 represents the equivalent of N(d2) which is the probability that an option will be exercised.

We now look at the formulas behind the various figures to get an intuitive idea of what is happening (Table 8.3).

	A	B	C	D
193	Current share price	100		
194	Volatility	0.2		
195	Drift	0.1		
196	Time period	1		
197	Exercise price	95		
198				
199		First	Second	Third
200		trial	trial	trial
201				
202	Generated share price	126.48	110.52	93.4
203	Intrinsic value of option	=MAX(B202-$B$197,0)	=MAX(C202-$B$197,0)	=MAX(D202-$B$197,0)
204	Discount factor	=EXP(-$B$197*$B$197)	=EXP(-$B$197*$B$197)	=EXP(-$B$197*$B$197)
205	Present value of option	=B203*B204	=C203*C204	=D203*D204

Table 8.3 Spreadsheet formulas behind option values

There are two important Excel functions we use. The first is the "=MAX" function. In the above case, we simply ask Excel to produce the maximum of two values $S - X$, which is the intrinsic value of the option (if it is in-the-money) or 0. It is this function or the inherent choice that makes options complex. The yes/no situation creates nonlinearity, and this in turn creates complexities too great for conventional risk measurement techniques.

The second is the "=EXP" function or the continuous compound discount factor. In cell C16 we use this continuous compound discount factor, which is the equivalent of exponential "e."

Generating the share prices

Unfortunately, generating the share prices in a Monte Carlo simulation is not a straightforward matter. There are number of characteristics that we need to address in order to develop a model which reflects the movement of share prices.

Expected share price

Consider a situation where an investor is undecided between putting money into shares or the bank. If interest rates are 10 percent, then investing £100 today will give about £110 at maturity. A rational investor will put £100 into the bank if the expected value of the share price in one year is below 10 percent. If the expected value of the share price is significantly above 10 percent then the rational investor would buy the share. We can conclude from this that if interest rates are 10 percent for the year, the market (which consists of rational investors!) expects the share price to rise by 10 percent.

Clearly, in reality, investors will seek a risk premium and some of the more risk adverse investors will look for a return of, say, at least 12 percent on the share (2 percent above the normal bank rate). In theory, however, it is possible to eliminate the market risk by constructing a portfolio of shares and options. The famous Black and Scholes model has used this approach when valuing options. They value their options by constructing a risk neutral or risk free portfolio (which contains options). By valuing this portfolio and working backwards, they come up with a formula that values option. A risk neutral portfolio is one whose value does not change as the share price changes. So, it is not totally unrealistic to assume that rational investors will simply seek a return equivalent to the risk free rate of interest. Our Monte Carlo structure, therefore, must be such that the generated share prices incorporate the current rate of interest or more correctly, the opportunity cost of capital.

Stochastic element

There will always be a random pattern to share prices. The greater the volatility of shares the greater is the randomness. This is the second factor that we must build into our model. If the volatility is high, we can expect the share prices to deviate away from its mean significantly and this in turn will have an impact on option prices. The level of volatility is greater as the time to maturity is greater. This is explained next.

Stochastic element and time period

The volatility of a share price or any other commodity is related to the square root of time rather than time itself. For instance, if the annual volatility for a share is 20 percent, then the volatility over a two-year period is represented by:

$$\sigma\sqrt{\Delta t}$$

This gives 20%*1.4142 = 28.28%.

Most practitioners have difficulty in understanding this relationship. The example that follows should help to enlighten them.

Risk exposure

Consider a situation where a shareholder buys a share in Company X and holds it for two years, and a second shareholder buys two shares in the same company and holds them for one year. Assume that the volatility on share X is 20 percent. Which investor is taking the greater risk?

The answer is that the second shareholder is taking on a bigger risk. This is due to the fact that the two assets in the second shareholder's portfolio have a correlation of 1. Therefore, the portfolio has a standard deviation of 2×20 percent = 40 percent. If the share was worth £100, the annual volatility of the two-share portfolio would be £40.

In the case of the first shareholder, we make an important assumption that a share's random path is independent of what happened previously. Therefore, if a share price has fallen in the previous year, it does not have any impact on what will happen in the current year. The correlation between the two time periods (year 1 and year 2) is, therefore, zero. We would expect a lower combined standard deviation in these cases. The volatility is simply 20 percent $\times$ 1.414 = 28.82 percent, and if the share is worth £100, the standard deviation is £28.82.

Normal distribution

The normal distribution curve is designed to cope with situations where the probability of a variable moving far away from the mean is remote and the probability that the variable stays close to the mean is quite high. If a share has a value of £100 we would expect, after a year, to see the share price relatively close to £100. The probability of finding a value of £10 or £1000 is very remote. Therefore, when generating random share prices, we must "alter" the theoretical Monte Carlo roulette wheel by making sure that extreme values have a very low likelihood of succeeding. As will be shown below, we achieve this by using the normal distribution curve in reverse.

Lognormal distributions

The final factor we must consider when generating random share prices is that it is not the share prices themselves but the return on the share prices that follows a normal distribution. More technically, a variable follows a lognormal distribution if its natural log follows a normal distribution. This is due to the fact that an absolute increase of £1 is easier to achieve, if the share price is £100 (a 1 percent move) than if the share price is £2 (a 50 percent) move. When we use normal distribution tables, therefore, we base our results on the continuous return (also known as the exponential).

Tailoring the roulette wheel

The benefit of mathematics is that all of the above can be captured in a small formula:

$$e^{(u\Delta t + \epsilon\sigma \sqrt{\Delta t})}$$

The above formula represents the expected value of a share in the future. Suppose that the above came to 1.23 and the current share price was £100, then the future share price would be £123. In the above formula:

u represents the growth rate or the risk free rate of interest

sigma represents the standard deviation

delta t represents the change in time

ϵ represents a "draw" from the normal distribution curve.

The examples that follow might help the reader to make more sense of the above.

In the previous example (Table 8.2), we generated the following share prices:

Example

	First trial	Second trial	Third trial	Fourth trial	Fifth trial
Generated share price	£126.48	£110.52	£93.40	£85.53	£135.97

Table 8.4 Generated share prices

Note that most of the share prices stay relatively close to the expected future share price of £110. This is due to the fact that we used the normal distribution curve to generate sensible and realistic prices. In theory, the average of the above figures should come to £110. In fact, they come to £110.38. However, this is more due to good luck than anything else. With only five trials, there is obviously the risk that the sample size will not be large enough and so we could just as easily have obtained a misleading mean.

Table 8.5 shows how the above figures were constructed.

	B	C
2	Current share price	£100
3	Volatility	20%
4	Drift	10%
5	Time to maturity	1
6	Exercise price	£95

Table 8.5 Option details

	B	C	D	E	F	G
8		First	Second	Third	Fourth	Fifth
9		trial	trial	trial	trial	trial
10	Random numbers	0.7500	0.5000	0.2000	0.1000	0.8500
11	Standard deviations	0.6745	0.0000	−0.8416	−1.2816	1.0364
12	Growth	0.2349	0.1000	−0.0683	−0.1563	0.3073
13	Exponential growth	1.26478	1.10517	0.93396	0.85529	1.3597
14	Generated share price	£126.48	£110.52	£93.40	£85.53	£135.97

Table 8.6 Procedure for generating share prices

First, we ask the computer to generate random figures between 0 and 1. In the first trial, the computer generates 0.7500. We then assume that this represents the area to the left of a variable under the normal distribution curve. The computer then calculates how many standard deviations above the mean are necessary to have 75 percent of the curve to the left of the line. The answer, which can be confirmed from the normal distribution tables by reading in reverse is 0.6745. Figure 8.1 illustrates this.

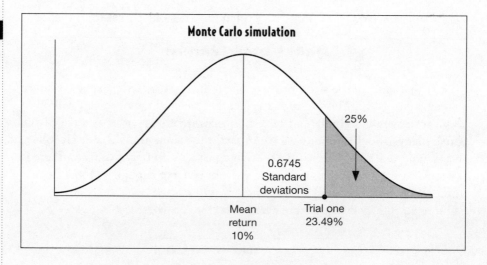

The figure of 0.2349 is simply the mean return 10 percent + 0.6745 × the standard deviation 0.20 to give a total of 0.2349. Fortunately, the time period is equal to 1, the square root of which is also 1 and this simplifies the calculation. Since we are dealing with lognormal returns, the actual return can be calculated (using the exponential function) as 1.26478. This means that we expect the share price to grow by 26.48 percent over the year. Since the original price is £100, the future price comes to £126.48.

In the case of the second trial, the computer generates a random figure of 0.50. Therefore, we must try and find a figure where the area to the left represents 50 percent. Obviously, this must be the mean itself and so there will be no standard deviations in our calculations. Therefore, the actual future price generated represents the mean price which is £110.52. Remember that the continuous growth function produces an increase slightly above 10 percent in this case.

For trials three and four, the computer has picked random numbers below the mean and, therefore, we end up with a negative number of standard deviations. Once we have an area under the curve below 50 percent, we would naturally expect the future value of the share to be below the mean of £110.52.

For readers who would like to model the above on Excel, we show the formulas we have used.

		B	C
2		Current share price	£100
3		Volatility	20%
4		Drift	10%
5		Time period	1
6		Exercise price	£95

Table 8.7 Option details

The random number can be obtained by using the function = rand(). This will produce a value greater than or equal to zero but less than 1.

	B	C
8		First
9		trial
10	Random numbers	=RAND()
11	Standard deviations	=NORMSINV(C10)
12	Growth	=$C$4+C11*$C$3*$C$5^0.5
13	Exponential growth	=EXP(C12)
14	Generated share price	=$C$2*C13
15	Intrinsic value of option	=MAX(C14-$C$6,0)
16	Discount factor	=EXP(-$C$4*$C$5)
17	Present value of option	=C15*C16

Table 8.8 Spreadsheet formulas to value options

Summary

This section briefly introduced how Monte Carlo simulations could be used to simulate future prices. When valuing an option we simply generate a number of possible share prices and then calculate the intrinsic value (if any) that the option will have in the future. The final step is in bringing it back to present value. Monte Carlo simulation is often used to price complex exotic options that are beyond the grasp of analytical models such as Black and Scholes. Risk managers and mathematical modelers find that Monte Carlo simulation is very flexible to suit their individual needs. What is important, however, is to recognize the "random walk" that share prices tend to take. Of utmost importance is the fact that it is the return on share prices, not the share prices themselves, that is normally distributed. Also, share prices seldom move to extreme values. In the vast majority of cases, the share price stays relatively close to the mean. All of these factors have been incorporated in the method displayed.

Applying Monte Carlo simulation to VaR

One of the main advantages of Monte Carlo simulation is that it can deal with portfolios whose options contain price dependent paths. Lookback options and average rate options are generally difficult to price in the conventional way. With Monte Carlo simulation, the process becomes easier. Given the trend toward more exotic and more complex options, structured Monte Carlo simulation is likely to grow in importance, not only as a pricing tool but also as a risk-measurement tool. Monte Carlo simulation can also be used to place a value on the other Greeks. For instance, changing the volatility and keeping the random numbers constant can reveal how much an option gains in value when volatility is changed, say from 20 percent to 21 percent. Price changes can, of course, also be incorporated.

The concept can be very easily applied to VaR. For instance, to calculate the VaR of the above option, we could run the simulation say 10 000 times and pick the five-hundreth lowest value. This represents the VaR at the 95 percent level. With computers becoming more powerful and easier to use, Monte Carlo calculations, even for, say, 10 000 runs are becoming less time consuming and easier to implement.

Random pricing

In the above example, we assumed for convenience that prices change once a year. The reality is, of course, that prices can change every five minutes and so, we would refine the technique above to reflect this. This involves breaking the time down into discrete sizes so that each trial is over t/n time periods, where n is the amount of smaller time periods. The example shown in Tables 8.9 and 8.10 illustrates how this would be achieved.

	First trial
Time period	0.001
Random numbers	0.1780
Standard deviations	−0.9229
Growth	0.0942
Exponential growth	1.09874
Generated share price	£109.87

Table 8.9 First trial

Time period	0.001
Random numbers	0.6598
Standard deviations	0.4119
Growth	0.0087
Exponential growth	1.00873
Generated share price	**£110.83**

Table 8.10 Second trial

In the above example, we have broken the year down into 1000 parts and generated a share price for each part separately. The process is the same as before except that we now put the change in time at 0.001. Obviously, the first share price is going to stay close to the original price because the time movement is very small. In the second time period, we use the share price calculated from the first simulation. Therefore, the figure £110.83 is simply £109.87 × 1.00873 = £110.83.

Correlation between assets

Monte Carlo simulation can deal with correlation between assets very effectively. This is achieved by manipulating the random selection process so that correlation relationships are preserved. Consider a situation where a bank has written an at-the-money call options on the dollar (against sterling) and at-the-money put options on the same exchange rate. If the dollar weakens, the put option becomes more valuable and the call moves out-of-the-money. Similarly, if the dollar gets stronger the put loses value and the call gains value. Therefore, a Monte Carlo simulation would simply generate future dollar/sterling exchange rates and use the same rate to price both a call and a put. In developing the random path, the "drift" in the exchange rate will depend on the difference between the sterling interest rate and the dollar interest rate. If the sterling interest rate was greater than the dollar interest rate, over a particular period, we would expect sterling to weaken and vice versa if the dollar interest rate exceeded the sterling rate. Obviously, when calculating the inherent risk of the options in this portfolio, we don't want the Monte Carlo structure to assume that calls and puts go up at the same time. In the above example, since both instruments use the same future exchange rate, this is quite easy to implement.

A more difficult situation arises when a call and a put option are written on two separate assets where both the assets themselves are correlated. Consider a situation where a bank writes a call option on a company producing heating oil, and writes a call option on one producing suntan lotion. Assume for the sake of simplicity that both companies have a negative correlation of –0.8. In this situation there is a low probability, that both options will be exercised. Without any adjustment, a Monte Carlo simulation approach would assume that a correlation of zero exists between the assets. This is clearly incorrect. Consider a second situation where the bank writes a put option on the suntan lotion company, a call option on the heating oil company and the weather turns out to be very cold over a period. The likelihood is that both options will be exercised. Again, in the absence of a correlation adjustment, a Monte Carlo simulation assumes that a zero correlation exists between both assets and this, of course, underestimates the true risk. Fortunately, a procedure known as Cholesky decomposition solves this problem.

Cholesky decomposition

When generating random numbers, the Cholesky process manipulates the randomness of the numbers by making sure that the correlation between assets is preserved. Suppose, for instance, that a random process was programmed to generate random numbers for two assets. The random numbers themselves are chosen as normal and based on this, we calculate the number of standard deviations as before. However, if the correlation is not zero, that is if there is some relationship between the variables, we make an adjustment to reflect this. The most popular method among VaR practitioners is the Cholesky method. Table 8.11 illustrates how this is achieved.

	Asset One	Asset Two
Time period	1	1
Random numbers	0.1042	0.7845
Standard deviations	−1.2580	0.7875
Cholesky adjustment	−1.2580	−1.2580
Growth	−0.1516	−0.1516
Exponential growth	0.85933	0.85933
Generated share price	£85.93	£85.93

Table 8.11 Cholesky adjustment where correlation =1

In this case, we have a portfolio of two assets. Both assets have a correlation of 1 with each other. This simply means that if Asset One goes up then Asset Two must go up as well. As before, we ask the computer to generate random numbers and then we use the normal distribution curve in reverse to make sure that figures close to the mean have a better chance of coming up compared to extreme values. This adjustment, however, is not enough. We must now make a Cholesky adjustment to reflect the correlation of one. As is evident above, the adjustment makes sure that when the first share price goes down, the second one goes down as well. Similarly, if the first share price went up, so too would the second.

Table 8.12 gives further insight into the way that Cholesky operates.

Random Numbers		0.1042	0.7845
Normal distribution adjustment		−1.2580	0.7875
Correlation			
	−1	−1.2580	1.2580
	0	−1.2580	0.7875
	1	−1.2580	−1.2580
	0.9	−1.2580	−0.7889

Table 8.12 Cholesky decomposition

Assume that the computer generates random numbers as before and we adjust them using the normal distribution table. If we ask for a correlation of −1, Cholesky will amend the figures so that if one asset is going up, the other must go down. If we specify a correlation of zero, then both assets are independent and so there is no need for any adjustment. If we specify a correlation of 1 then both assets will fall together. Finally, if we specify a correlation of 0.90, then Asset One falls, but Asset Two does not fall by as much.

Techniques behind Cholesky decomposition

The Cholesky factorization process is based on matrix algebra. For a full discussion on the subject, refer to JP Morgan's RiskMetrics documentation.

Conclusion

This chapter has illustrated the third technique of VaR risk measurement: Monte Carlo simulation. As the examples have shown, Monte Carlo can simulate optionality of whatever form and can deal effectively with even the most complex of exotic options. However, for a meaningful result, the number of simulations can often run into millions. For instance, there are many variables that affect option prices such as interest rates, underlying price, and volatility. Each of these must be varied in order to get a realistic risk measurement, so the number of simulations can be very high.

That said, the Monte Carlo simulation is likely to grow in importance. Risk modelers are currently developing ways to develop shortcuts which will preserve the quality of the Monte Carlo estimate, yet reduce substantially the amount of simulations involved.

Applying VaR Principles to Credit Control

Measuring credit risk more accurately

Introduction

For centuries, banks have built up considerable expertise in the evaluation and control of credit. Yet, it is only recently that banks have started to look at credit risk from a portfolio basis. At the present time, most banks manage credit risk by imposing limits on the amount of money that they lend to a counterparty. The procedure is analogous to the way that market risk was traditionally controlled, simply by putting limits on the amount of money that traders could put at risk. Today, the emphasis is on using the techniques developed by VaR systems to quantify the overall credit risk assessment on a portfolio basis which measures exposure to market, rating change, and default risk. The overall role and aim of this approach is to help portfolio managers to better identify those areas which are contributing most to credit risk and, like VaR, to examine possibilities for diversification.

In the past, risk managers relied heavily on their own intuitive feelings when making decisions on credit risk. Obviously, a credit portfolio model will not replace the quality of the decisions that experienced credit managers will make, but it will focus minds on the marginal credit risk that a bank is exposed to as opposed to the absolute risk.

Risk concentration

One dilemma facing banks is that while they want to build up expertise in lending to a particular sector, they do not want to overexpose themselves to that sector. For instance, a bank may concentrate its lending portfolio on the British building sector. The benefit of doing so is that by gathering up specialist knowledge it has a better understanding of the building industry and can, therefore, forecast troubled companies or troublesome loans more accurately. However, by over-exposing itself to one particular sector, there is the risk that the bank itself will collapse if the industry faces a downturn. In the past, banks have simply imposed counterparty limits as well as industry sector limits. Although such tactics control risk, they are unsatisfactory in that they prevent banks from exploiting lucrative and profitable opportunities. The ideal situation is where banks can build up their specialist knowledge and then diversify their risk away. In the past this was not possible, but now, with the emergence of credit derivatives, banks can apply their expertise in one sector and then "swap" credit risk with another bank in order to reduce its exposure, thus achieving diversification. VaR techniques have an important role to play for credit managers. In the first place, loan managers can identify those loans that contribute most to risk. Second, the risk manager can identify areas where credit derivatives can reduce his bank's exposure to risk.

The Monte Carlo approach to estimation of credit risk

Up to now, we have relied heavily on the normal distribution curve when measuring VaR. It features in the variance covariance method and in Monte Carlo simulation. However, with credit risk, the normal distribution curve may not be the most appropriate model. Most experts believe that market risk does not have an exact normal distribution profile, but the distribution is at least symmetric, and so is close to being normally distributed. Credit risk is not symmetrical, and, thus less suited to the normal distribution curve. This is shown in Figure 9.1.

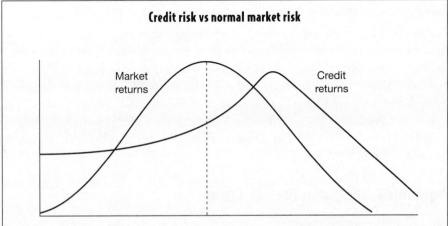

Credit risk vs normal market risk

Market returns

Credit returns

Fig 9.1

The normal distribution curve is the more symmetric of the two curves. This simply means that the returns of a portfolio have as equal a chance of going up as they do of going down. The curve for credit risk is, however, skewed. This means that in the majority of cases a portfolio will have above average returns. However, there are a few cases when the portfolio will make a loss and, although the probabilities of these losses are quite small, when they do occur, they tend to be quite large. So, although the probability of making losses is below 50 percent for credit risk, the probability that a portfolio will make a large credit loss is quite high. We can see, therefore, that traditional VaR methods (which rely on the normal distribution curve) will underestimate the possibility of making huge losses. The Monte Carlo simulation approach overcomes this weakness.

Credit event

There are two types of credit event:
- the borrower goes bankrupt
- the borrower suffers a credit downgrading from a credit agency.

In order to measure credit risk, we must first define a credit event. A credit loss is usually triggered by what is known as a credit event. Put simply, a credit event can take two forms. First the firm goes bankrupt, and second, the firm suffers a credit downgrading, in which case the value of the loan or bond declines. The value of a bond can be decomposed between interest rate changes and changes in credit quality. To assess credit risk we are not interested in the fact that an increase in interest rates may bring the price of a bond down. We are simply concerned with the loss in value of a bond or loan because the issuer or borrower has either defaulted or has suffered a credit migration; in such cases the probability of a default will increase.

Doubtful loan provisions

For profit and loss purposes, a more satisfactory approach to credit loss is to recognize when the quality of the loan has reduced and not to simply "book" the bad debt when it arises. This obviously creates less distortion in the profit and loss account and the actual profit or loss is measured with greater precision. Most banks now use VaR techniques when estimating the size of the loan provision. If over a year the quality of a loan suffered but did not reach default stage, then the loss in value, as a result of the greater risk, should be incorporated into the profit and loss account.

Probabilities of a change in credit rating

We can illustrate the probabilities that a particular bond will suffer either a credit migration or default. Tables as illustrated in Table 9.11 are generally available from credit reference agencies.

Rating	First issuer	Second issuer
Initial rating	BBB	CCC
AAA	0.03%	0.22%
AA	0.32%	0.01%
A	5.94%	0.23%
BBB	87.00%	1.29%
BB	**4.40%**	2.39%
B	**1.20%**	11.25%
CCC	**0.13%**	68.00%
Default	**0.98%**	**16.61%**
	100.00%	100.00%

Table 9.1 Probability of credit change

Assume that a bank has a portfolio of two bonds as shown above. The first issuer is BBB rated and the second issuer is CCC rated. The probability that the portfolio makes a loss is the total of the probabilities in bold type. For the first issuer this is 6.71 percent and for the second 16.61 percent. The first issuer has a credit rating of BBB, while the second one has a credit rating of CCC and a high probability of going into default.

Notice that if the bonds had a normal distribution, then the combined probability of making a loss for each bond would be 50 percent each. Figures 9.2 and 9.3 intuitively explain why the normal distribution curve is unsuited to measurement of credit risk. In Figure 9.2, the probability of not making a credit loss is very high at 77.8 percent and the probability of making a credit loss is 22.2 percent. In Figure 9.3, the probability of avoiding a loss completely is only 25 percent. The probability of making a loss will depend on the weightings of the bonds but in cases two, three and four, it is possible that a market loss can occur.

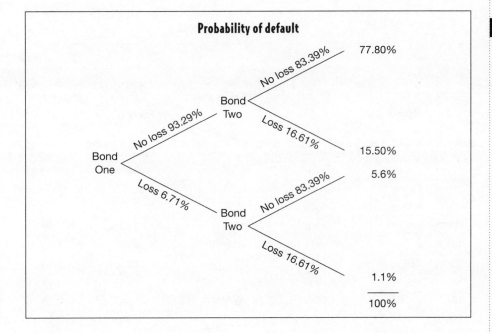

Fig 9.2

Before we generate random variables, we must adjust the figures in Table 9.1 to standard deviations. To do this, we simply assume that bond prices follow a normal distribution curve and calculate the number of standard deviations. Note that at this stage we are looking at the possibility that bond prices will change but are not, at this stage, trying to calculate the losses. Therefore, we can use the normal distribution curve to see how many standard deviations are necessary before an asset moves up or down to new credit ratings.

Fig 9.3

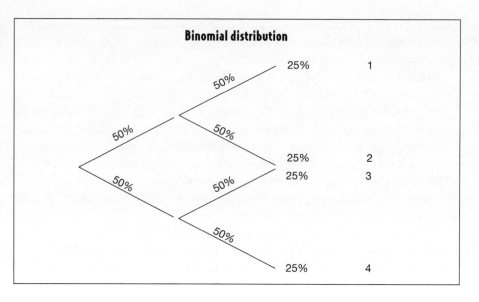

Binomial distribution

	B	C	D	E	F
114	Bond A			Number	
115				of	
116		Probability	Cumulative	standard	
117			probability	deviations	
118	Rating			From	To
119	AAA	0.03%			
120	AA	0.32%	99.97%	3.43	2.70
121	A	5.94%	99.65%	2.70	1.53
122	BBB	87.00%	93.71%	1.53	−1.50
123	BB	4.40%	6.71%	−1.50	−1.99
124	B	1.20%	2.31%	−1.99	−2.29
125	CCC	0.13%	1.11%	−2.29	−2.33
126	Default	0.98%	0.98%	−2.33	

Table 9.2   Probability of a change in credit rating for Bond One

Table 9.2 can be interpreted as follows. If the return of the asset moves, say, 2.5 standard deviations below the mean, its credit rating will be B (between −2.18 and −2.75). Alternatively, if the new return is two standard deviations above the mean, its new rating will be A.

The next step is to do simulation tables as follows:

	C	D
98		Probability
99		
100	AAA	0.03%
101	AA	0.32%
102	A	5.94%
103	BBB	87.00%
104	BB	4.40%
105	B	1.20%
106	CCC	0.13%
107	Default	0.98%

Table 9.3 Rating probability for first issuer

	B	C	D	E	F
114	Bond A			Number	
115				of	
116		Probability	Cumulative	standard	
117			probability	deviations	
118	Rating			From	To
119	AAA	0.0002			
120	AA	0.0033	=C120+D121	=NORMSINV(D120)	=E121
121	A	0.0595	=C121+D122	=NORMSINV(D121)	=E122
122	BBB	0.8693	=C122+D123	=NORMSINV(D122)	=E123
123	BB	0.053	=C123+D124	=NORMSINV(D123)	=E124
124	B	0.0117	=C124+D125	=NORMSINV(D124)	=E125
125	CCC	0.0012	=C125+D126	=NORMSINV(D125)	=E126
126	Default	0.0018	=C126	=NORMSINV(D126)	

Table 9.4 Spreadsheet formulas to calculate standard deviation for Table 9.2

For Bond B the relevant table is as follows:

	B	C	D	E	F
128	Bond B			Number	
129				of	
130		Probability	Cumulative	standard	
131			probability	deviations	
132	Rating				
133	AAA	0.22%		From	To
134	AA	0.01%	99.78%	2.85	2.83
135	A	0.23%	99.77%	2.83	2.60
136	BBB	1.29%	99.54%	2.60	2.11
137	BB	2.39%	98.25%	2.11	1.73
138	B	11.25%	95.86%	1.73	1.02
139	CCC	68.00%	84.61%	1.02	−0.97
140	Default	16.61%	16.61%	−0.97	

Table 9.5 Probability statistics for second issuer

The first step in risk estimation, using Monte Carlo simulation, is to generate random variables. This is the equivalent to using the random function on Excel, but because bonds are correlated with each other, we must "adjust" the randomness of the numbers to reflect this. Let's assume that the bonds have a correlation of 1. Then we can use the calculations in Table 9.6:

	Asset One	Asset Two
Random numbers	0.1042	0.7845
Standard deviations	−1.2580	0.7875
Cholesky adjustment	−1.2580	−1.2580
Rating	BBB	Default

Table 9.6 First Monte Carlo simulation

Table 9.6 can be intuitively interpreted as follows. Assume that the correlation between both assets is one. Asset One is a bond issued from Company X and Asset Two from Company Y. Both are in the same industry, and this explains the strong correlation between them. The second company is clearly the weaker because the asset starts off with a credit rating of CCC, which is close to default. The random number for Asset One is only 0.1042 and is well below the mean point of 0.50 (this is the point where the normal distribution curve is split in two). Therefore, the random generator has picked a scenario where the building industry has suffered. The random number for Asset Two looks brighter, but the Cholesky adjustment recognizes the fact that both assets move together. In other words, they have a correlation of 1; therefore, the random figure for Asset Two can be ignored. The figure −1.2580 applies to both bonds. This means that the returns of both assets have gone 1.2580 standard deviations below the mean. We then look up the tables for Bond A and Bond B. Bond A stays at credit rating BBB. From Table 9.2 we see that the movement −1.2580 falls between 1.50 and −1.53, and Bond B moves from CCC to default (−1.2580 is below −0.97 in Table 9.5).

The final step is to calculate the market value of each of these bonds after the simulation.

Services like JP Morgan's CreditMetrics and other credit reference agencies are able to produce tables similar to Table 9.7.

Category	Year one	Year two	Year three
AAA	4.00%	4.30%	4.70%
AA	4.35%	4.65%	5.05%
A	4.36%	4.66%	5.06%
BBB	4.71%	5.01%	5.41%
BB	4.72%	5.02%	5.42%
B	5.07%	5.37%	5.77%
CCC	15.42%	15.72%	16.12%
Default			

Table 9.7 Discount factors for bond ratings

This table simply tells us that investors require a higher risk premium if they are going to buy a risky asset. The table also reveals that the yield curve is upward sloping, that is, in the long term, interest rates are expected to rise. In fact, it could be an indication that trouble may lie ahead for the building industry or other similar types of industries.

For our purposes, we need this information to value our bond. Assume that the first bond has three years left to maturity; we can use the grid in Table 9.8 to value it for each of the credit categories.

	£10	£10	£110	MV
AAA	0.9615	0.9192	0.8713	£114.65
AA	0.9583	0.9131	0.8626	£113.60
A	0.9582	0.9129	0.8624	£113.57
BBB	0.9550	0.9069	0.8538	£112.54
BB	0.9549	0.9067	0.8536	£112.51
B	0.9517	0.9007	0.8451	£111.49
CCC	0.8664	0.7468	0.6387	£86.39
Default				

Table 9.8 Bond valuations for different credit ratings

To get the figure 0.9131 we take 4.65 percent for two years, that is $1/(1+r)^n = 0.9131$.

To calculate the market value, we simply discount each of the cash flows to their present value, that is for Bond AA £10 × 0.9583 = £9.583 and £9.583 +£9.131+£94.89 = £113.60.

A default bond is a little bit more difficult to deal with simply because there would be uncertainty about the recovery rate. Again, credit reference agencies provide details of possible recovery rates in the event of default. For the sake of completing our table, we will assume a default recovery rate of 60 percent, giving Bond B a future value of £60.

	Asset One	Asset Two
Time period	1	1
Random numbers	0.1042	0.7845
Standard deviations	−1.2580	0.7875
Cholesky adjustment	−1.2580	−1.2580
Rating	BBB	Default
MV	£112.54	£60
Nominal value holding	£7 000 000	£10 000 000
Future market value	£7 877 800	£6 000 000
Value of portfolio	£13 877 800	

Table 9.9 Valuation of a portfolio

This simulation could be done, say, 10 000 times and then we would take the five-hundredth lowest result to get the 95 percent confidence level. The difference between the current value of the portfolio and the "simulated" value of the portfolio would then be the credit at risk.

Summary

This section illustrates how we can apply VaR techniques in estimating the amount of losses we could make due to a credit event, namely a reduction in the value of the loan or a default by the issuer. As with VaR, diversification is important. A bank could reduce risk if it diversified its portfolio across a broad range of issuers instead of concentrating on just a few areas. There is a conflict, of course, in doing this. Banks can reduce risk if they concentrate on one specific sector and build up expertise in that sector. The side effect of such a policy is that the bank is overconcentrated. We will see later how a bank can attain both objectives: specialize and diversify. This could be achieved, first, by using a portfolio approach to credit risk in order to estimate exposure and second, using credit derivatives in order to reduce specific exposure levels.

Unfortunately, credit risk does not follow a normal distribution, so we must alter the VaR methodology in order to measure the amount of credit at risk. Unlike market risk, VaR cannot assume that a portfolio of bonds follows a normal distribution. Therefore, we must look at each of the bonds separately but still apply normal distribution methodology to measure the risk that a bond will default. Once this is achieved, we calculate the value of the bond. Finally, we use Cholesky's decomposition method to capture any correlation effects between bonds.

JP Morgan, the architect behind RiskMetrics, has introduced a new product – CreditMetrics – which is a framework for quantifying credit in portfolios of traditional credit products. As with VaR, the aim is to promote greater transparency of credit risk, and to provide a benchmark for credit-risk measurement.

Reducing credit risk

Overview

In the previous section we outlined the importance of measuring risk on a portfolio basis. In this section, we consider how we can use such measurements to reduce risk. Traditionally, banks set controls in two areas:

1 They considered the largest absolute size of the risk.
2 They considered the probability that a company would go into default.

Banks would, of course, have restricted the amount of money they lent to customers with a poor credit rating. The worst fear naturally is that banks lend large amounts of money to companies, only to find that they have suffered a credit migration.

Calculating risk on a portfolio basis allows us to measure how much an individual instrument contributes to the overall risk of the portfolio. This allows for better decision making. We can, for instance, identify those types of loans that contribute most to risk. With this knowledge, a bank can make better quality decisions on resource allocation, performance measurement, and regulatory requirements.

Regulatory requirements

Bank regulators have developed capital adequacy rules designed to penalize those banks which expose themselves to credit risk without implementing an appropriate hedge or control procedure. As with VaR, the purpose of portfolio risk management is to reassure the regulators that a particular bank is very aware of its credit exposures and has control procedures in place, thus reducing the possibility of closure. Obviously, it is in the interest of regulators to make sure that the portfolio risk management system is one that identifies not only the type of credit risk that a bank is exposed to, but also the effectiveness of the hedges used.

Portfolio mismanagement: ISDA vs the Bank of England

In January 1997, the International Swap Dealers Association (ISDA) raised concerns about how the Bank of England treated credit books for the purposes of calculating capital adequacy. The ISDA argued that credit derivatives used to reduce portfolio credit risk should be reflected in the capital adequacy calculation.

Consider a situation where a bank has £20 million in its loan book and £30 million in its swaps book. Its capital adequacy based on weighting of 20 percent and a rate of 8 percent would be as shown in Table 9.10.

Example

	Nominal amount	Weighting	Capital adequacy 8%
Loans	£20 000 000	100% £20 000 000	£1 600 000
Swaps	£30 000 000	20% £6 000 000	£480 000
			£2 080 000

Table 9.10 Capital adequacy calculation

A bank might use a credit default swap to control £6m of its loans. The correct economic treatment would be as shown in Table 9.11.

	Nominal amount	Weighting	Capital adequacy 8%
Loans	£14 000 000	100% £14 000 000	£1 120 000
Swaps	£30 000 000	20% £6 000 000	£480 000
			£1 600 000
Credit default swap	£1 000 000	£200 000	£16 000
	Total		£1 616 000

Table 9.11 Diversified capital adequacy calculation

In the above example, the credit default risk covers £6m of loans, but the nominal amount is substantially reduced to reflect the fact that the counterparty (the party underwriting the risk) has a very high credit rating.

The Bank of England nevertheless ignores the fact that the credit default derivative is being used as a hedge, and so calculates capital adequacy as follows:

Original risk	£2 080 000
Credit default risk	£16 000
Total	£2 096 000

Table 9.12 Undiversified capital adequacy calculation

Clearly, in adopting the above approach, the Bank of England has not considered a fundamental principle of portfolio management, that there is a correlation of −1 between the underlying asset and its hedge. Obviously, the Bank of England, and regulators in general, should encourage financial institutions to hedge against credit risk. As it stands, the Bank of England, by not taking a portfolio approach, is actually penalizing sensible management policies of credit risk.

Setting limits for the allocation of lending funds

If banks are fully aware of how to calculate the capital at risk, then they will be better able to make decisions on limits. An undesirable situation would be one where bankers were making decisions on credit limits, without a full understanding of the additional risks that those decisions created for their portfolios.

Deciding the appropriate risk premium that we should charge

Where the amount of capital at risk is high, we need to identify individual bonds and how much they contribute to that risk. Here, there are two types of risk measure that a firm should use. First, it could use a marginal statistic. This involves calculating the overall risk in a portfolio and then recalculating it after the introduction of an extra asset. The difference between both figures is the marginal risk. Obviously these marginal risks differ from portfolio to portfolio, and in order to measure these differences, correlation is very important. A bank that is lending to the building industry would calculate a higher marginal risk for an additional building loan compared to a portfolio that has no other building loans. Many experienced credit experts use portfolio analysis to calculate both marginal risk and absolute risk. An absolute risk calculation is necessary because if a bank were heavily exposed to one particular counterparty, unwinding a position, particularly after a credit default, would create liquidity problems.

Identifying prime risk exposures

Advanced portfolio credit risk management techniques can reveal important risk drivers. For instance, a bank may be exposed to an economic downturn in Belgium, and may also be heavily exposed to the electronics industry across the world. In these circumstances, it might be worthwhile to identify those clients which contribute most to risk within the electronics industry and which are based in Belgium and reduce that risk using credit derivatives.

Summary

The rationale for assessing risk on a portfolio basis is broadly similar to the rationale for measuring market VaR. To recap, we calculate VaR for four reasons:

1 regulatory requirements
2 setting market-risk limits
3 identifying the risk–reward relationship
4 identifing those areas of risk that need to be monitored more closely.

Although credit-risk measurements have some fundamental differences, VaR techniques can be incorporated for measuring and reducing exposure to credit risk.

Tools to reduce credit risk

The growth in the market for credit derivatives provides an incentive for banks to pay closer attention to portfolio risk assessment. In the past, measuring risk on a country-by-country or industry-by-industry basis was useful for the setting of limits. However, as with market risk, setting credit limits involved more individual intuitive decision making than a scientific or rigorous approach. Most credit experts would still argue in favor of this approach. Portfolio risk management techniques can, however, like VaR, enhance the quality of decision making, as well as coordinate the activities of various lending officers. Without this coordination, banks could unwittingly become overexposed to the same risk drivers and, without realizing it, place all their eggs in one basket. Portfolio risk assessment can highlight this. More importantly, banks can now use credit derivatives to reduce domestic exposure and reduce concentration risk. Today, credit experts in major banks can identify economies with different cycles and characteristics and then, using credit derivatives, make sure that they are not overexposed to one particular type of economy.

Distinguishing credit risk from market risk

One important contribution that credit derivatives have made is that they can distinguish credit risk from market risk. Consider a portfolio that has used interest rate futures to neutralize interest rate risk (which is market risk), and is left with a credit risk exposure. It is now possible to reduce this credit risk exclusively. In the past, banks were faced with a situation where they might have had to take on market risk alongside credit risk, by either buying or selling corporate bonds. Now this is no longer necessary.

Using credit derivatives to reduce credit risk

Total return swaps

Terminology

> **Total return swap** – A total return swap transfers credit risk by swapping the returns of one particular asset from one party to another. The party which receives the returns pays the current interest rate to compensate the party which pays the asset return.

Fig 9.4

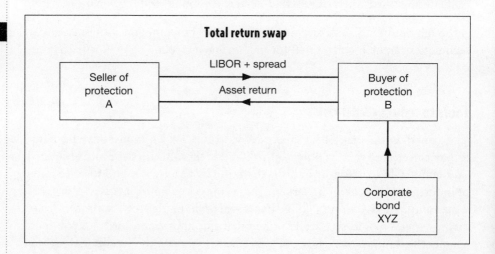

Bank B has purchased a corporate bond in Company XYZ and seeks protection in case the company defaults. Bank B, therefore, enters into a total return swap with Bank A whereby B pays over the coupon plus any capital gain less any capital loss, and in return receives the current floating rate of interest (LIBOR plus spread). An alternative is, of course, for Bank B simply to sell the corporate bond and put the proceeds into a bank to earn the current floating rate of interest. However, the transaction costs of selling the bond might be high. Also, if the bond is illiquid and Bank B holds a large quantity, its price could come tumbling down. Third, if instead of purchasing a corporate bond, Bank B gave a loan to XYZ, banking relations might suffer if XYZ knew that its loan was being sold on. The solution then is effectively to "lend" the asset to Bank A and in return receive LIBOR plus a spread.

The total return swap also offers benefits to the seller of protection, Bank A. Bank A may, for instance, believe that XYZ's credit rating is too high and that an upgrade is possible. To take a position on this, Bank A could simply buy the bond. However, transaction costs may be high, the bond may be illiquid, also, by buying the corporate bond, Bank A takes on an interest rate risk. A sensible solution to this, therefore, is to gain exposure to the credit change only, and this is what a total return swap allows the bank to do. If the underlying asset moves to a higher credit rating, Bank B gains from the increase in the economic value. If the bond suffers a credit downgrading or possibly a default, this will influence the asset return that Bank A receives.

Advantages of a total return swap over purchase/or sale of a risky bond or loan

- transaction costs are reduced
- illiquid nature of corporate bond could influence purchase price
- confidentiality – client is not aware that lender is purchasing protection.

Illustration of a total return swap

Figure 9.13 illustrates a term sheet for a total return swap.

Bank A pays	Total return on asset with time adjustments on coupon where appropriate
Bank B pays	6 month LIBOR + 80 basis points
LIBOR	USD LIBOR
Principal	$5 000 000
Initial price of asset	$102
Maturity	5 years
Early termination	Credit event as determined by independent party
Termination payment	Capital profit or capital loss
Capital profit or loss	Market value at termination date less initial price of $102
Market price	To be established by the calculation agent
Business day convention	30/360
Documentation	ISDA

Table 9.13 Specifications for a total return swap

Reference asset	
Name	XYZ Corporation
Grade	BBB bond
Type	Senior bank loan
Coupon	10%
Maturity	5 years
Payment	Coupon paid per annum
Day count convention	30/360

Table 9.14 Details of bond issuer

The above is fairly straightforward. Bank B is the protection seller and so assumes any capital profit or loss on the reference asset. In return, Bank B pays A LIBOR plus the spread. In effect, Bank B is borrowing the asset from A and paying LIBOR plus the spread to compensate. Each year Bank B will receive the coupon and pay Bank A the floating rate of interest, until either the total return swap terminates or a credit event occurs. A credit event might be either a significant downgrading of the reference bond or an actual default. When this happens, an independent party, "the calculating agent," decides the market value and Bank B pays over the difference. If, for instance, the calculating agent decides the market value to be $60, Bank B must pay to Bank A the capital loss $5 000 000/$100*($60-$102) = $2 100 000. Sometimes it makes sense to avoid having to calculate the market value and simply deliver the asset. Disputes in such cases are minimized.

Uses in portfolio risk management

Consider a situation where Bank A is exposed to a lot of companies within the electronics sector in Belgium. The bank could suffer huge losses if there is an economic downturn in Belgium, together with a fall in demand for electronic products. A sensible strategy for Bank A, therefore, is to obtain credit protection on the bulk of those customers who fall within these risk criteria.

Default swaps

While a total return swap is the equivalent to a future or forward, a default swap is the equivalent of an option. In return for a premium, the protection seller undertakes to compensate the protection buyer in the event of a credit default. We saw earlier that in VaR models those derivative products that have "optionality" have a nonlinear relationship with the underlying asset. For writers of default swaps, risk measurement is more difficult and normally Monte Carlo simulation techniques would be used.

Figure 9.5 illustrates the cash flow of a default swap.

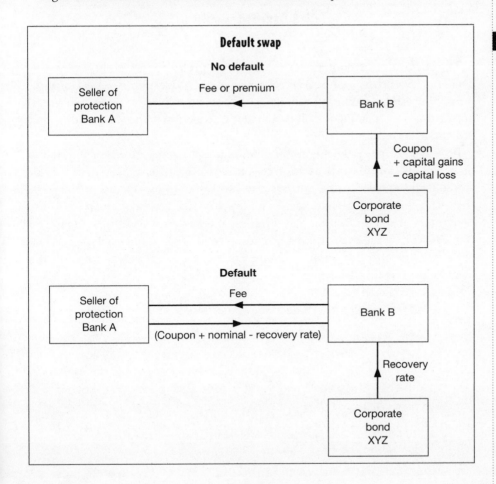

Fig 9.5

Bank B in this case benefits if there is an improvement in the credit rating of corporate bond XYZ. However, if there is a credit default, then Bank A must pay over the difference. Whatever happens, Bank B is perfectly hedged. In the case of Bank A, the maximum profit that can be earned is the premium paid while losses are unlimited (although technically linked to the current value of the bond). Bank B is effectively granting an option to purchase the asset if it falls below a certain value. The specifications of a default swap appear below.

The protection buyer pays	Premium of 800 basis points semi-annually
Nominal amount of reference asset	£8 000 000 XYZ Corporation
Early termination	Credit event or in 4 years' time
Termination payment	Notional × (market price at inception – final value)
Final price	Prevailing market price at date of payment
Materiality	Price falls below 90% of today's value subject to interest rate movements
Business days	30/360
Documentation	International Swaps and Derivatives Association

Table 9.15 Default swap details

The buyer of protection undertakes to pay a premium that in this case is calculated at 800 basis points. The reference asset in question is XYZ Corporation. In return for paying a premium, the protection buyer receives four years' protection from a credit default or a material reduction in the value of the bond because of a credit migration.

If no default or credit migration takes place, the seller of protection makes no payments over to the protection buyer. However, if, as a result of default or a credit migration, the asset suffers a fall in value of greater than 90 percent then a credit event is deemed to take place. Note that the fall in the price of the bond must be due to a credit deterioration and not due to a change in interest rates. Normally the calculation agent responsible for coming up with the final price will refer to government bonds and price the corporate bond on the assumption that throughout the period of the default swap, the risk free interest rates have remained constant.

Table 9.16 illustrates how a default swap differs from a total return swap.

Instrument	Interest rate increase Credit spread increase	Interest rate reduction Credit spread increase
Corporate bond (for party long the asset)	Market loss (VaR) Credit loss	Market gain Credit gain
Total return swap (protection seller)	Credit loss	Credit gain
Credit default swap (protection seller)	Credit loss less premium received	Premium

Table 9.16 Comparison between credit instruments

Credit linked notes

Credit linked notes are simply bonds whose performance is related to the credit exposure of an underlying asset. They are normally used by investors as a convenient way of gaining access to credit exposure either to a single issuer or to a combination of issuers. The procedure operates as follows:

- A special purpose vehicle (SPV), the equivalent to a trust, is set up and investors are invited to subscribe for medium-term notes.
- The funds generated from the issue are then used to enter into total return swaps, default swaps, or a combination of the two, depending on the risk profile that the SPV wants to assume.
- If there is no credit event, the investors, in addition to receiving the risk free rate of interest, will also receive the premium (if a default swap is used) and capital gain (if a total return swap is used).
- If there is a default, the investor's return is net of any protection payments made.

Role of diversification in credit linked notes

VaR calculations are very important in credit linked note structures. Investors, who want to gain credit exposure will pay very close attention to two factors – the level of diversification and the level of gearing. As with banks, SPVs will set limits on certain concentrations, such as industrial sectors, geographical location, product type, etc. In the past banks used subjective judgments to decide on the limits. SPVs will more than likely combine subjective judgment with statistical packages that are designed to exploit diversification. If they succeed, then their simulations will reveal relatively low volatility in their earnings. Investors will therefore not demand so high a credit risk premium. In addition, if diversification can be exploited to the full, then the managers of the SPV can consider alternative means of enhancing earnings. A popular technique for instance is to use geared pool structures. This effectively provides greater leveraged access to the return on a pool of assets. For the investor who wants exclusive credit exposure, the benefit of an SPV is that he can obtain relatively high earnings (through gearing) coupled with diversification. Of course, there is a high correlation between the losses due to high gearing and credit default. An increase in interest rates, for instance, will have a significant impact on the building industry, and if an SPV is both highly geared and has a high concentration within the building industry then a VaR calculation will reveal a relatively high exposure.

Conclusion

The growth in the use of credit derivatives has given banks more resources with which they can influence the level of exposure to credit risk that they are prepared to tolerate. Credit managers can thus achieve better control over their portfolios if they understand the areas of risk that they are exposed to. Once this is known, banks can use specific derivatives to control that exposure. The growing use of market derivatives and the substantial losses that banks have made in the past from using such derivatives, means that credit control, even among top-ranking rate financial institutions, is of growing concern to banks. Portfolio risk measures can identify the overall exposure and can provide valuable information to lenders when deciding to invest in new securities, or what credit derivatives they should use.

Estimating Volatility for Profitable Trading and Risk Reduction

Volatility and its measures

Exponentially weighted moving average (EWMA) vs time series

GARCH: changing variance and correlation between current and past events

Conclusion

Volatility and its measures

Introduction

Academics in the financial world have carried out exhaustive research on how to estimate future volatility based on historical results. While a lot of this research is purely academic and of little practical use, financial engineers have found ways to tailor this research to make it more practical, useful, and profitable. The result is that VaR models are, in theory, able to predict volatility with more precision and so enhance the quality of the VaR models. A bank that trades in highly volatile assets is obviously taking more risks than a bank which does not. However, as we shall see below, it is a mistake to assume that volatility remains constant. Certain assets that display low volatility now, will become very volatile in the future and vice versa. To make risk information more precise, risk managers need to develop and utilize models that allow for the fact that volatility is itself not stable.

Traders, of course, can exploit this information when identifying profitable trades. Many traders have no particular view of the direction of a particular market, but do have views on volatility. In Chapter 7 we illustrated how traders, with option-trading strategies such as straddles, strangles, and butterflies, can make substantial profits if their estimates of volatility prove correct. For now, we build on the traders' understanding of volatility and show how risk managers and traders forecast volatility. Clearly, no trader can predict volatility with 100 percent accuracy but he or she can develop a system that minimizes errors, by developing a better understanding of volatility characteristics.

What is volatility?

Most traders and risk managers, of course, know what volatility means – it is the statistical measure of the price variation of an instrument. Table 10.1 gives an indication of what exactly we are measuring.

In Table 10.1 we calculate standard deviations 1 and 2 using two variations of the formula (shown below) and the Excel function. Naturally, they all converge to produce the same figure.

$$\sigma = \sqrt{\frac{\Sigma\,(xi - x)}{n}}$$

and

$$\sigma = \sqrt{\frac{\Sigma x_i^2 - (\overline{x})^2}{n}}$$

In earlier chapters we said that VaR was a measure of volatility, which in turn is a measure of standard deviation. The table illustrates three different approaches. Note that it is the norm to take the standard deviation of the continuous returns of the stock rather than the stock price itself. If we were to use the actual prices to measure the standard deviation, we would get inconsistent results since the actual standard deviation changes as the price grows. The lognormal standard deviation, or the standard deviation based on the continuous growth rate, is practically more useful for risk estimation. The figure 0.04879 represents the continuous growth rate between 20 and 21, and is obtained by talking the natural log of 1.05 (21/20). The mean is calculated in the conventional way. We take the total of all the continuous growth rates and divide by the number in the sample. In each of the cases, we compare the actual continuous growth rate against the continuous growth rate and record the difference, in other words, 0.02610 and 0.06818, etc. We then square them and add them up to get 0.014832. Finally, we divide this by the number in the sample, 6, to get 0.002472. The square root of this figure gives us a measure of the standard deviation, 0.04972.

	B	C	D	E	F	G	H
5							Asset
6	Day	Asset	Continuous	Mean	Difference	Difference	price
7		price	growth			squared	squared
8			rate				
9							
10	0	20					
11	1	21	0.04879	0.02269	0.02610	0.00068	0.00238
12	2	23	0.09097	0.02269	0.06828	0.00466	0.00828
13	3	24	0.04256	0.02269	0.01987	0.00039	0.00181
14	4	25	0.04082	0.02269	0.01813	0.00033	0.00167
15	5	23	−0.04256	0.02269	−0.06525	0.00426	0.00181
16	6	22	−0.04445	0.02269	−0.06714	0.00451	0.00198
17							
18	Totals		0.136132174			0.01483272	0.01792
19							
20	Standard deviation 1		0.049720417	0.00247212			
21	Standard deviation 2		0.049720417	0.00247212			
22	Standard deviation 3		0.049720417				

Table 10.1 Measures of volatility

In a turbulent period, we would expect stock prices to jump up and down considerably. This has implications for option pricing, particularly if the volatility is based on historical volatility as shown above. Needless to say, when the standard deviation increases, so too does the price of options, which is based on the asset. The "time value" of both calls and puts rises when there is a lot of volatility. The time value represents the difference between the premium and the intrinsic value of the option. Where volatility increases, so too does VaR.

Formulas behind standard deviation

For the sake of completeness, Table 10.1 shows two other ways of calculating standard deviation. Standard deviation 2 is the most preferred method of calculating in practice. This process simply involves squaring the continuous returns and then summing them. The figure 0.04879 squared, for instance, gives 0.002380, and when all the squared terms are added we get 0.01792. Finally, we divide this by the number in the sample by 6 and subtract the mean squared $(0.02269)^2$ to get 0.002472. The third standard deviation is simply obtained from the Excel function $=(\text{STDEVP } D11:D16)$.

	B	C	D	E	F	G	H
5							Asset
6	Day	Asset	Continuous	Mean	Difference	Difference	price
7		price	growth			squared	squared
8			rate				
9							
10	0	20					
11	1	21	=LN(C11/C10)	=$D$18/$B$16	=D11-E11	=F11^2	=D11^2
12	2	23	=LN(C12/C11)	=$D$18/$B$16	=D12-E12	=F12^2	=D12^2
13	3	24	=LN(C13/C12)	=$D$18/$B$16	=D13-E13	=F13^2	=D13^2
14	4	25	=LN(C14/C13)	=$D$18/$B$16	=D14-E14	=F14^2	=D14^2
15	5	23	=LN(C15/C13)	=$D$18/$B$16	=D15-E15	=F15^2	=D15^2
16	6	22	=LN(C16/C15)	=$D$18/$B$16	=D16-E16	=F16^2	=D16^2
17							
18	Totals		=SUM(D11:D17)			=SUM(G11:G17)	=SUM(H11:H17)
19							
20							
21	Standard deviation 1		=E21^0.5	=(G18/(B16))			
22	Standard deviation 2		=E22^0.5	=H18/6-E16^2			
23	Standard deviation 3		=STDEVP(D11:D16)				

Table 10.2 Spreadsheet formulas for Table 10.1

The original data, namely the share prices, are contained in cells C10 to C16.

Degrees of freedom

Readers with a background in statistics will realize that when the sample is small we should consider degrees of freedom. Note that in all the calculations above we have deliberately omitted the adjustment for degrees of freedom. In simple terms, when calculating the standard deviation, we should divide not by the number in the sample, but by one less, that is by 5 instead of 6 in this case. The reason is that when we use six variables we are effectively studying five differences (not six) between the variables, and this is what the standard deviation measures. The omission is for two reasons: (1) we want to present a consistent approach for the calculation of standard deviation; (2) the adjustment for degrees of freedom is not necessary when we are dealing with large numbers of data. When risk managers and traders are calculating volatility, they tend to use vary large series of data. Hence, any adjustment would only have a minimal impact.

Volatility vs position trading

The introduction of derivatives allows traders to engage in two types of trade: position trading and volatility trading. Position trading involves taking a position which will profit if the asset moves in a certain direction. A person who is long a particular asset is not necessarily the owner of that asset, but nevertheless profits if the asset increases in value and suffers if the asset falls in value. By buying the asset itself, the trader takes a long position but he could just equally take a short position if he buys a future on the asset or alternatively either writes a call or buys a put. A short position is sometimes more difficult to achieve in the underlying cash market; one has to hold the asset to begin with. However, with derivatives a trader can quite easily short future, write calls, or buy puts. In all of these three cases the trader benefits if the asset falls in value.

The second type of trader is known as a volatility trader. This trader does not necessarily have a view on the direction of a particular asset but expects the volatility of the asset's return to either increase or decrease. Traders normally face two choices when dealing with volatility. They can assume that volatility remains constant or they can assume that there is a term structure to volatility, in other words, that it is conditional on past events or on time. In practice, many risk managers assume that volatility and correlation are constant in the sense that if it is going to jump up or down the deviation will be, relatively speaking, constant. Unfortunately, studies in volatility have proved otherwise. Volatility tends to come in bursts and clusters. This means that highly volatile periods are often interspersed with tranquil periods. Traders and risk managers should therefore be able to both make money and control risks if they have a better understanding of how volatility is forecast. In the methods presented below, we build up from a basic and simplified approach, illustrating unusual features and characteristics of volatility and how the models are dealing with these.

Time series analysis

Most forecasting methods are an extension of time series analysis. This topic is probably very familiar to students with a statistical, mathematical, or even business studies degree. We start with a simple example to illustrate how it works.

Example A company selling "seasonal" products, such as ice-cream, needs to forecast its sales in the future and like the risk manager trying to calculate future volatility, makes predictions based on past results. The problem with seasonal data is that they display characteristics which prevent a visible trend from emerging. Table 10.3 illustrates this. A seller of umbrellas, for instance, will find that sales peak in the winter months and are below average sales in the summer months. An ice-cream salesman will experience the exact opposite. In relation to stocks, similar characteristics may be present in volatility forecasting. At the year end, for instance, many companies close out their positions, and so trading volumes may increase. There is also the prospect that certain companies may manipulate prices at December 31 in order to give a favorable light to year-end valuations for accounting purposes. The London Stock Exchange for example, has recently implemented a system which detects this activity. Such anomalies can distort volatility, so traders do need to be aware of them.

Fig 10.1

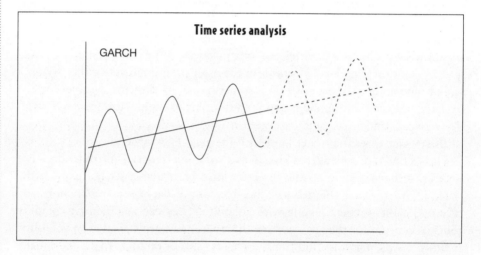

Time series analysis

GARCH

The moving average approach can, to some extent, reduce distortion by establishing a de-seasonalized trend line, which can then be used to forecast future sales or future volatility levels.

Table 10.3 illustrates how future sales are forecast. We first take the "raw" data and de-seasonalize them by taking the average. The figure of 2480, for instance, is the total of the first four figures, and the figure 620 is simply 2480/4. To get the next average, we drop 680 from the "window" and include the fifth figure of 620. The net result of this is that the new total drops by 60 to 2420, bringing the overall average down to 605. The final adjustment (not necessary in all cases) is to simply take the midpoint of two averages so that we can relate the result to a specific quarter. The first eight figures in the final column are "estimates" based on past data. The figures beneath (in the box) are forecasts based on past estimates. The calculation of the forecasts is discussed below. At this stage it is important to distinguish between "estimates" and "forecasts." Estimates are calculated from historical data, and once these estimates are known, we make forecasts of future data. Calculating volatility from past data is intuitively straightforward, shown in Table 10.1. However, calculating volatility from past data involves the use of samples, and obviously different samples produce different results. Generally, the old rule of statistics prevails: the larger the sample, the more accurate the estimate.

Calculating forecasts from estimates

Once we have de-seasonalized the data, we can establish a trend. In this case, the total growth from (612.5 to 667.5) is 55 giving an average growth of 55/7 = 7.86. We then make the assumption that this will be the growth rate for the forecast period. The figures in the box (675.36, 683.21, and 691.07) reflect the fact that the growth rate is on *average* 7.86 per period. The final step, (not shown on the table) is to seasonalize the data. This involves taking the forecasted trends and adjusting them to reflect the actual forecasts for each season, rather than the average forecast. We normally have to make assumptions when using past estimates to calculate future volatility. Unfortunately, this topic is more than just academic when calculating VaR. For instance, bond prices tend to mean revert, simply because interest rates are under pressure to mean revert. Loosely speaking, mean reverting in this context means that interest rates cannot stay unusually low for an extended period, nor can they stay unusually high. Also, various exchange mechanisms will affect volatility and, therefore, should influence our forecasts. When Britain, for instance, was a member of the Exchange Rate Mechanism, risk managers forecasting volatility recognized the fact that, over an extended time period, volatility was not related to time. All of these factors will be discussed in more detail later.

The spreadsheet used to construct the data above is shown in Table 10.4. The "raw data," namely 680, 700, 400, etc. are contained in cells E32 to E43.

We will see later that VaR packages such as RiskMetrics, when estimating data, rely on a form of time series analysis. We will expand on this later. Before that, we outline the two ways of estimating (as opposed to forecasting) data and the relative advantages and disadvantages of each.

Implied vs historical data

The estimates outlined above are based on historical data. Most traders would correctly question why it is necessary to use this approach. A more sensible technique is to calculate the implied volatility based on option prices. The Black and Scholes model, for instance, calculates option prices based on five inputs: the current asset price, the time to maturity, the strike price, interest rates, and the volatility. The first four are easy to obtain, the last one – volatility – as the previous section has shown is difficult to estimate accurately. A sensible approach, one that is more accurate and less time consuming, is to look at the price of exchange-traded options and then work the Black and Scholes model in reverse. This would involve setting up the Black and Scholes model on a spreadsheet, and then estimating the "implied" volatility.

	C	D	E	F	G	H
28						Mid-point
29				Moving	Moving	moving
30	Year	Quarter	Volume of sales	total	average	average
31						
32	1995	1	680			
33		2	700			
34		3	400	2480	620.0	612.50
35		4	700	2420	605.0	622.50
36	1996	1	620	2560	640.0	640.00
37		2	840	2560	640.0	642.50
38		3	400	2580	645.0	648.75
39		4	720	2610	652.5	657.50
40	1997	1	650	2650	662.5	663.75
41		2	880	2660	665.0	667.50
42		3	410	2680	670.0	675.36
43		4	740			683.21
44						691.07
45			Average growth		7.86	
46			per quarter			

Table 10.3 Moving average table

Weaknesses of options models in measuring volatility

Weaknesses of implied volatility

- **Weaknesses of the models.** Models like that of Black and Scholes place too much reliance on the normal distribution curve, which underestimates the prospects of achieving extreme events. This gives rise to the "volatility smile" concept. Also, most models assume that volatility remains constant. In reality, volatility itself is volatile.

- **Transparency of the data.** Only exchange-traded options provide transparent data and, generally, there is not enough of them to rely on implied volatility all the time.

- **Profit margins.** Implied volatility is likely to be much higher than actual volatility because option writers add on the cost of implementing their hedge, as well as their own profit margins. Using such information without adjustment can lead to an overpricing of options and risk-minimizing strategies that rely on a volatility figure which is too high.

	C	D	E	F	G	H
28						Mid-point
29				Moving	Moving	moving
30	Year	Quarter	Volume of sales	total	average	average
31						
32	1995	1	680			
33		2	700			
34		3	400	=SUM(E32:E35)	=F34/4	=(G35+G34)/2
35		4	700	=SUM(E33:E36)	=F35/4	=(G36+G35)/2
36	1996	1	620	=SUM(E34:E37)	=F36/4	=(G37+G36)/2
37		2	840	=SUM(E35:E38)	=F37/4	=(G38+G37)/2
38		3	400	=SUM(E36:E39)	=F38/4	=(G39+G38)/2
39		4	720	=SUM(E37:E40)	=F39/4	=(G40+G39)/2
40	1997	1	650	=SUM(E38:E41)	=F40/4	=(G41+G40)/2
41		2	880	=SUM(E39:E42)	=F41/4	=(G42+G41)/2
42		3	410	=SUM(E40:E43)	=F42/4	=H41+$G$45
43		4	740			=H42+$G$45
44						=H43+$G$45
45			Growth per quarter	=(H41-H34)/7		

Table 10.4 Spreadsheet formulas behind time series analysis

The case profile that follows, illustrates that models themselves can misprice options and so overreliance on them can produce misleading volatility figures. There are two reasons for this: (1) implied volatility is for fixed time periods and often, perhaps because of the volatility smile, it is difficult to "interpolate" volatility for longer time periods; (2) pricing models, as the pofile shows, often fail to accept that volatility itself varies and so ends up underpricing options.

Case profile

The Black and Scholes model

There are numerous examples of banks losing a lot of money because they use models religiously, without being aware of inherent weaknesses. The result is that they either underprice or overprice, leaving themselves exposed to the market, which is ruthless when it comes to mispricing.

There is one important difficulty with implied volatility, and this relates to the weakness of the valuation models. The Black and Scholes model, together with some binomial pricing models, assume that volatility is constant. This can be a serious flaw not only for risk management, but also when pricing options. Generally, for linear instruments, such as futures, making assumptions about the static nature of volatility may not pose too many problems. If volatility increases, one party benefits and the other suffers. The opposite can, nevertheless, equally apply. Generally speaking, we do not take on too much risk by making the assumption of constant variance. For options however, the constant variation assumption can lead to incorrect option valuations. A trader who is long an option is also long volatility. If volatility increases, the trader stands to make more money. If volatility falls, the value of the option falls, but it never goes below zero. Thus, the trader who is long an option hopes that volatility itself is not constant. The writer of an option who is unaware of this suffers because he could end up undervaluing an option on an asset whose volatility changes constantly.

Mathematicians will know that in the partial differential equation (upon which Black and Scholes is based) theta pays for gamma, which means that the higher gamma is, the higher is the rate of decay of the option's premium. Since there is no mention of vega in the Black and Scholes' partial differential equation, the writer is not rewarded for a change in vega. For nonmathematicians, the following intuitive explanation should suffice. If the relationship between the asset price and the underlying share price fluctuates rapidly, the writer of such an option is taking a heavy risk and is rewarded by the fact that as the option approaches maturity, the premium reduces at a very fast rate. However, if volatility fluctuates rapidly, the writer of an option is once again taking on a lot of risk, but is not rewarded for this. The net result of this is that the Black and Scholes model tends to undervalue options.

Profit margins

Academics have uncovered other problems with implied volatility. When traders are building volatility into their pricing models, they normally calculate the historical volatility, and then increases this to reflect profit margin. Most traders are aware that for deeply out-of-the-money options and for deeply in-the-money options, the precarious nature of the normal distribution curve and in particular "fat tails" means that the historical volatility must be increased. Second, traders often build in their cost of hedging and a profit margin. The result is that the implied volatility is almost always too high. Risk managers must make a distinction between historical volatility, which is what they are trying to measure, and implied volatility, which is what they get if they use option-pricing models. As a safety precaution, risk managers will take a prudent approach and assume the worst. However, if the true volatility is a lot lower, then the risk strategy may not always give the best hedge.

Observable prices

A final weakness with implied volatility is that there are a limited number of exchange-traded options from which to estimate volatility. Using over-the-counter (OTC) option prices is, of course, close to useless. OTC option prices often reflect the bargaining power of both parties and often have little to do with volatility. Also, OTC option prices are not transparent. This leaves the risk manager with exchange-traded options and, because the number of exchange traded options is limited, the implied data are of limited use.

Implied or historical – which should we use?

Most academics have formed the view that the quality of data obtained from implied volatility is superior to simple historical procedures and should be used where available. Nevertheless, studies by Kroner, Kneafsey, and Claessens (1995) argue that a new procedure to calculate historical based forecasts (GARCH) has produced results which are superior to implied volatility. GARCH (generalized autoregressive conditional heteroskedasticity), which we discuss later, is a very complex procedure measuring for volatility risk and runs the danger of being difficult intuitively to understand. This setback lends itself to operational risks. RiskMetrics however, has come up with an approach known as the "exponentially weighted moving average," which is much simpler than GARCH, but (as RiskMetrics designers argue) it retains the accuracy and precision that GARCH offers.

Exponentially weighted moving average (EWMA) vs time series

Introduction

In trying to reach better precision on the forecast of future volatility, practitioners have experimented with the idea of adjusting the time series method described earlier to forecast future volatility. The idea behind exponential weighting is to apportion weights to data contained in the moving-average window. The example in Table 10.2 gives each of the variables equal weighting. Exponential smoothing, however, tends to give more recent data a higher weighting than "old" data.

There are generally two problems that risk managers must try to solve when estimating volatility:

- They must keep the sample frame as wide as possible: the wider the window, the greater the number of variables and so the more accurate the result. If the frame is kept narrow then the risk of sampling error is greater.
- They must recognize that more recent data bound to have a more important influence on future volatility than past data. This is because volatility tends to happen in clusters. If there is a stock market crash on, say, Monday, then volatility will remain high for the next two weeks or perhaps the next two months. After a while, volatility tends to return to sensible levels.

The difficult task facing risk managers is to come up with a weighting system which reflects the importance of more recent data, but at the same time keeps the sample frame wide enough to avoid sampling error.

HSBC

The Asian crisis that erupted in October 1997 caused considerable volatility in HSBC shares. In the days which followed the crash, the share price, which up to then had remained volatile, went from £19 to £12.94 and over the next five months gradually crept up to £20. In the days immediately following the crash, the "time value" of HSBC options increased significantly. In fact, most traders believed them to be overpriced. Within a few months, however, actual volatility and implied volatility had returned to normal levels. There are various studies which back up the view that volatility tends to happen in clusters. The Brady Commission Report (Hull, 1995) examining the stock market crash of October 1987 revealed that programed selling accounted for an unusually high proportion of total sales in the period following the crash. The conclusion to be drawn from this is that high volatility can in some instances lead to even higher volatility. So if volatility is unusually high, models should be predicting high volatility in the short term.

Shadow features

Consider the moving average calculation in Table 10.3. We repeat the table in Table 10.5, but this time we introduce an unusual shock. Table 10.5 illustrates the shadow effect of such a shock. For period four, we have increased sales significantly from 700 to 2700 to see the effect it has on the averages. The increase may be due to a one-off order. However, the moving average calculation has assumed that sales for the next four periods will increase as a result. Such a conclusion is, of course, inaccurate. It would make more sense either to eliminate the unusual increase altogether or to use a weighting system which would reduce the impact of the shock on other periods.

The shadow-effect problem can just as easily apply to volatility. Suppose a risk manager tries to reduce sampling error as much as possible by using a large sample frame, namely calculating a 100-day moving average (as opposed to four used opposite). There is the problem that a stock market crash in, say, July can have an impact on the volatility 100 days later, in October. A one-off crash, therefore, can increase the forecasted volatility for a long period ahead and this can cause problems because it does not reflect what happens in reality. A possible solution to this problem is to weight the moving average so that future forecasts are heavily dependent on the most recent data and not influenced too much by old or very historic data. The system of the exponentially weighted moving average overcomes this problem.

The exponential weighting system

Table 10.6 illustrates how an exponential weighting system operates.

Year	Quarter	Volume of sales	Moving total	Moving average	Midpoint moving average Shock	Midpoint moving average No shock
1995	1	680				
	2	700				
	3	400	4480	1120.0	**1112.50**	612.50
	4	**2700**	4420	1105.0	**1122.50**	622.50
1996	1	620	4560	1140.0	**1140.00**	640.00
	2	840	4560	1140.0	**892.50**	642.50
	3	400	2580	645.0	648.75	648.75
	4	720	2610	652.5	657.50	657.50
1997	1	650	2650	662.5	663.75	663.75
	2	880	2660	665.0	667.50	667.50
	3	410	2680	670.0	675.36	675.36
	4	740			683.21	683.21
					691.07	691.07
	Growth per quarter			−63.57		

Table 10.5 Shadow effect of a shock

Recent observations

Table 10.6 illustrates how the exponential weighting scheme allocates weightings to the past data. The ordinary or equally weighted moving average allocates an equal weight to each figure. So for a twenty-point moving average each figure would have a weighting of 0.05. Thus, if there had been a major shock 20 days ago, this would still be reflected in the forecast for today. The exponential weighting places more emphasis on yesterday's volatility and less emphasis as the data get older. For instance, the last figure one day ago was −13.98 percent. The square or variance of this return is 1.95 percent. This would carry 6 percent of the total weighting if the exponential factor was 0.94. On the other hand, if the weighting was 0.70 the last figure would carry a weighting of 30 percent, and if the exponential factor was 0.50, the weighting of the latest data would be 50 percent. We can conclude from this that if the chosen weighting exponential is high, the current variance will have only a small impact on the total variance. On the other hand, if the weighting exponential is low, the current data will have a significant impact on the total weighting. Consider a case where the exponential is 0.50: the most recent data will heavily influence the volatility forecast for the future. The rate of decay in the weighting is quite high because as each day passes the weighting halves. Therefore, if there was a crash 20 days ago, it would hardly register on volatility calculated for tomorrow or afterwards.

Old observations

Table 10.6 also reveals that old data have very little impact when the exponential weighting is quite low. This is because the rate of decay is higher if the weighting is low. In fact, when the weighting is 70 percent or 50 percent, then the earliest data have absolutely no influence on future data. Table 10.6 reveals that data are very important when the exponential weighting factor is high, and not important when the weighting factor is low. Starting from day one, the weighting is (1–0.94) when the factor is 0.94 and (1–0.7) when the exponential factor is 0.70. As each day passes, we multiply the current weighting by the decay factor. Therefore, 0.06 multiplied by 0.94 gives us 0.0564, and when this is multiplied by 0.94 we get the next figure, 0.053. This process is repeated right up to day 20.

The spreadsheet setup for the first four rows in Table 10.6 is set out in Table 10.7.

	B	C	D	E	F	G	H
74	Day	Share	Continuous	Return	Decay	Decay	Decay
75	number	price	return	squared	factor	factor	factor
76					0.94	0.7	0.5
77	20						
78	20	21	4.88%	0.24%	0.01852	0.00034	0.00000
79	19	22	4.65%	0.22%	0.01970	0.00049	0.00000
80	18	23	4.45%	0.20%	0.02096	0.00070	0.00000
81	17	21	–9.10%	0.83%	0.02229	0.00100	0.00001
82	16	22	4.65%	0.22%	0.02372	0.00142	0.00002
83	15	23	4.45%	0.20%	0.02523	0.00203	0.00003
84	14	24	4.26%	0.18%	0.02684	0.00291	0.00006
85	13	25	4.08%	0.17%	0.02856	0.00415	0.00012
86	12	26	3.92%	0.15%	0.03038	0.00593	0.00024
87	11	27	3.77%	0.14%	0.03232	0.00847	0.00049
88	10	28	3.64%	0.13%	0.03438	0.01211	0.00098
89	9	29	3.51%	0.12%	0.03657	0.01729	0.00195
90	8	30	3.39%	0.11%	0.03891	0.02471	0.00391
91	7	31	3.28%	0.11%	0.04139	0.03529	0.00781
92	6	32	3.17%	0.10%	0.04403	0.05042	0.01563
93	5	25	17.44%	3.04%	0.04684	0.07203	0.03125
94	4	22	–12.78%	1.63%	0.04984	0.10290	0.06250
95	3	20	–9.53%	0.91%	0.05302	0.14700	0.12500
96	2	23	13.98%	1.95%	0.05640	0.21000	0.25000
97	1	20	–13.98%	1.95%	0.06000	0.30000	0.50000

Table 10.6 Exponentially weighted moving average

	B	C	D	E	F	G	H
74	Day	Share	Continuous	Return	Decay	Decay	Decay
75	number	price	return	squared	factor	factor	factor
76					0.94	0.7	0.5
77		20					
78	20	21	=LN(C78/C77)	=D78^2	=(1-F$76)*F$76^($B78-1)	=(1-G$76)*G$76^($B78-1)	=(1-H$76)*H$76^($B78-1)
79	19	22	=LN(C79/C78)	=D79^2	=(1-F$76)*F$76^($B79-1)	=(1-G$76)*G$76^($B79-1)	=(1-H$76)*H$76^($B79-1)
80	18	23	=LN(C80/C79)	=D80^2	=(1-F$76)*F$76^($B80-1)	=(1-G$76)*G$76^($B80-1)	=(1-H$76)*H$76^($B80-1)
81	17	21	=LN(C81/C80)	=D81^2	=(1-F$76)*F$76^($B81-1)	=(1-G$76)*G$76^($B81-1)	=(1-H$76)*H$76^($B81-1)

Table 10.7 Spreadsheet formulas for exponentially weighted moving averages

Ghost factors vs sample error

Keeping the exponential factor low (i.e. 0.50 and 0.70) has the advantage of reducing the problem of ghost or shadow features. However, if it is kept too low, the sampling error problem arises because the forecast is based only on very recent data and not on old data. On the other hand, if the exponential factor is too high, the problem of ghost features emerges. Indeed, it is possible to augment the problem of ghost features if the exponential factor is too high.

RiskMetrics exponential weighting

In Table 10.7 the first weighting factor was deliberately chosen at 0.94. RiskMetrics use this figure because they believe that this is the most optimal weighting for daily data. They believe that it not only produces good forecasts, but also the decay factor is consistent with the properties of covariance matrices calculations. As explained earlier, the RiskMetrics system tries not only to calculate with reasonable precision, but also tries to ensure ease of implementation. This, of course, eases intuitive understanding and avoids the "black box" approach whereby risk managers buy a state-of-the-art system, but are unsure of how it works. The operational errors of implementing a complex VaR measurement system can often outweigh a system that is very close to accurate, yet easy to understand and implement.

In trying to come up with a good exponential weighting factor, RiskMetrics have relied heavily on a statistical technique known as the "root mean squared error." Loosely speaking, RiskMetrics have tried to find the smallest root mean squared error over different values of exponential factors. In other words, they looked for a decay factor that produces the best forecast. The conclusion that they reached was that the best decay factor for daily data is 0.94, and the best decay factor for monthly data is 0.97.

Their approach has come under heavy criticism. Carol Alexander (1996) suggests that using a exponential weighting of 0.97 may actually augment the original ghost features and not diminish it. This suggests that the weighting factor is too high because it places too much emphasis on earlier data, and not enough on later data. The result of this is that a stock market crash will stay in the fore-casting system for a longer period of time.

Fig 10.2

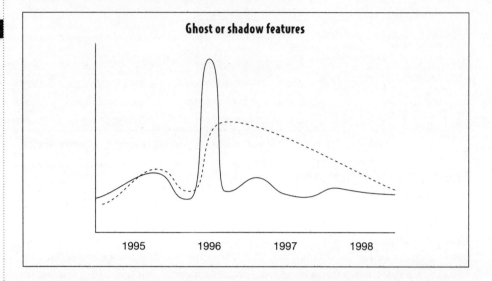

Figure 10.2 illustrates the problem of "ghost features" that all risk managers try to avoid. The solid line illustrates actual data and the dotted line indicates a moving average forecast. Note that the forecast volatility stays high and takes some time before it actually leaves the system. With a low exponential factor however, more emphasis is placed on recent events and so by choosing a decay factor of, say, 0.94 or 0.92, this problem is reduced. However, there are other factors to consider, apart from the ghost features. Sampling error is also impor-tant and can arise if the decay factor is too low.

GARCH: changing variance and correlation between current and past events

RiskMetrics maintain that their exponentially weighted moving average approach closely resembles the precision and accuracy of the GARCH (gener-alized autoregressive conditional heteroskedasticity) technique. Nevertheless, the EWMA approach is easier to operate, adding only a minor adjustment to the equally weighted time series approach. The GARCH model has grown in popularity because it recognizes that the variance is not constant. As stated ear-lier, volatility tends to have quiet periods of low volatility interspersed with clusters of very high volatility. The conclusion to be drawn from this is that volatility is itself dependent on past volatility and is, therefore, unlike Brown-ian motion models which assume that future price fluctuations are not influ-enced by past events.

Definition

Heteroskedasticity means changing variance. A process is said to be autoregressive if there is a non-zero correlation between current events and past events.

The research into volatility suggests that autoregression exists. The GARCH method recognizes this.

Figure 10.3 illustrates the problem of volatility.

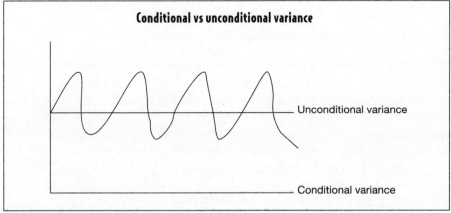

Conditional vs unconditional variance

Unconditional variance

Conditional variance

Fig 10.3

The straight line indicates unconditional volatility. If volatility is unconditional, then it is completely random, and so becomes easier to model. If, on the other hand, volatility is conditional upon some event, the assumption of complete randomness is incorrect. This is why, as explained earlier, many option-pricing models are slightly flawed. They fail to recognize the changing characteristics of volatility. There are many variations of the GARCH model. Engle developed the original ARCH model in 1982. This is a simple equation which places weightings on the previous error terms and a constant. The difficult part is trying to determine these weightings. The ARCH model is designed so that all the coefficients are positive, so that the variance itself is always positive. In simple terms, the conditional heteroskedasticity of past returns is captured. Thus, if there were large movements in the stock market a few days ago, current volatility would be a little higher than usual.

From ARCH to GARCH

Engle's student, Bollerslev, further developed the ARCH model to include autoregressive terms on past volatilities. These terms were included with the original terms of squared errors. The GARCH model is as accurate as an infinite ARCH model and retains the exponentially declining weights. It is, therefore, suitable for measuring volatility in financial markets where quiet periods of volatility are followed by periods of high activity. The GARCH model is nevertheless, more flexible. The coefficients can be structured so that unusual events such as a stock market crash or a currency crisis can leave the forecasting system very quickly if necessary. Similarly, the coefficients in front of the mean errors can be designed so that forecast volatility is quick to react to past market movement.

IGARCH (or integrated GARCH) is a variation of the GARCH models that allow the weighting on the past volatility and the weighting on the squared errors to equal one. This is the model that RiskMetrics simulate with their exponentially weighted moving average (EWMA). The EWMA is similar to the IGARCH model when the first term of the IGARCH model is equal to zero.

Practical considerations with volatility forecasting

There are a number of practical matters that risk managers need to take into consideration when forecasting future volatility. Recent developments in the Exchange Rate Mechanism will, for instance, influence the way that future volatilities are forecast for exchange rates. Most currencies, for example, must operate within a band of, say, 2.25 percent. This, of course, means that volatility, as estimated by a GARCH model, is unrealistic if it is too high.

Conventional models assume that volatility is related to the square root of time. This model is correct as long as we assume that there is no autocorrelation and that there are no other barriers affecting volatility. In reality, however, the presence of autocorrelation does impact on the rule that volatility is related to the square root of time.

A second problem is that events, such as that concerning the Exchange Rate Mechanism, impose maximum restraints on volatility. If, for instance, the Irish punt is expected to stay within 2.25 percent of an agreed exchange rate, the rule that volatility is related to the square root of time only applies up to a certain level. Forecasters of volatility must, therefore, reflect real world events along with mathematical models and assumptions.

Definition

Exchange Rate Mechanism – The Exchange Rate Mechanism was devised in 1989 in order to encourage European economic integration. Its aim is to stabilize the exchange rate between member states with a view to introducing a single European currency. The system has attracted many critics because its success requires direct government intervention and this often imposes restrictions on economic policy. In 1992, for instance, the British government was forced to push up interest rates in order to keep sterling within an agreed target. Eventually, with interest rates so high, Britain was forced to withdraw from the ERM. The date of withdrawal is often refered to as "Black Wednesday."

Estimating volatility

Consider a situation where a trader buys two shares in Company X and retains them for two years, and a second situation where a trader buys a single share in Company X and retains it for four years. To calculate the standard deviation in the first case, we simply multiply the annual volatility by two. This is because both shares, being from the same company, have a correlation coefficient of 1. Using the method described earlier to calculate the volatility of a portfolio, we multiply the annual standard deviation by two. For the second case, in the absence of any autoregression, it would be safe to assume that volatility is related to the square root of time. In other words, we multiply the annual volatility by the square root of time in order to get volatility for four years. This is the convention when pricing options. However, the procedure is inaccurate if autocorrelation exists. Autocorrelation suggests that the relationship (i.e. the correlation coefficient) between two volatilities is not zero, but somewhere between zero and one.

Conclusion

With more and more emphasis being placed on volatility trading and risk management, research into volatility estimating and forecasting is likely to continue. Volatility tends to happen in clusters, so it would be dangerous to assume that it remains constant all the time. A second factor to consider is the "shadow" or "ghost" nature of volatility. Where we use a time series to estimate volatility, we must give more weighting to recent events as opposed to older events. Two of the more popular methods of estimating volatility are EWMA and GARCH. While GARCH is more accurate, it is fairly difficult to implement in practice. EWMA is more practical and can very often achieve the accuracy of GARCH. Nevertheless, the success of the EWMA system depends, to a large extent, on obtaining the most optimum weighting factor. The academic world is currently divided on whether RiskMetrics (users of EWMA) have come up with the most optimum weighting for the purposes of volatility forecasting.

Real-life Application of Models

Should we rely on VaR?

Introduction

As we said earlier, most risk managers, if given the choice between having a state-of-the-art model to measure risk or having a less accurate model, but one that is easily understood by all the risk team, would choose the less accurate model. Unfortunately, in the complex world of risk management, it is not possible to have a "black box" which will produce a figure that everyone can rely upon. Every model has its weakness. Models which are complex but accurate are often difficult to "trace," and so the risk team becomes too dependent on it. This is probably the greatest risk of all. In this chapter, we discuss in detail the limitations of VaR models. From a practical point of view, we examine how VaR can be linked into a bank's accounting system so that weighting matrices can be constructed with acceptable accuracy.

A standard model

For the immediate future, banks are likely to use models which, although not completely perfect, guide the risk-management team toward reducing risk, but not eliminating it. Over the next few years, risk managers will be faced with a choice on which model to apply. To make a correct decision, they must be aware of the strengths and limitations of each. Unfortunately, while there are many models on the market, only JP Morgan's RiskMetrics reveals all the technicalities and assumptions upon which the model is based. For this reason, not surprisingly, it therefore attracted the widest amount of criticism. While their critics have proposed other methods, they have not given detailed guidelines of how they operate and so constructive criticism is close to impossible.

The likelihood is that RiskMetrics will become a standard risk-measurement device. Like the Black and Scholes option pricing model, it contains many flaws, but as long as risk managers are aware of these limitations, it will probably achieve the same success in the risk world that the Black and Scholes model has achieved in the option pricing world.

The main fear among many risk practitioners is that people will take VaR for granted. This means that they will overrely on a single VaR figure. If this is low, they will assume that everything is OK, and will not ask too many questions. On the other hand, if it is too high then, like a budget that has gone out of control, they will investigate and take the necessary corrective action. Obviously, overreliance on models can be dangerous. Sometimes the model is simply not applicable. Banks have lost money because some of their employees used risk-measurement models which were inappropriate for the situation. The greatest safeguard against a model being used incorrectly is to make sure that as many users as possible understand the model in detail and are aware of its limitations.

Criticisms of VaR: the level of confidence

When calculating VaR, JP Morgan uses the 95 percent confidence interval. This means that the model calculated the maximum expected loss 19 days out of 20. Some experts believe that this figure is too low. If VaR is to become the industry standard, it should provide information on extreme events because this is what the regulators are interested in. Instead of 95 percent, therefore, some experts argue that the confidence level should be set at 98 percent or 99 percent. Obviously, the higher the level of confidence, the higher the amount of the loss, and regulators would need to assure themselves that banks are capable of surviving the big losses and not the day-to-day losses. The 1987 crash, the European currency crises, and liquidity problems in the world's bond markets all produced situations where banks were capable of making losses well above the maximum losses 19 days out of 20. One inherent danger, therefore, with calculating VaR at 95 percent is that a bank underestimates losses in extreme events and mistakenly believes that it is capable of dealing with a crisis.

Users of RiskMetrics

JP Morgan nevertheless argues that its intention never was to say that capital requirements should equal VaR at 95 percent. Instead, capital would be a function of VaR. Regulators would, therefore, decide upon a scalar and then multiply this by the VaR figure in order to decide upon the capital requirement. The RiskMetrics system does not even attempt to define what this scalar should be. It leaves this up to the regulators. Potential users of RiskMetrics should, therefore, bear in mind that the RiskMetrics model is not designed purely for regulators. Instead, it is a risk-measurement tool designed for management use. The model is not designed for extreme events because it wants to examine the risk–reward relationship so those managers can make internal decisions which will reduce risk. To claim that a model can satisfy both regulators and internal decision makers is trying to be all things to all people. The situation is similar to what accountants face when they prepare accounts. Financial accounts are prepared for external publication and must comply with certain rules and regulations. These published accounts give shareholders a guideline of the company's profitability. However, for internal decision making, accountants prepare management accounts, which basically compare marginal revenue with marginal costs. JP Morgan's RiskMetrics is designed for internal use and, like management accounts, it compares the additional revenue that a project generates against the marginal risk (as opposed to marginal costs). It would be pointless to measure expected returns against extreme risk because this would be meaningless for regulators, and even more meaningless for internal decision making.

Liquidity risk

Another criticism of RiskMetrics is that it does not deal with liquidity risk at all. There is no point in "marking to market" as RiskMetrics does if, in an extreme situation, liquidity becomes difficult. This has an important impact on determining the most appropriate horizon for exposure risk measurement. Giving one-day and one-month measures of exposure for trading and market making activities is inappropriate if a bank finds it difficult to liquidate that asset. Critics of VaR models (and RiskMetrics) believe that, although measuring liquidity risk is difficult, some appreciation of how quickly liquidity can dry up is essential. Some information can be obtained from the bid–ask spread. If there is a relatively wide gap between the bid price and the ask price, this should be regarded as a warning signal that, in the event of a crash, such instruments will be difficult to convert into cash. Isolating market risk from liquidity risk can be misleading and dangerous because the model underestimates the amount of risk involved.

Case profile

NatWest – market weakness

In 1996 NatWest's systems and procedures failed to prevent significant losses arising on its derivative trades. OTC options present unique operational and liquidity difficulties which a risk manager must be aware of. A single trader, Kyriacos Papouis, was accused of causing over £50 million worth of losses in National Westminster Bank when he priced and traded OTC interest rate options. Of concern to the risk profession is the fact that Papouis was able to work within NatWest's risk procedures and still amass those losses. He persuaded his immediate bosses that his procedure for calculating volatility and valuing options was working properly. As has been the case in many other disasters of this type, the person responsible was initially considered to be a star trader who had established a glowing record, which eventually turned out to be rather less glowing than anticipated. Unlike Nick Leeson (the Barings trader), Papouis did not commit a fraud to cover up his losses, neither did he gain personally from NatWest's disaster. The problem, therefore, could be classified as a systems or operations failure. Even if OTC options are priced correctly, there are certain liquidity difficulties which must be overcome.

All of Papouis' trades were correctly accounted for and were regularly examined by risk managers. Yet, despite this, there was a clear breakdown somewhere. The problem was partly due to the fact that OTC option price validation is very difficult and places considerable pressure on the risk departments within various banks. Often, risk managers will not have enough technical knowledge to price options correctly and so overrely on what the trader says.

Over-the-counter options

NatWest's problem highlights the additional complexities that over-the-counter options have over exchange-traded options. OTC options are tailor-made contracts that banks often offer companies. Exchange-traded options, on the other hand, are "standardised" contracts traded on a recognized exchange. Clearly, OTC options are more profitable, but from a writer's point of view they have a number of problems:

- They are difficult to value.
- They are generally illiquid.
- A margining system does not apply, so counterparties are exposed to a credit risk.

Valuing models

Valuing exchange-traded options is relatively straightforward. Since such options are relatively liquid, the screen price is perfectly valid. With OTC options, however, traders rely on models such as Black and Scholes as well as Cox, Ross, and Rubenstein. All of the models are based upon assumptions, and if these assumptions prove inaccurate, then so too will the prices. Option prices are very volatile to begin with and if an inexperienced trader misprices an option, the more experienced traders from other banks will have no hesitation in exploiting any arbitrage opportunities that may arise from the mispricing. Value at Risk models, of course, cannot measure the risk of overrelying on option valuation models, as NatWest discovered.

Liquidity

Nonliquidity is also something that a VaR model cannot cope with. In extreme cases, where the markets crash, traders need to offload and close out their instruments very quickly. OTC or tailored items are more difficult to close out. Currently, VaR modelers are undertaking research into incorporating liquidity risk into VaR by looking at the bid offer spreads. For the moment, however, liquidity risk is difficult to measure, and once a risk manager has discovered losses on a position, he can expect those losses to increase if he tries to close his position at a time when the markets are illiquid.

Margining

Since OTC options are difficult to value, it is not easy to apply a margining system, which and this means that losses can creep up without the risk manager being aware that such losses exist. One benefit of exchange-traded options over OTC options is that a margining system applies. If a trader is making losses on exchange-traded options, he must send funds to the exchange within 24 hours to cover those losses. Provided the risk manager does the appropriate reconciliation, he or she can tell the amount of losses the bank has suffered on the previous day by looking at the margin account. With OTC options, of course, no margining system applies, so the risk manager must develop alternative means to measure the losses. Such measures can only produce estimates of losses and not actual losses. A risk manager could, for instance, telephone the counterparty and ask for a recommended value of any open positions. In practice, this is done quite a lot for OTC options, but does not always prove accurate. Generally, most VaR models cannot cope with OTC options. Although developments in Monte Carlo simulations could improve valuation techniques, different simulation systems could very easily produce different values, and so both parties may have difficulty in agreeing on how much margin should be paid.

Volatility

According to the *Financial Times* (1997), NatWest investigators believe that Kyriacos Papouis overestimated the value of the options he sold and bought. This meant that he would have paid too high a price for the options and, of course, many traders would have exploited this. Risk managers who may not have fully appreciated the intricacies of option pricing, would have accepted Papouis' valuations, and this would have diluted an important trading control – independent pricing checks.

The *Financial Times* went on to say: "Most traders tend to use more sophisticated models than the controllers who check their books. This phenomenon has become known as 'model risk' – a risk that traders can use their own computers to justify inflated prices."

Volatility smile

Many traders are aware that models based on the normal distribution curve (such as Black and Scholes and many VaR systems) underestimate the probability that a price will fall or rise dramatically. To overcome this, traders push up volatility for options, which are deeply in-the-money or deeply out-of-the-money. The result of this is that the implied volatility for at-the-money options is a lot lower than those that are deeply in or out-of-the-money. This gives rise to the "volatility smile" curve. Again, most VaR systems cannot pick this up. Yet, if they could, NatWest might have realized sooner that it was in trouble and could have stemmed the losses.

Like the Barings collapse, the NatWest incident has proved to be worrying for risk managers.

> The most frightening aspect of the case for many bankers is likely to be its very simplicity. There was no grand deception or hiding of trades in secret accounts. Nor has any collusion between Mr Papouis and other traders being discovered. One of the bank's key traders appears simply to have blinded his managers with science and a volatility smile. (*Financial Times*, 1997)

Criticisms of VaR methods

Options trading

In Chapters 6 and 7 we outlined the complexities of options. Of the three VaR measures, only the Monte Carlo simulation can deal with such complexities. However, because of its complex nature, operation problems with Monte Carlo are likely to arise. With vanilla options, and even more so with exotic options, there is a difficult interplay of parameters and also multidimensional nonlinearity. In short, there is no simple way of tracking all the complex risk parameters within a VaR framework.

Estimating covariances and volatility

In Chapter 10 we outlined the dangers of assuming that volatility remains constant. As the case profile on NatWest has shown, volatility has unique characteristics and requires complex modeling procedures. Ignoring such complexities can mean that instruments are undervalued and, in extreme situations, losses from misinterpreting volatility can occur.

Value at Risk methods rely heavily on the covariance or correlation between assets. Like volatility, however, these can vary quite a lot and in extreme or stress situations can act in a manner which is totally different from the norm. Regulators and practitioners disagree on the degree of correlation that should be allowed in risk measurement. Ignoring correlation altogether can lead to extreme values of VaR and could mean that hedges are not recognized as hedges. Integrating a variance covariance and correlation matrix on the other hand could seriously underestimate the capital at risk, particularly in stress situations, which is what VaR is trying to measure.

A standard model, a standard system

People with an accounting background will recognize the importance of having, as far as possible, a standard system of calculation procedures for risk measurement. Without such a standard system, certain banks might use the equivalent of creative accounting tactics, that is to say they might be tempted to adopt a system that produces the least VaR and so minimize capital adequacy. A standard model, however, can encourage all banks to measure risk in the same way, diversify in the same way and so hold similar portfolios. The difficulty here is that if there is a market crash all banks will act in a manner similar to each other, which will cause considerable instability in the marketplace. The problem is equivalent to what economists term "Goodharts Law," namely, by trying to observe and correct a relationship, that relationship breaks down. In the 1970s, for instance, the Bank of England looked at the relationship between the supply of money and inflation and then tried to control inflation by reducing the supply of money (assuming that there was a correlation between the two). Once it implemented the policy, the correlation broke down and the policy proved ineffective.

Lognormal distribution

One main concern among practitioners about VaR is the belief that the returns on asset prices follow a lognormal distribution. In reality, there are normally more extreme price changes than the normal distribution curve suggests. This suggests that the normal distribution curve underestimates situations of extreme risk (which is what VaR tries to measure). Various studies in this area reveal that although the normal distribution curve is the best representation of an asset's distribution, in reality there are more days with small distributions, fewer days with intermediate distributions, and more days with larger distributions. This is summarized in Figure 11.1.

Fig 11.1

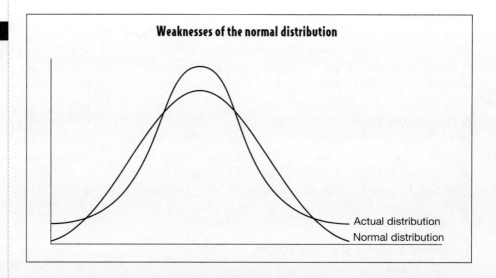

Weaknesses of the normal distribution

Actual distribution
Normal distribution

Terminology

Skewness – where a distribution is lopsided, that is whose right tail is longer than the left or vice versa, that distribution is said to be skewed to the left or the right. Asset prices themselves suffer from skewness, but this is corrected if, instead of taking the asset prices themselves, we take the return on the asset prices (the lognormal distribution).

Kurtosis – a distribution experiences positive kurtosis if the mean is tall and narrow compared to the normal distribution (as shown in Figure 11.1). The Black and Scholes model and the RiskMetrics version of VaR both suffer from kurtosis that is difficult to correct. The result of this is that the

Black and Scholes model underestimates the price of far out-of-the-money and far in-the-money options. The RiskMetrics model underestimates the possibility of a major disaster, such as a stock market crash.

Continuous trading

Diffusion – trading follows a diffusion process if there are smooth and continuous changes from one period to the next with no gaps between prices. Intuitively this means that we can graph an asset's price movement without lifting pen from paper.

Jump process – this is where a price follows a step pattern, that is a share price could be at £9 on Friday evening and then suddenly jump to £11 by the start of business on the following Monday morning.

When central banks change interest rates, they tend to change by fixed amounts, for example, half of one percent. The process is not gradual and so central banks' policies tend to encourage a jump process. Similarly, with exchange rates, where governments "lock" into a fixed exchange system, intervention is required, and this often displays "jump" as opposed to "diffusion" characteristics.

When developing pricing or risk-measurement models, most designers assume that markets follow a continuous or diffusion process. The problem is very acute for option traders. Consider a trader who shorts a straddle with, say, a month to maturity. A "gap" in the market would cause him to lose money, and although the gap may recover, the probability of doing so in the short term is very remote. Where optionality is concerned, therefore, the presence of "gapping" can enhance the value of an option.

VaR is particularly weak when it comes to "gapping" simply because it fails to recognize that gapping exists. When a trader is short gamma, he is very exposed to "gapping," yet, as we have seen, many VaR methods are incapable of capturing gamma risk. Also, a trader may sell options and delta hedge his portfolio. VaR recognizes and rewards such delta hedging, but fails to pick up the risk of a major price change at, say, the weekend. The problem is particularly severe when options are close to their expiry date.

Constant elasticity of variance

Most risk-measurement and option-pricing models make the assumption that volatility characteristics are the same whether a price rises or fall. In reality, most traders accept the fact that assets may be more volatile when falling than rising or vice versa, depending on the asset. We can conclude, therefore, that the volatility of a market is not independent of the price of the underlying contract. New models such as the constant elasticity of variance model have incorporated this into option pricing and strictly speaking, these complications should be taken on board when measuring risk. Most VaR measurement systems, however, are incapable of making this distinction.

Merrill Lynch

Banks like Merrill Lynch believe that the use of mathematical risk models alone may provide a greater sense of security than warranted and, therefore, reliance on these models should be limited. Its risk management division uses several risk-technology tools, including a risk-inventory database, a trading-limit monitoring system and stress scenarios. A special risk-inventory database gives details of daily consolidation of securities exposure. This analysis is carried out by product, credit rating, country, etc. Mathematical risk models are incapable of quantifying large-scale potential financial events with any precision. For this reason, models like VaR are not exclusively relied upon. Instead, mathematical models supplement other risk-management projects.

Although we have featured products in detail throughout this book and have examined the inherent risks with these projects, the primary risk is not in the product itself, but in the way the product is managed. In the Barings' case, breaches of discipline and lapses in supervision are the prime reasons behind banks making huge losses. A VaR system or any other mathematical system is incapable of picking up such risks.

Ten years ago, Merrill Lynch implemented a risk process throughout the bank, which was based on the belief that there is more to risk management than identifying and measuring risk. The bank has developed a philosophy based on several principles, notably:

- The most important tools in any risk process are experience, judgment, and constant communication with risk takers.
- Vigilance, discipline, and an awareness of risk must be continuously emphasized throughout Merrill Lynch.
- The process must be flexible to permit adaptation to changing environments, including the evolving goals of Merrill Lynch itself.
- Merrill Lynch also believes that the key objective must be to minimize the possibility of incurring unacceptable loss. Such losses usually arise from unexpected events that most statistical and model-based risk methodologies cannot predict.

▶

To implement this philosophy, Merill Lynch's risk-management process relies on three key elements:

- communication
- controls and guidelines
- risk technology.

In order to encourage better communication, risk management is organized along geographical and product lines to ensure direct and frequent communication with specific trading areas. The risk-management team also performs regular and formal risk reviews with the senior trading managers.

Conclusion

Most books which espouse the theory of VaR are heavy in mathematical content and many of those new to risk management may form the view that risk measurement and control is a science that can be controlled with mathematical formulas. Clearly, understanding intuitively what VaR models are trying to do is an important tool that a risk manager needs when making important risk decisions. However, most experienced risk managers believe that there are other variables that are more important. Perhaps, the most important attribute is common sense. Those risk managers who abide religiously by VaR risk-measurement models are almost certainly doomed to disaster. There will never be a simplified risk-measurement system that we can follow religiously. However, it does make sense to appreciate the complex nature of risk management and the extent to which VaR can contribute towards the measurement and control of such risk.

Appendix 11.1
INTERNAL REPORTING – RISK REWARD

In this Appendix we outline the difficulties of reconciling trading and risk measurement information with that of the accounting system. Obviously, all of the weighting matrices developed for VaR measurement must come from the general ledger. However, reconciling trader valuations and accounting valuations has always been a difficult and complex procedure. This has given risk to inadequate control and has also made the task of installing a VaR system more difficult. One important function of VaR is to measure the risk–reward relationship. This is obviously difficult if accountants are valuing reward (profit) on one basis, and risk managers are measuring risk on another.

Different horses for different courses

Traders and risk managers tend to value financial instruments differently from accountants. This has given rise to reconciliation problems between the front office and the back office. These reconciliation complications can of course lead to greater misunderstanding and operational risk. Accountants don't always mark-to-market financial instruments. In other words, they don't show on their balance sheet the current market cost of the instrument they are dealing with. Very often companies will issue generous options to staff and newly appointed directors. Only when these options are exercised are they reported on the balance sheet. Clearly, a more accurate treatment is to value such options on the date that they are granted and then reduce the profit and loss account accordingly.

Warren Buffett criticizes accountants

> Warren Buffett, the American investment guru who runs Berkshire Hathaway, has attacked the conventional accounting treatment of derivatives: "Earnings have been overstated because companies have followed the standard – but in our view dead wrong – accounting practice of ignoring the cost to a business of issuing options." (*Financial Times*, 1998)

The reason that derivatives are not shown on the balance sheet is that accountants have always relied on historical cost. There is justification for doing this. Using the historical approach is consistent. If directors were allowed to impose current values then in subjective cases, where instruments are difficult to value, directors would be free to use their judgment and this, of course, gives rise to "creative accounting." Directors might be tempted to keep an eye on earnings per share when valuing instruments. Thus, they could artificially inflate profits.

Today, with banks and companies using derivatives more and more, accountants have had to reexamine the historical cost convention and the likelihood is that in the future, where market values exist, these will be shown in the accounts. To estimate current market values, accountants would have little difficulty where the prices are quoted. Obviously, valuing exchange-traded products would be much easier than over-the-counter products since the exchange-traded market is very liquid. Where quoted prices are not available, accountants could attempt to make estimates based on similar products. A customized interest rate swap, for instance, could be broken down between a fixed and floating bond and each part valued separately.

If finding a similar product proves difficult, accountants could look for a quote from a broker. Obviously, such valuations cannot be overrelied upon, particularly if the broker has built up a very close relationship with the trader.

The accountant could also consider using models such as Black and Scholes and/or discounted cash flows. However, models are based on assumptions and these may prove inaccurate. In addition, accountants must estimate variables like volatility. This, of course, gives directors a license for creative accounting.

Gains and losses

Even if accountants get the valuation right there is still the issue of when and how he should recognize profits and losses. Clearly, if a swap is being used for hedging purposes then any profit or loss on the instrument should not be recognized as such, since the swap is being used as a hedge instead of for trading purposes.

Statement of total gains and realized losses

The US-based Financial Accounting Standards Board recommends that all instruments should be marked to market. If an instrument is held for trading purposes, any increase or decrease in value should be recognized in the profit and loss account immediately. Where an asset is held for hedging purposes, any gain or loss on that asset should be held temporarily in the STRGL reserve account and gradually released into the profit and loss account.

	B	C	D	E	F	G	H
6	Fixed rate	9%					
7	Nominal value	£100					
8	Term in years	5					
9							
10	Year	1	2	3	4	5	Total
11	Rate	7%	13%	8%	10%	13%	
12	Discount factor	0.763	0.693	0.857	0.909	1.000	
13	Profit and loss interest	9	9	9	9	9	
14	Annuity factor	3.387	2.361	1.783	0.909	0.000	
15	Value	£107	£91	£102	£99	£100	
16							
17	STRGL						
18	Debit/(credit)	–£7	£16	–£11	£3	–£1	£0
19	Closing balance (Dr)/Cr	–£7	£9	–£2	£1	£0	

Table A11.1.1 Treatment of a fixed loan

In Table A11.1.1, the company has elected to pay a fixed loan for five years at 9 percent. Therefore, the charge to the profit and loss account must be £9 per year. However, the actual rate of interest has changed throughout the loan. When interest rates are lower than the fixed rate, the present value of the loan commitment is £107. This increase in liability produces a loss of £7, but because we are dealing with a hedge (as opposed to a trade), the difference is reflected in the STRGL account as opposed to the profit and loss account. Obviously, whatever happens to the interest rate during the five years, the value of the loan drops to the principle £100 on the day before the loan matures. Therefore, the STRGL account must return to zero.

	B	C	D
6	Fixed rate	0.09	
7	Nominal value	100	
8	Term in years	5	
9			
10	Year	1	2
11	Rate	0.07	0.13
12	Discount factor	=(1+C11)^(C10-$C$8)	=(1+D11)^(D10-$C$8)
13	Profit and loss interest	=$C$6*$C$7	=$C$6*$C$7
14	Annuity factor	=(1-C12)/C11	=(1-D12)/D11
15	Value	=C14*C13+$C$7*C12	=D14*D13+$C$7*D12
16			
17	STRGL		
18	Debit/(Credit)	=C19	=D19-C19
19	Closing balance(Dr)/Cr	=$C$7-C15	=$C$7-D15

Table A11.1.2 Spreadsheet formulas for Table A11.1.2

Floating debt to fixed swap

Year	1	2	3	4	5	Total
Rate	7%	13%	8%	10%	13%	
Value of floating bond	£100	£100	£100	£100	£100	
Value of fixed payors						
Swap (Cr)/Dr	−£7	£9	−£2	£1	£0	
STRGL						
Debit/(credit)	−£7	£16	−£11	£3	−£1	
Closing balance(Dr)/Cr	−£7	£9	−£2	£1	£0	

Table A11.1.3 Accounting treatment of swap

Appendix 11.2 NORMAL DISTRIBUTION TABLES

Z Value	0.0000	0.0100	0.0200	0.0300	0.0400	0.0500	0.0600	0.0700	0.0800	0.0900
0	0.5000	0.5040	0.5080	0.5120	0.5160	0.5199	0.5239	0.5279	0.5319	0.5359
0.1	0.5398	0.5438	0.5478	0.5517	0.5557	0.5596	0.5636	0.5675	0.5714	0.5753
0.2	0.5793	0.5832	0.5871	0.5910	0.5948	0.5987	0.6026	0.6064	0.6103	0.6141
0.3	0.6179	0.6217	0.6255	0.6293	0.6331	0.6368	0.6406	0.6443	0.6480	0.6517
0.4	0.6554	0.6591	0.6628	0.6664	0.6700	0.6736	0.6772	0.6808	0.6844	0.6879
0.5	0.6915	0.6950	0.6985	0.7019	0.7054	0.7088	0.7123	0.7157	0.7190	0.7224
0.6	0.7257	0.7291	0.7324	0.7357	0.7389	0.7422	0.7454	0.7486	0.7517	0.7549
0.7	0.7580	0.7611	0.7642	0.7673	0.7704	0.7734	0.7764	0.7794	0.7823	0.7852
0.8	0.7881	0.7910	0.7939	0.7967	0.7995	0.8023	0.8051	0.8078	0.8106	0.8133
0.9	0.8159	0.8186	0.8212	0.8238	0.8264	0.8289	0.8315	0.8340	0.8365	0.8389
1	0.8413	0.8438	0.8461	0.8485	0.8508	0.8531	0.8554	0.8577	0.8599	0.8621
1.1	0.8643	0.8665	0.8686	0.8708	0.8729	0.8749	0.8770	0.8790	0.8810	0.8830
1.2	0.8849	0.8869	0.8888	0.8907	0.8925	0.8944	0.8962	0.8980	0.8997	0.9015
1.3	0.9032	0.9049	0.9066	0.9082	0.9099	0.9115	0.9131	0.9247	0.9162	0.9177
1.4	0.9192	0.9207	0.9222	0.9236	0.9251	0.9265	0.9279	0.9292	0.9306	0.9319
1.5	0.9332	0.9345	0.9357	0.9370	0.9382	0.9394	0.9406	0.9418	0.9429	0.9441
1.6	0.9452	0.9463	0.9474	0.9484	0.9495	0.9505	0.9515	0.9525	0.9535	0.9545
1.7	0.9554	0.9564	0.9573	0.9582	0.9591	0.9599	0.9608	0.9616	0.9625	0.9633
1.8	0.9641	0.9649	0.9656	0.9664	0.9671	0.9678	0.9686	0.9693	0.9699	0.9706
1.9	0.9713	0.9719	0.9726	0.9732	0.9738	0.9744	0.9750	0.9756	0.9761	0.9767
2	0.9772	0.9778	0.9783	0.9788	0.9793	0.9798	0.9803	0.9808	0.9812	0.9817
2.1	0.9821	0.9826	0.9830	0.9834	0.9838	0.9842	0.9846	0.9850	0.9854	0.9857
2.2	0.9861	0.9864	0.9868	0.9871	0.9875	0.9878	0.9881	0.9884	0.9887	0.9890
2.3	0.9893	0.9896	0.9898	0.9901	0.9904	0.9906	0.9909	0.9911	0.9913	0.9916

Z Value	0.0000	-0.0100	-0.0200	-0.0300	-0.0400	-0.0500	-0.0600	-0.0700	-0.0800	-0.0900
0	0.5000	0.4960	0.4920	0.4880	0.4840	0.4801	0.4761	0.4721	0.4681	0.4641
-0.1	0.4602	0.4562	0.4522	0.4483	0.4443	0.4404	0.4364	0.4325	0.4286	0.4247
-0.2	0.4207	0.4168	0.4129	0.4090	0.4052	0.4013	0.3974	0.3936	0.3897	0.3859
-0.3	0.3821	0.3783	0.3745	0.3707	0.3669	0.3632	0.3594	0.3557	0.3520	0.3483
-0.4	0.3446	0.3409	0.3372	0.3336	0.3300	0.3264	0.3228	0.3192	0.3156	0.3121
-0.5	0.3085	0.3050	0.3015	0.2981	0.2946	0.2912	0.2877	0.2843	0.2810	0.2776
-0.6	0.2743	0.2709	0.2676	0.2643	0.2611	0.2578	0.2546	0.2514	0.2483	0.2451
-0.7	0.2420	0.2389	0.2358	0.2327	0.2296	0.2266	0.2236	0.2206	0.2177	0.2148
-0.8	0.2119	0.2090	0.2061	0.2033	0.2005	0.1977	0.1949	0.1922	0.1894	0.1867
-0.9	0.1841	0.1814	0.1788	0.1862	0.1736	0.1711	0.1685	0.1660	0.1635	0.1611
-1	0.1587	0.1562	0.1539	0.1515	0.1492	0.1469	0.1446	0.1423	0.1401	0.1379
-1.1	0.1357	0.1335	0.1314	0.1292	0.1271	0.1251	0.1230	0.1210	0.1190	0.1170
-1.2	0.1151	0.1131	0.1112	0.1093	0.1075	0.1056	0.1038	0.1020	0.1003	0.0985
-1.3	0.0968	0.0951	0.0934	0.0918	0.0901	0.0885	0.0869	0.0853	0.0838	0.0823
-1.4	0.0808	0.0793	0.0778	0.0764	0.0749	0.0735	0.0721	0.0708	0.0694	0.0681
-1.5	0.0668	0.0655	0.0643	0.0630	0.0618	0.0606	0.0594	0.0582	0.0571	0.0559
-1.6	0.0548	0.0537	0.0526	0.0516	0.0505	0.0495	0.0485	0.0475	0.0465	0.0455
-1.7	0.0446	0.0436	0.0427	0.0418	0.0409	0.0401	0.0392	0.0384	0.0375	0.0367
-1.8	0.0359	0.0351	0.0344	0.0336	0.0329	0.0322	0.0314	0.0307	0.0301	0.0294
-1.9	0.0287	0.0281	0.0274	0.0268	0.0262	0.0256	0.0250	0.0244	0.0239	0.0233
-2	0.0228	0.0222	0.0217	0.0212	0.0207	0.0202	0.0197	0.0192	0.0188	0.0183
-2.1	0.0179	0.0174	0.0170	0.0166	0.0162	0.0158	0.0154	0.0150	0.0146	0.0143
-2.2	0.0139	0.0136	0.0132	0.0129	0.0125	0.0122	0.0119	0.0116	0.0113	0.0110
-2.3	0.0107	0.0104	0.0102	0.0099	0.0096	0.0094	0.0091	0.0089	0.0087	0.0084

REFERENCES

Alexander, Carol (1996) *Risk Management and Analysis*. London: John Wiley & Sons Ltd.

Financial Times (1997) "When the smile is wiped off."

Financial Times (1998) "US profits overstated by a third, says report," 17 April.

Hull, John (1995) *Introduction to Futures and Options Markets*. New York: Prentice Hall.

Kroner, K., K.P. Kneafsey and S. Claessens (1995) "Forecasting volatility in commodity markets," *International Journal of Forecasting*.

BIBLIOGRAPHY

1 Decovny, S. (1992) *Swaps*. London: Woodhead-Faulkner.
2 Fabozzi, F. and A. Konishi (1997) *The Handbook of Asset Liability Management*. Chicago: Irwin.
3 Fabozzi, F. and F. Modigliani (1996) *Capital Markets*. Upper Saddle River, New Jersey: Prentice Hall.
4 Galitz, L. (1996) *Financial Engineering*. London: Pitman.
5 Ho, Thomas (1997) *Fixed Income Solutions*. Chicago: Irwin.
6 Hull, J. (1995) *Introduction to Futures and Options Markets*. Englewood Cliffs, New Jersey: Prentice Hall.
7 Jarrow, Robert and Stuart Turnbull (1996) *Derivative Securities*. Cincinnati, Ohio: Thomson Publishing.
8 Jorion, P. (1997) *Value at Risk*. Chicago: Irwin.
9 Morgan, J.P. (JPM) (1994–5) *RiskMetrics. Technical Documentation Releases 1–3*. New York: JP Morgan.
10 Ritter, L. and W. Silber (1993) *Principles of Banking and Financial Markets*. New York: Basic Books.
11 Sharpe, W. F. (1995) *Investments*. Englewood Cliffs: Prentice Hall.

GLOSSARY

Abandon An option holder allows the option to expire without exercising it.

American An American option gives the holder the right, but not the obligation, to exercise before maturity.

Arbitrage Profiting from pricing anomalies. A trader can buy an instrument on one exchange and sell it on another at a higher price. The difference is known as arbitrage profit.

Asset allocation Allocating an investment fund into different assets to achieve maximum return on diversification.

At-the-money An option whose strike price equals the current market price of the underlying instrument.

Bank bill A bill of exchange acceptable by a bank.

Basis This is the difference between the futures market price for a given commodity and the cash or spot price for the commodity or security.

Basis point 1100th of 1%.

Basis swap Similar to interest rate swap.

Bear A trader or investor who believes the market is about to fall.

Bear market A market whose prices are falling.

Bid The price paid by the market taker for the purchase of a security, such as an option or a futures contract, at a specified price.

Black and Scholes The option pricing model written by Myron Black and Fischer Scholes in 1972 and used by many market practitioners.

Bond A security sold by governments and corporates in order to raise capital. Bonds normally provide the buyer with an income flow plus the return of the initial capital on the maturity date of the bond.

Broker An intermediary between buyer and seller.

Bull One who believes that prices are heading higher; an up-trending market.

Bull market A rising market.

Call money A bank loan repayable on demand.

Call option An option giving the holder the right, but not the obligation, to buy an underlying instrument (i.e. a share, a bond, or a quantity of foreign currency) at a pre-agreed exercise price (strike price) on or before a specific future date.

Cash market The market for a cash commodity where the actual physical product is traded.

Cash settlement A purchase and sale is made for cash. This is unlike a derivative, which is simply an agreement for a purchase or sale, and which derives its value from the underlying asset.

Closing price The price at which the last sale is agreed, prior to the exchange's closing for the trading period.

Collar (interest rate) This strategy gives the buyer protection against interest rate rises, but at a reduced premium. The holder has bought a cap at one level and, in order to recoup some or all of its cost, has sold a floor at a lower level.

Coupon A regular cash payment which an investor receives on a bond (i.e. a bond with a coupon of 12% per annum pays £12 per year regardless of the interest rate), until the bond matures.

Credit risk The potential loss that a creditor makes from defaults by a counterparty.

Default Failure to make a payment when due or to deliver an instrument, despite agreeing to do so.

Delivery The process of giving or receiving a commodity or security.

Derivative An instrument, contract, or agreement which is based upon an underlying commodity, exchange rate, stock, bond, or other traded market.

Differential swap This is similar to a cross currency swap except that both payments on the swap are made in a single currency. It is used by a company wishing to gain exposure to foreign interest rates without incurring an exchange rate risk.

Discount The difference between the current price and the future price of an instrument (including a sum of money receivable in the future) to reflect the opportunity cost of capital, that is interest rates.

Disintermediation The process where borrowers deal directly with sellers without passing through an intermediary such as a bank.

Dollar rate A variable amount of a foreign currency as quoted against the US dollar.

EDSP Exchange delivery settlement price. The price that is used for cash settlement when a security is delivered under a futures contract.

ERM Exchange Rate Mechanism.

Eurobond A bond denominated in a currency different to the currency of the country in which the bond is issued.

Eurocurrency Deposits and loans denominated in a currency other than that of the country in which the deposit is held or the loan made.

European style An option which may be exercised on the expiry or maturity date only.

Exchange-traded contract A contract traded on a recognized exchange such as LIFFE by exchange members. Exchange-traded contracts tend to be standardized and this makes them more liquid or easier to unwind.

Exercise A call option is exercised when the holder takes delivery of the underlying contract and pays the exercise price. A put option is exercised when the holder receives the exercise price and takes delivery. Options are only exercised when they are in-the-money.

Exercise price The price at which a person can purchase or sell the underlying instrument upon exercise of an option. The exercise price is also known as the "strike."

Exotic options The new generation of option derivatives, including lookbacks, barriers, baskets, ladders, and differentials. They are often tailor-made and are generally more complex than the plain vanilla options.

Expiration date Maturity date.

Fair value This is the theoretical price of a future or option. The theoretical price of options is calculated by option pricing models. An example is Black and Scholes. For futures, the theoretical price is the level where the contract should trade, taking into account cost of carry.

Fixed interest security A bond that pays a fixed sum of money at periodical intervals.

Floating exchange rate The exchange rate that applies when the value of a currency against another currency is determined by market forces, such as supply and demand.

Floating rate security This is a bond, or other security, on which the income payments move in line with the market rates of interest.

Floor A floor is an option which protects the holder against a downward movement in the price of a security or derivative.

Forward contract This is an agreement to buy or sell a given quantity of an asset (e.g. currency) at a specified future date at a pre-agreed forward price.

Forward rate agreement (FRA) An agreement where a client can, today, fix the rate of interest that will be applied to a notional loan or deposit in the future.

Futures contract This is similar to a forward contract except that it is standardized, as opposed to tailor-made, and dealt with through an exchange.

Holder The purchaser of an option.

In-the-money An option is in-the-money if it is profitable to exercise immediately and out-of-the money when the intrinsic value is zero and the strike price does not equal the underlying price.

Interest rate cap This is an option product where the holder (buyer) is guaranteed a maximum interest rate charge over a specified term at a rate of his choosing. Since it is an option, a principal is payable.

Interest rate collar An interest rate collar involves the simultaneous purchase of an interest rate cap and the purchase of an interest rate floor. The holder (buyer) is guaranteed a maximum and minimum borrowing cost over a specified term at a rate of his choosing. A premium may be required, but may net to zero.

Interest rate risk Interest rate risk represents the loss a portfolio can suffer when there is an adverse change in interest rates.

Interest rate swap A process by which a fixed rate liability can be converted into a floating rate liability or vice versa.

Intrinsic value The intrinsic value is the difference between the option strike price and the underlying price of an in-the-money option. Alternatively, it is what the holder receives if he exercises the option immediately.

ISDA International Swaps and Derivatives Association.

LIBOR The London Inter-Bank Offered Rate. This is the interest rate charged when one bank lends money to another.

Liquidity risk The money lost when a trader tries to realize cash for a security where the market is thin. It is the difference between the market value and the cash value (when unwound).

Long A person is long an asset if he profits when that asset increases in value.

Margin A variation margin is a payment or receipt to an exchange in respect of some options and futures which is designed to protect the exchange from default by a trader. Each day the market value of a trader's position is calculated. If there is a loss compared to the previous day, the trader makes up the difference with a margin payment. If there is a profit, the exchange pays over this profit to the trader.

Marked-to-market A derivative or instrument is 'marked-to-market' when it is valued on the basis of closing prices. The 'marked-to-market' value represents the amount of money that a trader can expect to receive or pay when he unwinds a position.

Maturity Period to the redemption of a financial claim.

Offer price The price at which an investor can buy an instrument.

Option A contract which gives the holder the right to purchase (call) or sell (put) the underlying futures contract or security at a specified price within a specified period of time.

Out-of-the-money An option whose strike price is worse than the current market price of the underlying instrument (i.e. an option that is not worth exercising).

Over-the-counter (OTC) A tailored transaction, usually between a client and a bank, negotiated privately between the parties. This is the market for securities or derivatives created outside organized exchanges by dealers trading directly with one another or their counterparties by telephone, screen or telex.

Physical or cash market The actual physical product, as opposed to the futures or derivative market.

Premium The market price of an option.

Price transparency A product or instrument is price transparent if traders have access to the last price agreed between buyer and seller.

Put option A contract which give the holder the right to sell a futures contract or an underlying contract at a specific price within a specified period of time.

Put–call parity The relationship which holds between the price of a call and the price of a put. If this relationship is broken an **arbitrage** opportunity exists.

Security A term used to describe investments, e.g. stocks, bonds, bills.

Short position A short position is one where the trader or investor profits if the asset price falls, and suffers if the asset price rises.

Speculator A trader who tries to profit by, first, taking a view and then taking a position on the underlying market.

Spot foreign exchange A transaction to exchange one currency for another at a rate agreed today (the spot rate) for settlement in two business days' time.

Spread (bid/offer) The spread is the excess of the ask (offer) price or interest rate over the bid price or interest rate. It is the market maker's or banker's margin. The bid price is always lower than the offer for a market maker.

Strike price The same as exercise price.

Swaps An obligation between two parties to exchange (usually interest or foreign exchange) payments over a specific term at a predetermined rate.

Swaption A swaption is an option into a swap transaction with predetermined characteristics. The holder of the option has the right, but not the obligation, to become a counterparty to a payor's or receiver's swap.

Theoretical value The value of a future or option as determined from the "cost of carry" pricing mechanism or an option pricing model.

Tick The standard minimum price movement on an exchange-traded futures or option contracts (0.01%).

Time to expiry This is the length of time between now and the maturity date. The longer the option has to go to until expiry, the more valuable it is.

Time value The time value of an option is the difference between the premium on an option and the intrinsic value.

Traded option An option contract bought or sold on a recognized exchange.

Translation risk Exchange rate risk arising from the fact that a transaction is priced in a foreign currency.

Treasury bill A debt instrument issued by the government for raising short-term finance.

Treasury bond A long-term security issued by the government.

Value at Risk Value at Risk is a single number that identifies a statistically probable maximum change in profit or loss within a given time interval and a stated confidence interval.

Volatility Volatility is a measure of the degree to which price fluctuations have occurred in the past or can be expected to occur in the future. Securities and commodities that vary considerably from their mean value prices are said to be very volatile.

Writer The writer is the seller of an option (the party who receives the premium).

Yield The rate of return on a security.

Yield curve The curve that expresses the relationship between the maturity of a security and the rate of return it provides.

INDEX